TRANSFORMATIONAL LEADERSHIP

TRANSFORMATIONAL LEADERSHIP

Value-based Management for Indian Organizations

Edited by

Shivganesh Bhargava

Los Angeles | London | New Delhi
Singapore | Washington DC | Melbourne

First published in 2003 by

SAGE Publications India Pvt Ltd
B1/I-1 Mohan Cooperative Industrial Area
Mathura Road, New Delhi 110 044, India
www.sagepub.in

SAGE Publications Inc
2455 Teller Road
Thousand Oaks, California 91320, USA

SAGE Publications Ltd
1 Oliver's Yard, 55 City Road
London EC1Y 1SP, United Kingdom

SAGE Publications Asia-Pacific Pte Ltd
3 Church Street
#10-04 Samsung Hub
Singapore 049483

Published by Vivek Mehra for SAGE Publications India Pvt Ltd, typeset at InoSoft Systems in 10 pt. CG Times.

Library of Congress Cataloging-in-Publication Data

Transformational leadership: value-based management for Indian organizations/ edited by Shivganesh Bhargava.
  p. cm.
  Selections of papers presented in a national seminar on leadership and human values at the Indian Institute of Management, Lucknow during April 12–14, 2000.
  Includes bibliographical references and index.
  1. Leadership—Moral and ethical aspects—India—Congresses. 2 Organizational change—India—Congresses. 3. Values—Congresses. 4. Management—India—Congresses. I. Bhargava, Shivganesh, 1959-

HD57.7T728   658.4'092—dc21   2002   2002026888

ISBN: 978-07-619-9722-1 (PB)

SAGE Team: Shyama Warner, Ritu Singh, R.A.M. Brown and Santosh Rawat

To
My late father
Raghav Ram Bhargava

Contents

Preface

Today, organizations are finding it increasingly difficult to respond successfully to the constantly evolving global, technological, economical, and social challenges. Unprecedented competition, a very fast changing market, and uncertainty of product lines demand a new kind of leadership as a recognized strategic tool for organizational excellence. The need arises for globally competent corporate leaders with human values, confidence, and professional commitment. The emergence of such leaders, who can transform and renew organizations with global vision and foresight is the need of the day. The present work is an endeavor to recognize the reality of the leadership crisis, particularly in Indian organizations in almost all sectors.

This book consists of 15 research papers, out of 54 presented in a national seminar on leadership and human values held at the Indian Institute of Management, Lucknow, during 12–14 April, 2000, dealing with the skills, knowledge, abilities, and other characteristics that are related to the effectiveness of a leader. Attempts have been made to integrate within the framework of the value-based leadership the emerging business strategy of the 21st century.

A dynamic leadership steers the nation towards the achievement of sustainable development. The papers presented in this book vary in their framework, methodology, and analyses, and attempt to explore, understand, and explain the dynamics of effective leadership. The book is meant for scholars of management and behavioral sciences, catalysts, organizational change agents, business leaders, entrepreneurs, human resource development managers, and others who wish to enhance the excellence and scope of their organization.

Acknowledgements

I would like to thank Pritam Singh, Director of the Indian Institute of Management, Lucknow, who provided me with the opportunity to coordinate a national seminar on value-based leadership—the outcome of which was this book. I wish to thank all the 54 contributors who participated, and my colleagues at IIM Lucknow for all their help. I also thank my sons Abhinav and Animesh, my wife Aruna, and my mother Dhurpati who were of great help throughout this project. Finally, my sincere thanks to the Response team for all their help in making this book a reality.

Introduction

Value-based Leadership and Organizational Excellence

New Economy: Challenges before Management Scientists

Knowledge, technology, and globalization are the main drivers of the new economy. Its success requires skill development, knowledge management, and voluntary involvement of people. Organizations therefore have no option but to apply all possible intangible resources and capabilities for value creation. This points to the need for an effective leadership. In fact, the impact of leadership on organizational performance has never been as critical as it is today. Rapid global changes are forcing organizations to introspect on their success/failure experiences and rethink their long-term strategies of managing people for enhancing performance, since successful strategies of the past will have only only short-term effectiveness in this era. Management scholars agree that through developing a leadership that suits the requirements of an organization and the cultural temperament of its people is extremely difficult, such leadership has long-term implications on enhancing organizational performance.

Leadership

Leadership in organizational behavior is perhaps one of the most extensively researched and studied topics. Research has shown that managers rank leadership abilities as the key to success (Bain, 1995). However, leadership has been a very difficult issue and has a somewhat tarnished reputation (Gardner and Avolio, 1998).

Leadership is the ability to influence colleagues, achieve desired results, and give purpose, clarity, and direction to an organization. Evidence suggests that effective leadership stimulates and inspires the members of the organization. Management literature too defines leadership as the ability to influence people, not only by what it is, but also by what it does: that it is both being and action. It empowers, motivates, and organizes people to achieve a common objective and provides moral guidance.

Leaders can create an environment in which others are motivated to put in their best. Therefore, it is necessary for a leader to have a pragmatic as well as an understandable operating philosophy that provides for open communication between the leader and members without an organization cannot achieve its objectives. An effective leader always, keeps in mind that though it is not easy to respect another person's point of view, it is essential to do so for developing and maintaining relationships with others.

Effective leadership stems from the moral authority and integrity of the leader, and his or her credibility among the followers on whom leadership can count. Note that this does not refer to yes men but to good followers. The art and science of effective leadership can be learnt through a consistent and committed emulation of critical thinking and not simply by being a 'yes' person. One must be hardworking and disciplined, humble and patient, and able to receive and offer constructive criticism.

A leader identifies and chooses the best strategies to achieve the objectives of an organization but without being an effective manager these cannot be achieved. It is important to realize that leadership is basically a developmental process that requires training and the desire to learn continuously.

Theoretical Aspects of Leadership

It is established that leadership skills can be learnt and developed in accordance with individual aptitude. Observing leadership behavior and analyzing the underlying attributes of leaders are the two major ways of distinguishing a successful and effective leader from an unsuccessful and ineffective one.

There are several theories for analysing leadership leadership effectiveness: starting from the traditional trait theory (Stogdill, 1974) to behavioral theories that lead to the development of contingency theories (Fiedler, 1967). These theories have identified several forms of leadership: attri-butional leadership (Pfeffer, 1992), charismatic leadership (Conger and Kanungo, 1988), transactional leadership (Burns, 1978), transformational leadership (Bass, 1985) and visionary leadership (Nanus, 1992; Saskin, 1992).

Indian Interventions

Most of the theories of leadership effectiveness developed in the West and have been copied in the East. Their success has precluded the need to evolve a different framework. Surprisingly, an approach when applied by one leader is effective but ineffective when applied by his or her colleague. Similarly, an organization in a region benefits by one kind of leadership while another organization in the same region does not. This results in short-term success only. As evident, the effectiveness of the organizational life cycle in India is far less than that in the West and Indian organizations today are struggling to survive, despite the application of effective leadership.

Research and analysis has led to the conclusion that probably the leadership styles of organizations in India are efficient in terms of improving productivity but they have no longevity because they do not belong to people. There is a wide gap between the leadership style applied and desired. Though people share some common universal values, they have a distinct set of their own values, and a uniqueness that separates them from others. This demands a leadership that belongs to them and is their own as well as indigenous.

Stemming from the recognition of the need, several leadership models have been developed: nurturant task leadership (NTL) by Sinha (1980), pioneering and innovative leadership by Khandwalla (1982), participative and democratic leadership by Singh and Bhandarker (1984) and subsequently transformational leadership (1989), and visionary leadership by Chakraborty (1999). These models provide guidelines and directions for developing an effective leadership style and enhancing organizational performance.

NURTURANT TASK LEADERSHIP

J.B.P. Sinha (1980) is the first Indian social scientist to propose a model of leadership that suits Indian culture. Keeping certain common Indian value systems in mind, he proposed the Nurturant Task Leadership style based on empirical data on middle-level management. This style advocates that the leader be a nurturant leader and a taskmaster at the same time. It showed its success in some organizations and obtained attention of the scholars. More than a dozen Ph.D. students in India have examined its merits. Other contemporary models of leadership such as the pioneering and innovative leadership style of Khandwalla (1982) and the participative and democratic leadership style of Singh and Bhandarker (1984) and subsequently transformational leadership (1989) emerged in the same line.

Sinha's model enjoys the support of theorists but not of managerial professionals. I too, feel that his model largely represents the middle of the road of the managerial grid. Interestingly, however, H.R. Prasad, Joint MD, Gabriel India Limited believes that a leader should be 'tough but fair with people', 'set and demand standards of excellence', and have 'the ability to set priorities'. This supports the external validity of Sinha's framework in the Indian context.

TRANSFORMATIONAL LEADERSHIP

Present times call for a new brand of leadership: namely, transformational leadership. Following the major work of Bass (1985) on transformational leadership, extensive research worldwide has revealed that transformational leaders are those who are value driven, courageous and lifelong learners, and have the ability to deal with ambiguity, complexity, and uncertainty. They are visionaries who transform the values, beliefs and needs of their followers to align with the demands of the organization. Such leaders have to be highly realistic and practical when it comes to taken action, focusing on structure, strategy, environment, implementation, experimentation, and adaptation. This kind of leadership stimulates interest and an awareness of the mission and vision of the firm, ensures the development of employees, and encourages placing group interests before individual interests. A transformational leader makes decisions quickly, seizes opportunities and modifies systems to revitalize the organization. Some characteristics of such leaders are vision, passion, perseverance, values (conviction, character, care, courage, and competence), and respect for individuals. In India, Singh and Bhandarker's (1989) extensive empirical work on this style of leadership has provided certain directions to facilitate organizations to develop transformational leaders.

Generally, three activities are associated with transformational leadership:

Creation of vision
Mobilization of commitment
Institutionalization of change

CREATION OF VISION

Management without visionary leadership lacks the vitality to survive. A transformational leader articulates his intuitions effectively and prepares methodically for the future. A leader with a vision is imperative for affecting the necessary transformation in the face of the overwhelming need for change

MOBILIZATION OF COMMITMENT

Transformational leaders make the vision happen. They mobilize the organization to accept the new commitment and work towards fulfilling it. Major changes in organizational structure and human resources management need to be coupled with fundamental changes in the basic political and cultural systems of the organization and its members. The mission is to transform their mindset and direct them towards a broadening of vision, insight and understanding. The mission must take into account the changing communication, decision-making, authority and performance processes.

The focus should therefore be on transforming the old economy mindset and creating a work culture and systems for new management. This ultimately clarifies purpose, makes behavior congruent with beliefs and values, and leads to activities that endure in the long run.

INSTITUTIONALIZATION OF CHANGE

Transformational leaders translate their vision into reality, mission into action, and philosophy into practice. At a deeper level, institutionalization of change necessitates shaping and reinforcing new knowledge, competence and behavior to weld with the transformed organization. It is critical that the new realities, action, and practices are shared throughout the organization. For this the right teams comprising the best and brightest people need to be identified by the transformational leader.

In these activities, leaders employ one of the four I's.

Idealized influence
Inspirational motivation
Intellectual stimulation
Individualized situations

VISIONARY LEADERSHIP

The twenty-first century leader will have to be a visionary, a change agent, a change leader, and a knowledge manager. It is for the leader to create the organization's vision and align it with the corporate strategy so it shares the company's customer-centric value proposition with employees across all levels and facilitates internal cohesiveness. In other words, a visionary leader needs to achieve strategic alignment by integrating the shared vision and the strategy with performance objectives. He or she should be able to identify and take advantage of emerging opportunities well before the competition. Thus the leader's success in actualizing the organization's vision and strategy is a function of her/his ability to build and nurture a learning organization. Chakraborty (1999) has made a significant contribution to popularizing this concept.

Without a visionary leadership development plan, organizations will be at a disadvantage in the current-day environment of globalization. Leaders must provide vision and direction, and be responsible for accomplishing the purposes for which the organization exists. For many non-governmental organizations (NGOs) mission has been the driving force around which they have mobilized their financial and personnel resources. They are task oriented, with little focus on the development of those who manage and lead the organization. Consequently, the organization's personnel resources may not be used in the most effective and sustaining manner. This is where the absence of visionary leadership is most often felt.

Journey from Productivity–Efficiency–Effectiveness to Excellence

The last five decades have witnessed a sea-change in management objectives in terms of achieving goals. Roughly, it was the era of productivity till the 1950s, the era of efficiency till the 1970s, and the era of effectiveness till the 1990s. Today is the era of excellence, marked by rapid market and environmental changes.

Society is transforming and moving rapidly towards a new age. This requires a new kind of leadership, capable of giving guidance, inspiration, and a new vision. It is therefore incumbent upon managers to be emotionally and intellectually equipped to tackle the challenges being thrown up by a progressively industrializing society: the highly competitive market conditions, the dramatic advancements in technology, consumer pressure groups, and the volatile socio-political environment.

Organizations cannot be satisfied with just doing well. Perhaps an organization's productivity graph is high, its efficiency ratio is also high, and its people are not resisting change. But what should not be forgotten is that above all there exists the external environment and competitors who are doing much better. Therefore, in this era of global competition organizations have to ensure excellence in all aspects, and that is possible if leaders are aware and vigilant. So, organizations have to target their strategies at customers, product (cost as well as quality), motivation (building a committed workforce), social obligations, and gaining competitive advantage. They have to concentrate on managing differently their assets, capital, delivery system, reward and compensation system, quality, research and development, sales, and relationship with stakeholders. All this warrants a value-based leadership.

Value-based Leadership

Globalization, decentralization, and dynamic markets are forcing organizations to evaluate their strategies of managing physical and human resources. Undoubtedly, financial health and state-of-the-art technology are still dominant in organizational performance. Achieving excellence, however, is possible through a positive mindset of the people of the organization, which only an effective leadership can effect.

Unlike the past, leadership, today is aligned with corporate strategy and organizations are realizing the need for a change in their management practices. A leader can be charismatic, participative, democratic, directive, visionary, transactional, or transformational, but the sustainability of his or her effectiveness is possible only if the leader's values are reflected not just in personality, action, decision, and outcomes but emanate from the heart. This is what is value-based leadership.

Value-based leadership is the voluntary relationship of the leader—without showing or exercising authority or power—with his or her people. This automatically becomes the guiding and driving force for them in pursuing their tasks/responsibilities/assignments as a challenge for the organization. Value-based leadership goes beyond transformational leadership. Such a leader does not have to set the vision or target; people will realize and understand through her/his actions and behavior.

Need for Value-based Leadership

For organizations to create and sustain high performance is a major challenge in the present-day business scenario. It can be achieved only by confronting the growing global competition and applying the value-based leadership model. This requires going beyond traditional piecemeal incremental changes and having a transformational leader. Aligning all human and physical resources with the strategic goals of the organization is the key to success.

Organizational Excellence through Value-based Leadership

Values and trust are key to the growth of societal capital in business. The role of government in society is diminishing, with corporations carrying out many functions for long considered the sole preserve of the government. For sustainable performance and excellence, organization can therefore not afford to ignore the social, cultural, and global realities of the times. This requires a leadership that is distinct from that of the past and suits today's environment and requirements. Value-based leadership is the alternative to it.

Value-based leadership is all about creation of socially conscious managers. It integrates leadership skills in a value-based system and society. So, value-based leadership is the vision, motivation, organization, and action of the leader. It gives a sense of power and hope, provides guidance, direction and inspiration, and empowers people to realize their leadership potential. It is not merely an extension of transformational leadership; rather, it is beyond it. A leader does not have to act consciously to emerge as a value-based leader, but will be naturally perceived as one through his or her actions, reactions, and achievements. Such leadership will lead not only to continuous growth of return on investment, output, and involvement of people, but to greater overall effectiveness.

Globalization, communication, and technology have altered the course of business and society. A metamorphic change is coming about in the way we communicate and promote ideas. The shift from being artisan driven to being knowledge driven is a business reality now. It is being increasingly realized that to cope with the emerging challenges, managers of the new economy need wider knowledge, a broader perspective, and vision, newer skills and greater understanding of people, processes and technology. Here, leadership can prove to be a strategic tool for achieving organizational excellence.

Thus, corporate leaders with human values, confidence and professional commitment, who can transform and revitalize organizations with vision, foresight and a human touch is the demand of the time and the challenge for professionals.

Leadership and Human Values

According to the philosophy of values, the universe is self-sufficient, free from supernatural cause or control. In line with this some behavioral scientist argue that all moral values are ephemeral and of human origin, while others endorse ethical relativism, that is, that there are no universally valid principles, since all moral principles are valid relative to cultural or individual values. In fact, ethical relativism assumes that organizations should lay emphasis on the values of the personnel if all values are relative. But some behavioral scientists contradict this, endorsing hedonistic ethical values, that is, that individuals seek their own pleasure and that the highest good for oneself is the most pleasure with the least pain. Therefore, organizations should encourage their personnel to be more accepting of their hedonistic tendencies, as human beings are basically hedonistic and reward seeking.

Positivism assumes that since knowledge is limited to observable facts, scientific theories can be shown to be true on the basis of evidence only. Hence, scientists can be objective and impartial observers and their empirical observations will eventually lead to a complete understanding of reality. In this way, logical positivists make a sharp distinction between facts and values and regard values as intellectually meaningless.

The foregoing discussion demonstrates the importance of studying values for managing people more effectively. Most Indian organizations have so far tended not to incorporate their personnel's values into quality of work life, productivity and performance. However, there is a growing realization that to achieve organizational goals, value systems must be owned and practised by all the personnel. In fact, organizations must view their personnel's core values as a potential resource and leverage on them.

But the question is, why only values? That is because values are what we care about most and what motivate us. When we incorporate our deepest values in our work we work harder because the outcome matters to us. We become more committed and get greater fulfilment from what we give and from what we accomplish. The most effective leaders are those who know their own values and act by them and are able to help others do the same. In fact, self-regulation based on values and attitudes has become an alternative to modern bureaucratic ways of regulation and behavior control in society as well as in business. Value-based leadership is not restricted to the human aspect alone. Value-added business processes convert process inputs into value-added output, eliminating the non-value adding ones and maximizing the value-added ones. Philosophically, everything we do is value based. We believe we are doing the right thing when we anticipate satisfaction from an enterprise. For example, when we buy something it is because of the value we perceived in it (usefulness, style, price, quality, and so on).

How an organization can inculcate value systems, particularly the spiritual ones, among personnel to enhance their quality of work life and productivity has been the concern of much research and has been demonstrated also (Singh, in press).

Value-based Leadership in the Twenty-first Century

Leadership is essential in all spheres of management, social, political, business, governmental, or non-governmental. In the present era of globalization, value-based leadership assumes an important dimension, particularly in its impact in the areas of finance (EVA) and marketing (value-based-marketing). However, to achieve sustainable development and to reap competitive advantage in the first evolving socio-economic scenario, value-based leadership requires special emphasis.

It is believed that the spiritual values of personnel can enhance organizational performance (Singh, in press) and healthy organizations can be developed only when they transmit such values among personnel. It is the responsibility of the organizations to explore personnel values, especially spiritual values, to promote growth and well-being.

Promoting Value-based Governance

Spiritual values and beliefs affect personnel's goals and lifestyle, and their physical, social and mental health. Organizations should let personnel know that values have physical, emotional and spiritual consequences and help enhance quality and productivity. Among developing countries, Japan is now a developed country by virtue of its value-based governance. This shows that governance plays a very important role in steering the firm towards its goals. However, a set of values need to be followed whatever be the mode of management.

In value-based administration, productivity embraces efficiency and effectiveness as well as quality of thought and action. Attitudinal changes are essential. Reflecting on value in administration, the interaction with the environment has to be kept in mind. For good organizational governance, manager should have clarity of thought, a positive attitude, tolerance, honesty and integrity, sincerity, respect for individuals, self-control and self-confidence, and a concern for self-development.

The ethical and effective approach for organizations is to assess the values of its personnel and to adopt a valuing style. The spiritual valuing style may be the most effective way to optimize the health of the organization and consequently to improve the quality of the work life of its employees. Teaching and modeling spiritual values is desirable for healthy organizations. Trainers should realize that they are value agents and try to model and teach value systems to personnel. Organizations should assess the values of the personnel during in-job training but values should not be imposed at this juncture. Personnel should be encouraged to have their personal value systems and disagree with their superiors on certain issues. Organizations should help them utilize their values in self-development.

Value-based Leadership: Strategic Tool of the Twenty-first Century

Excelling in the twenty-first century is possible only for those who take and make decisions within the framework of certain values known to their people. Certainly, value-based leadership is an alternative to bureaucratic regulation of behavior in society and in organizations and it can put society on to the path of equity, prosperity, and sustained progress. It is difficult here to prescribe the values that guarantee the success or excellence of a leader—values that are acquired along the course of family, school, and organizational socialization—but it is possible to know the value framework of everyone. A good team of followers can be built by leading with energy and enthusiasm, giving a sense of purpose and direction, planning strategically for success, applying positive strokes of praises and encouragement, creating opportunities, demonstrating confidence and faith in employees' abilities, and encouraging achievable tasks, and developing a vision for the future.

The success of the economy as a whole will be largely determined by the quality of the top leadership.

Conclusion

What differentiates a winner from a loser is the right mindset. Innovation and trial are the only ways to accomplish breakthroughs and to advance. Successful leaders and managers are those who are able to transform at relevant points. Managing people is the key element and hence leadership is more about guiding and facilitating the efforts of people. Resistance to change can be overcome through transformational value-based leadership, not transactional managers. Implied in these changes is the need for a paradigm shift in management thought and practice.

The emotional intelligence of leaders drives performance and their moods and behavior drive the moods behaviors of others in an organization. Thus leaders' emotional intelligence creates a certain culture or work environment. High levels of emotional intelligence create an environment wherein information sharing, trust, healthy risk taking, and learning flourish.

The current-day environment is replete with pioneers, who with their vision are transforming the way businesses are run and wealth is created. Thus, they are constantly moving on the leadership cycle. A new brand of leadership is necessary which would strike the right balance between ideation and implementation, and value-based leadership could be that alternative.

The basic principles of leadership have evolved over centuries and are well accepted, proven, and applied worldwide. A dynamic leadership steers the nation towards sustainable development. In today's knowledge society, flat, hierarchyless structures, virtual teams, and connected workers will create a milieu for success. It is becoming increasing clear that to have a cutting edge, apart from analytical and professional competence, a manager must have sound value-based leadership qualities.

India, despite its rich intellectual and natural resources, has not been able to make a place for itself in the world because of the leadership crisis in all sectors. Organizations worldwide finding it more and more difficult to respond successfully to the constantly evolving global, technological, economic and social challenges. Stiff competition, rapidly changing markets, and uncertainty of product lines demand a new kind of leadership as a strategic tool for organizational excellence. Today's organizations need people who can learn quickly on the job, who can make smart decisions and are quick with execution.

In 'Why Some Companies Make the Leap... and Others Don't'; Jim Collins (2001) suggests moving from 'good to great' as a strategy for twenty-first century managers. One cannot move from bad to good if the image of a leader has not been reflected. A leader has a certain distinct set of ideals and values that guide him/her in the process of performing his/her responsibility. This is possible if one is a dynamic, visionary, innovative, and achievement oriented transformational leader but one has to be a value-based leader to excel.

Leadership is still studied as a dependent, independent, as well as intervening variable, and therefore the multiplicity of themes. It is clear that transformational leadership is taking on an extended meaning. New kinds of employment relationships, changes in the measures and criteria of performance, market uncertainties, global competition, and other compelling work and family factors are forcing organizations to opt for a leadership that has a transformational flavor with a different kind of human touch for managing people at the workplace. In this volume this has been referred to as value-based leadership. As the essays here will show, successful executives worldwide are placing greater value on improvisation and learning, where value-based leadership for enhancing excellence has its unique place. Organizations aspiring for excellence have no choice but to rush for it.

Caution

In recent years, there has been significant growth in responsibility among corporates as well as in society. To manage a business is to integrate economic, environmental and social practices in the formulation and implementation of strategy. Demands for objectivity, quality, transparency, and accountability have also increased over the past few years. Therefore, people today talk not only 'trust me' but also 'tell me', even 'show me'. This implies that poor performing corporations cannot survive for long. However, there are different ways of looking at the problem of performance.

It is difficult to say what direction this century's corporate leaders are going to take but it is a matter of great concern how prospective leaders are on their values. Change has been occurring and successful organizations have been sensitive to it. Knowledge does not follow from one person nor can decisions be taken by one individual on behalf of all. Everyone has a say and empowerment goes together with teamwork.

Bureaucratic leadership provides a base for equality but leads to inefficiency. Democratic leadership gives scope for fresh ideas to emerge from others and for openness, but accountability gets diluted. Participative leadership encourages involvement of people but leads to dependency. Directive leadership leads to innovation but is always full of uncertainty. Visionary leadership thinks too far ahead; as a result the gap between the goals set and those achieved increases. Executive leadership can achieve goals through set standards but without much gain. Strategic leadership applies knowledge to exploit situations effectively but there is little guarantee of success across situations. Transactional leadership believes in winning the race by introducing and manipulating different kinds of rewards with established rules. Transformational leadership assumes that resolution of problems lies with the leadership itself. Thus the leader becomes the basis for others to follow in achieving goals but does not guarantee the goals that will be achieved. Therefore, there is need to go beyond transformational leadership by integrating the merits of all, assessing situations, and choosing the best possible strategy for the system.

Organization of the Book

The present volume attempts to provide a framework for the emergence of a new kind of leadership that will enable organizations to face the contemporary challenges.

In Chapter 1, 'Leadership in Unpredictable Times', Dr Dharni P. Sinha shows that in the fast-changing techno era managerial tasks have become increasingly complex and business leaders have to be on their toes all the time. He argues that the unsettling economy has created a flux in business worldwide and as a result multinationals are another challenge to developing economies as well as to established businesses. He advocates measures that will prevent chaos, conflict, and instability in the Indian economy and society, and within enterprises and institutions that have been carefully nurtured since Independence. For facing such challenges requires resilient leaders, he proposes, leaders who are like a plant with a fresh, green and living core; when stepped on, it bends, but soon springs back. Resilience calls for elasticity, buoyancy, adaptability, and strong life energy. He concludes that resilient leaders create resilient organizations, learning organizations, networked organizations, flat, and flexible organizations. They cultivate a resilient workforce, create resilient systems, and uphold values, work with others and create resilience among them, and contribute to excellence in the organizations they serve.

In Chapter 2, 'Leadership in the 21st Century: Towards Renaissance Leadership', Pritam Singh and Asha Bhandarker demonstrate that success in the future will come only to those who equip themselves in accordance with the requirements and demand of the changing time. Those who are not able to do so will not be able to survive in the corporate world. The authors also argue that much from within Indian traditions, culture and history has been applied by the West and has led to success. It is high time therefore that we concentrate on building systems that are guided by the values and framework that are our own. In this context, they recommend a leadership that starts from the transactional and moves to renaissance through the transformational. They stress that organizations will have to become leaner, faster, open, change oriented, and entrepreneurial, taking advantage of the opportunities thrown up by the changes to create new products and services; they will have to work from a global perspective; redefine the meaning of quality and customer service; they will need to work with people in creative and new ways to involve, inspire, and facilitate their functioning; above all they will need to build a new mindset on everything—strategy, technology, process, people, and products

In Chapter 3, 'Value-based Corporate Governance', M. Radhaswamy and Vineet Basotia demonstrate that value-based corporate governance is essential in today's corporate scenario. Good governance is stated as a combination of two aspects, namely, higher values and effective functioning. They highlight the business and spiritual views that can be adopted by corporates for good governance. Here the authors' spiritual views are backed by dictums from ancient Indian texts.

In Chapter 4, 'Value-based Leadership: Perspectives from Indian Ethos', N. Sivakumar and U.S. Rao present guidelines for value-based leadership derived from various Indian scriptures. They cite contemporary scholars on leadership to substantiate the all-time relevance of these guidelines. They conclude that value-based leadership is the safest means of ensuring social welfare and the spiritual growth of people worldwide long tormented by violence, strife, and deprivation.

In Chapter 5, 'Leader–Member Exchange as a Function of Leader Effectiveness: A Path Analytic Assessment of its Effect on Organizational Climate and Burnout', Vaishali and Mohit Kumar give an empirical analysis of leadership effectiveness. They examined the relationship between organization climate, leader–member exchange, and burnout. The authors concluded that twenty-first-century leaders are going to be those who show greater empathy and concern for people's issues and who do not rely on position or rank for their status.

In Chapter 6, 'Transformational Leadership and Organizational Structure: Role of Value-based Leadership', Garima Garg and Venkat R. Krishnan in their empirical work show that transformational leadership and value-based leadership are positively related to each other and that both are positively related to decentralization; their results also reveal that when value-based leadership is controlled, transformational leadership is no longer related to decentralization. The authors highlight the importance of value-based leadership in transforming organizations and individuals.

In Chapter 7, 'An Emotionally Intelligent Leadership Style', Mohit P. Kumar and Shivganesh Bhargava demonstrate on the basis of their empirical data the need for an emotionally intelligent leader in this century.

In Chapter 8, 'Leadership in High Performing Organizations', Shailendra Singh empirically demonstrates that high performance is the need of the times and is possible only through emotionally intelligent leadership.

In Chapter 9, 'Transformational Leadership, Values, and Effectiveness: Towards Creating a Context for Value-based Leadership', Sumita Rai and Arvind K. Sinha used factor analysis to derive the dimensions of transformational leadership and show that transformational leadership has a meaningful and significant relationship with aspects of personal effectiveness. They also argued that the realization of certain values adds to the strength of association of transformational leadership with some of the aspects of personal effectiveness.

In Chapter 10, 'Knowledge Management for Sustainable Innovation', Archana Shukla and R. Srinivasan examined the knowledge management programme as an integrated process of managing organizational change. It is argued that the emphasis is on acquisition and creation of new knowledge through sharing of current practices rather than creation of new practices, and products or services. Therefore, it is needed to be recognized that new learning and knowledge is acquired when there is an interaction between experience and new information. The chapter focuses on how to make knowledge management programmes foster innovation and creativity in organizations.

In Chapter 11, 'Team-based Leadership for Non-Government Organizations', Mary P. Sebastian and Shivganesh Bhargava examined the role of leadership on effective management of non-government organizations (NGOs) for sustainable development. They emphasize why team-based leadership is a powerful strategy in improving the effectiveness of NGOs through a case analysis.

In Chapter 12, 'Managerial Leadership and Power', G.S. Das analysed a case to demonstrate the relationship between power and leadership in the context of enhancing organizational performance.

In Chapter 13, 'Effect of Empowerment in Indian Industries: An Empirical Analysis', K.S. Gupta empirically examined the state of empowerment in Indian organizations.

In Chapter 14, 'Building a Value-based Corporate Character: The Wipro Experience', R. Padmaja and Manisha Singh emphasized the importance of value-based corporate governance.

In Chapter 15, 'Meaning to India of Emerging Global Concepts of Ethics and Leadership Effectiveness', R.C. Sekhar presented the Indian perspective. He pointed out that the post-modernist fear that any leadership, structure or system might turn out to be oppressive and should therefore, be done away with is a cry of desperation and not a credible alternative.

In the last chapter, U. Pareek on 'India Transiting to the New Millennium: Kurt Lewin Remembered', re-examined the past and demonstrates the contribution of great scholars like Lewin in the study of such social aspects of organization as leadership and organizational performance.

This volume provides a holistic perspective of how to be an effective leader in this century. One has to carefully see the contexts and environment before finalizing a strategy.

References

Bass, B.M. (1985). *Leadership and Performance Beyond Expectation*. New York: Free Press.

Bennis, W.G. and B. Nanus (1985). *Leaders: The Strategies for Taking Charge*. New York: Harper and Row.

Chakrabarty, S.K. (1999). *The Wisdom Leadership*. Delhi: Wheeler.

Conger, J.A. and R.N. Kanungo (1988). *The Charismatic Leadership*. San-Francisco: Jossey-Bass.

Collins, J. (2001). *Good to Great*. New York: HarperCollins Publishers.

Gardner, W.L. and B.J. Avolio (1988). 'The Charismatic Relationship: A Dramaturgical Perspective'. *Academy of Management Review*. 23(1), 52–58.

Ghosh, A. (2000). 'Leadership Effectiveness: Issues and Challenges'. Paper presented at the National Seminar on Leadership and Human Values held at the IIM, Lucknow (12–14 April, 2000).

Khandwalla, P. (1982). *A Turnaround Strategy*. Vikalpa.

Nanus, B. (1992). *Visionary Leadership*. New York: Free Press.

Pfeffer, J. (1992). *Managing with Power*. Boston: Harvard Business School.

Saskin, M. (1988). 'Visionary Leader'. In J.A. Conger and R.N. Kanungo (eds.), *The Charismatic Leadership*. San-Francisco: Jossey-Bass.

Singh, P. (in press). *Contours of 21st Century Leadership*.

Singh, P. and A. Bhandarker (1989). *Transformational Leadership*. New Delhi: Wiley.

Sinha, J.B.P. (1980). *The Nurturant Task Leadership*. New Delhi: Concept.

1

Leadership in Unpredictable Times

DHARNI P. SINHA

We are living in a world characterized by discontinuous and speedy change; unprecedented global reach because of the internet revolution; and an *unsettling of the economy* where traditional businesses are losing their attraction and new businesses are yet to establish themselves.

The speed of change is best illustrated by the way technology has reached human homes; radio reached fifty million homes in fifty years, the telephone in thirteen years, and the internet in four years. Today news reaches billions of people worldwide instantly. The information revolution has at the same time contributed to faster obsolescence of technology, system and management practices. Managerial tasks have consequently become more complex requiring business leaders to stay on their toes all the time.

Unprecedented reach because of the internet and the convergence of technologies such as audio, video and computers has enlarged markets beyond domestic boundaries, and opened up opportunities for a company to become global very quickly. Interestingly, one of the portals on business schools launched by COSMODE, Bizkool.com, had 250,000 visitors in seventeen days—not even the world's largest shopping mall can accommodate so many visitors in such a short time! This phenomenal reach presents unbelievable potential for those who have the leadership skills to exploit them!

The unsettling economy has created a flux in the landscape of business all over the world. Multinationals are invading developing economies, established businesses are losing their hold; large companies are disappearing because of pressures from larger ones, leading to acquisition and mergers; and restructuring of corporations is creating a larger pool of unemployment, thus destabilizing the balance between economy and manpower utilization. India, too, is witnessing all these trends; Hindustan Lever has acquired and merged Brooke Bond, Lipton, Kissan, Tomco and Kwality and emerged as a mega corporation, retaining its leadership in the FMCG sector; HDFC has acquired Times Bank; Gujarat Ambuja has acquired a sizeable equity of ACC which has enhanced its available capacity; the Tatas have divested several businesses such as cement and soap, to remain focused; IOC, Reliance and GAIL and many other companies are expanding through acquisition and ensuring sustainability through divestment and downsizing. All this has had tremendous impact: both positive and negative. To avoid chaos, conflict and instability in the economy and society it is imperative to address these squarely.

Resilient Leaders

To meet the challenges of these unpredictable times, what is needed, among other initiatives, is resilient leaders. Resilience calls for elasticity, buoyancy, adaptability and strong life energy. When JJ Irani became CEO of TISCO, the steel gaint, it was in the dumps. Under his resilient leadership TISCO became and showed record performance. Lack of resilience manifests in paralysis, defensiveness, cynicism and despair, among individuals as well as organization. Binny, a one-time leading textile company has almost disappeared; so have Remington Rand, Hindustan Teleprinters and Hindustan Photo Films. Martin Burn, Andrew Yule and others have met a similar fate. Many public enterprises have had paralytic strokes; some closed down, others downsized or privatized. Ambiguity and uncertainty in an organization causes paralysis; if not coped with well, business declines and there is insecurity among employees. Further, it debilitates the organization's energy and ability to find creative solutions.

COSMODE's continuing research on corporate leadership in India has enhanced our understanding of the role of leadership in organization development; strategic leadership for growth; leadership for creativity and innovation; sectoral leadership such as political leadership, academic leadership, business leadership; and leadership for institution building. The latest research has led to the configuration of the profile of leadership in uncertainty.

Research has shown that resilient leaders have a definitive personal profile which integrates seven characteristics and is reflected in their behavioral pattern. These characteristics are:

1. Clarity of purpose embedded in values
2. Strong personal identity
3. Self-driven; self-motivated
4. Commitment to life-long, continuous learning
5. Active personal and professional networks
6. Well-articulated internal standards
7. Action orientation

Let me deal with these one by one.

Purpose

Resilient leaders are guided by a larger sense of purpose, and are driven by values. The purpose gives them a direction, if not destination, helps them to determine their dos and don'ts, and keeps them focused even in turbulent times. Tempered by values, the purpose may not coincide with their company's mission; but there is an alignment between their purpose and the organizational process.

Resilient leaders are guided by the larger perspective that purpose provides, which in turn makes them proud of making contribution to the organization they serve. Dr Anji Reddy, CEO of Reddy's Lab, is a scientist whose purpose in life has been to discover new molecules which will contribute towards healthy human life and he has relentlessly pursued this goal. The most profitable pharmaceutical company in India, Reddy's Lab has emerged as a leading pharmaceutical organization with a global presence.

Personal Identity

Resilient leaders have a strong sense of personal identity, and are distinctive. They are self-aware: they know what they are and what they are not; and they know how they succeeded and why they failed; and, more important, they work consistently towards validating their personal worth. They do not merge their personal identity with their career identity, but recognize that they are more than what they do at work; they are aware that they are part of a larger whole: the community, the region, the nation.

They can negotiate both placid as well as turbulent situations, and deal with ambiguous and complex realities. They have multiple internal gears, even the reverse gear, which may be required to reach the destination. Of the many resilient leaders, one who personifies this quality in abundance is Purnendu Chatterjee, a financial wizard, who has been part of George Soros Group and who is known for making and unmaking many national economies. Chatterjee raised a billion dollars to establish a global institute of technology in India. He, along with many NRIs, wanting to repay their debt to the country of their origin. The bureaucracy, however, was sceptical about the project and they were thus forced to abandon it. But Chatterjee has not given up; he is determined to overcome the bureaucratic constraints and reach his destination. Thus resilient leaders have conviction, a strong identity and the courage to navigate in a turbulent environment.

Self-driven

There was a time when leaders relied on the organization to chart out their career path. But resilient leaders create their own career path, which may not necessarily be linear. They are self-driven, prepared to move sideways, up and down, accept new assignments or even change their career. They exude self-confidence; they are not prone to dependence, counter-dependence or even independence, they recognize interdependence with others within and outside the organization and believe that working together helps them achieve personal goals as well as organizational objectives. Colonel S.P. Wahi who has been credited for building India's largest public enterprise, the Oil and Natural Gas Corporation (ONGC), is an outstanding example of a self-driven leader. He began his career in Avadhi Tank Factory; driven by the urge to construct the largest steel plant in the public sector, he moved to Bokaro Steel when it was in the project phase. Not satisfied with his achievement, he moved to Bharat Heavy Electricals Limited where he did a commendable job and earned the challenging assignment of head, ONGC. During the global oil crisis he enhanced oil production to nearly 40 million tonnes, meeting almost 50 per cent of India's oil requirements.

Continuous Learning

Resilient leaders are continuous and life-long learners. Getting out of portals of learning such as this does not put a stop to learning; in fact it opens up new vistas to acquire new knowledge, new skills and new behavior to meet new challenges. Resilient leaders learn from experience, seek feedback and engage in introspection, reflection and honest self-appraisal. They are motivated by success as well as failure; their learning is challenged by uncertainty, ambiguity and change. They do not get paralysed by them; rather, they get energized to learn new and different ways of dealing with realities. BPL's T.P.G. Nambiar is a perfect example of a resilient leader who has scaled new frontiers of business during the last fifteen years. A technocrat, he kept up with developments in technology, learnt entrepreneurship and created a growing and diversified conglomerate. Recently he joined hands with the Tatas, Birlas and AT&T, to create a mega company providing cellular and basic teleservices. He has established a competitive edge from continuous learning, innovating and applying.

Resilience and learning go hand in hand. The pace of change puts resilient leaders on a high learning curve. Those who can adapt and align to these changes find new opportunities. Those who get immobilized in the face of change get lost. Continuous learning keeps them going.

Personal and Professional Network

Resilient leaders are not concerned about job security; they build security by networking within and outside the workplace professionally and personally. They believe that their viability depends more on the quality of their professional network rather than on their position in the organization they serve. Recent research has shown that networking is correlated with high performance. High performers understand the importance of building a network; they offer their own knowhow to others before seeking their help. The interpersonal competence of the leaders enables them to build support groups, and creates synergy with the work group within the organization and professional colleagues outside it. Among those who have perfected the art of professional networking to meet the challenges of change is Yogi Deveshwar, chairman of ITC. ITC lost its credibility when its former chairmen were discredited for allegedly defrauding the state. Deveshwar, who came to ITC from Air-India where he had served as chairman, also headed the ITC Hotels Division where he had extensive opportunity to network locally and globally, with industry and government, with stakeholders and competitors. In a short span he has restored the company's credibility as a corporate citizen.

Personal Standards

Leaders are traditionally recognized by their status symbols and the wealth they acquire. However, the identity and success of resilient leaders is assessed by the high standards they set for themselves and their expectations of themselves. Their flexibility standards stipulate innovative behavior, and creativity. They are not averse to taking risks and seeking alternative career options. Two resilient leaders who have set high personal standards, without concern for status symbols are Narayan Murthy of Infosys and Azim Premji of Wipro. Murthy lives a simple life, drives his own car and gives himself a small salary compared to others in his position. He symbolizes simplicity, stretch, creativity and innovation which have become hallmarks of Inofsys culture. Premji, the wealthiest Indian, travels economy class. Another resilient leader who fits this frame is Rajat Gupta, CEO McKinsey and Company, the world's largest consulting company. He is acknowledged as a role model in his profession, and with the high standards of personal performance, he has earned the respect of all those who work with him and those in his profession worldwide.

Action Orientation

All the foregoing characteristics are hallmarks of a resilient leader. The most defining characteristic of resilient leaders is action orientation. Resilient leaders act, even in chaos or conflict; they transform ambiguity to clarity through action. All other characteristics help them to set direction, and create enabling conditions, but their action orientation contributes to performance. Resilience comes through action—and this is the real hallmark of a resilient leader. In our study, everyone who was profiled was action oriented, achievement oriented, have emerging unscathed through the ups and downs in their business and industry.

Resilient leaders create resilient organizations, learning organization, networked organization, flat and flexible organizations, cultivating a resilient workforce and creating resilient systems. Resilient leaders are not loners; they uphold values, work with others, create resilience among them and contribute to excellence in the organizations they serve.

2

Leadership in the Twenty-first Century: Towards Corporate Renaissance

PRITAM SINGH • ASHA BHANDARKER

The desire to look into the future is as old as the impulse that made human beings read the stars to divine the shape of things to come. The oracle of Delphi in Greece is a testimony of this human urge to peep into the future. Likewise, the oldest civilizations—Babylonian, Harappan, Chinese—had oracles which used various astrological and occult techniques to predict the future.

The importance of looking into the future and creating future context cannot be undermined. Context provides' meaning to thought and action; thus, without mapping the context, there can be misplacement of priorities, misdirection of energies and, invariably, paralysis of action. Chanakya, the great strategic thinker of ancient India, stated that strategy for good governance has to be built according to time, place and people, since these create the context for strategic thinking and action. This chapter proposes to sketch the contours of the twenty-first century corporation to enable the new generation leaders to face the challenges forcibly.

The twentieth–twenty-first century contrasts are discussed around the following dimensions:

- Emergence of intelligent society;
- Dehumanization at work;

- Strategy: Top down to bottom up;
- Growth: Wealth extracting to wealth creating;
- Organization: Pyramid to web;
- Style: Stability to change;
- Reach: Domestic to global;
- Structure: Thick boundary to thin boundary;
- Operations: Vertical to virtual;
- Product: Mass Production to mass customization;
- Financial disclosure: Quarterly to real time;
- Inventories: Months to hours;
- Quality: Affordable best to no compromise;
- People: Employees to nomads;
- Job expectations: Job security to employment security;
- Leadership: Transactional to renaissance.

Emergence of the Intelligent Society

Futurologists have for long been predicting the large-scale technological changes which human societies will be confronted with. Many predictions, which sounded like science fiction at one time, are now unfolding before us, triggered by the IT revolution and more specifically the internet revolution: robotics, intelligent sensors, digital imaging, superconductivity, nano-technology, gene therapy, and biotechnology.

Micro-chips will make computing capability very cheaply available and this will trigger infinite application possibilities, endowing common objects around us with capacity for intelligent functioning; for example, intelligent clothing, intelligent household goods and households with self-regulating capabilities, cars which can auto-drive—these are only some of the probable applications in day-to-day life. The rise of the bionic human—the chip with phenomenal computing power lodged in the brain—will further accelerate human capacity to perform certain kinds of intellectual tasks. Genetic cloning, genetic engineering to extend the human life-span will alter the lives of human beings and the structure of societies in many ways. The scope to replace ageing body parts with cloned organs and genetic engineering to cure diseases are among the numerous possibilities being talked about.

An important current trend likely to get further accelerated in this century is on the dimension of information and knowledge. The net will be the major paradigm shifting force for societies as well as organizations and will transform the way we live, work, communicate and relate with each other. In the future language will not be a barrier, at least for net communication. The possibilities that will be opened up for people all over the world are mind-boggling. Some of the consequences of these shifts are:

- Global business will explode once language barriers are technologically dealt with. This will facilitate more people to get into the global loop, conduct business, and establish contacts without deep pockets and muscle power.
- The ubiquitous global access to the net will facilitate everywhere connectivity and this will mean that work will happen round the clock without adhering to any guidelines of working hours.
- With the mobile device becoming the single point of communication, the net-line will virtually become one's lifeline, connecting up with all personal information as well as facilitating personal and business transactions.
- Greater dependence on technology will perhaps also bring in greater physical isolation from each other, although there will be more virtual contact with people. People will live more in the virtual world than in the physical world.
- There will probably not be a clear distinction between work life and personal life, since connectivity will facilitate access and reach of people to each other.
- With the rise in automation in both manufacturing and office activities, full-time jobs will decline drastically.
- The profile of the customer, levels of awareness, tastes, choices and expectations will change. The concept of service and the concept of time to market will take on new meaning in the age of instant connectivity.
- With so much virtual living one wonders what will happen to emotional and spiritual lives; will the human capacity to empathize, socialize, hold humanistic values and ethical considerations lie dormant? With everything around us going intelligent, will human beings mimic the machines that they are surrounded by?

Dehumanization of Work

The ascent of technological changes and shifts in societal and organized work life (as delineated above) coincides with increasing dehumanization. It is a form of self-alienation where the person feels estranged from himself, his needs and potential. This robs him of his ability to become a more complete human being, with the ability to experience and explore not only the material and sensory side of his nature but also the psycho-emotional as well as spiritual part of himself. The Darwinian dance of heightened competition will lead to increasing survival challenges for both organizations and individuals. In such a scenario of struggle for survival, dehumanization trends in organizations will get further exacerbated.

Various factors contribute to dehumanization at the workplace. Some of these are: the temporal nature of jobs owing to the trends of downsizing; job insecurity and workaholic behavior emanating from downsizing and mergers, reward systems within companies, and fall in community connectedness.

Research has also found that downsizing leads to loss of trust and lowered commitment to work. At the emotional level, those within the company have been found to display reactions like fear, withdrawal and paralysis. Jobs are disappearing only to be replaced by intelligent machines. Initially it happened on the shop-floors of manufacturing companies; then it spread to white-collar jobs. If in the industrial age people felt they were mere cogs and components in the wheel of organizational activity, in the information era, they feel dispensable and redundant.

The phenomenon of job insecurity affects both those who keep their jobs as well as those who have to leave them. In fact the mere announcement that people in an organization are leaving simulates anxiety. An air of uncertainty, a certain lack of trust will pervade, adding to the general sense of psychological unease. The latter experience lower sense of self-esteem and self-worth since these are intimately related to social identity and well-being. This will be heightened in societies where paid work is the major contributor to social identity and individual self-worth. Those who keep their jobs are also anxious and insecure because they try to stretch themselves and work long hours to hold on to the job. People become workaholics; actually, workaholism is becoming more and more pervasive in business organizations. In this century people will be workaholics not only out of choice (as in the case of entrepreneurs who thrive on challenges) but to cope with the increased job demands and pressures.

Rewards in companies are primarily monetary and material in nature. People work for such rewards with the expectation that more money will bring them greater societal appreciation, greater happiness and a better quality of life. However, money does not provide the satisfaction of the higher level needs for affiliation, self-esteem, a sense of purpose and meaning. As such people experience free-floating discontent and dissatisfaction.

The work and organizational community can potentially substitute the above, since people spend most of their lives at work. However, even this source of affiliation will get eroded, for three reasons:

- The changing employment patterns with people hopping jobs will lead to the formation of transient communities.
- Downsizing and retrenchment will lead to lack of full-time employment and will create a psychic vacuum at the individual level.
- Companies will be in the growth and survival mode, and the pace of work will get accelerated to cope with the demands. Consequently corporations will pay less attention to people's community needs.

The combination of these factors will result in people experiencing greater self-alienation as well as alienation from the community.

Strategy: Top-down to Bottom-up

The twentieth century corporations were well known for their large headquarters where corporate plans and strategy were evolved. In the true tradition of departmentalization, thinking and planning were also given a specialist status and the planning department aided the strategy-building process of the CEO. CEOs along with planning departments used to develop business strategy keeping at least a one-year time horizon. Thus, business strategies of the twentieth century organizations were built in a top-centric fashion, and subsequently percolated top-down for implementation. People on the scene of action—marketing, operations, finance, human resources and industrial relations—were not tapped for inputs and information to enhance the quality and acceptance of strategy. As a result, many strategic plans while being powerful blueprints could not be adequately implemented. Thus many companies experienced a gap between strategic thinking and strategic action. In fact, a major preoccupation of top management was to push strategy implementation. This approach worked quite weil in the less turbulent twentieth century since product life-cycles were longer and strategic planning was for incremental improvement.

Towards the end of the twentieth century, business experienced fierce competition, uncertainties and complexities, necessitating a paradigm shift in strategy formulation. The twenty-first century will see these phenomena in full-blown form, with the business environment getting much more turbulent, chaotic and discontinuous. Emergence of shareholders' democracy, proliferation of knowledge workers, co-partnership between suppliers and the organization, changing customer tastes, customized requirements and technological developments, are just some of the emerging factors that will cause complexity.

Interaction of these multiple forces will create complex dynamics, forcing twenty-first century corporations to redraw their process of strategy formulation to keep it relevant to their business needs.

The strategy formulation process, devoid of close involvement and constant feedback from all the relevant stakeholders, would be an unproductive exercise. In the twenty-first century there is a need for strategy building through a synthetic and syncretic approach. Neither the purely top-down, nor the purely bottom-up approach will be adequate. Over-reliance on the people-driven, bottom-up approach will render the strategy devoid of future perspectives, knowledge of the latest technological developments and a holistic approach. Overemphasis on the top-driven approach results in a distancing from the ground realities of markets and demands of customers. The need is to synthesize both approaches: top-down and bottom-up. Above all, the need will be to extract the underlying patterns from the apparent chaos and complexities.

Growth Model: Wealth Extracting to Wealth Creating

Companies of the old economy operating in the latter decades of the twentieth century grew by continuous improvement. They used techniques such as Business Process Engineering (BPR) downsizing, rightsizing, cost cutting, six sigma, financial restructuring, mergers, acquisitions, which helped them derive the maximum possible benefits from their businesses. Companies adopted the strategy of business restructuring by vacating non-core businesses. Growth was more through optimal and efficient utilization of resources.

These strategies helped twentieth century organizations to extract the wealth from the company. However, for companies to grow and create wealth in the twenty-first century, a shift is needed from the wealth-extracting model to a wealth-creating one.

The emerging opportunities in the current business environment (fuelled by technology, net and convergence) offer tremendous scope for new, wealth creating products and services. The pace at which products (and services) are going extinct and demand for new ones is increasing indicates the gap and the opportunities that exist therein to create new products and services. To tap these opportunities a new business model and an entrepreneurial approach will be needed. Imaginative and innovative approaches will provide the scope to release wealth, rather than merely extracting from old business models which bring only diminishing returns. By using the wealth-creating route companies can create second-curve thinking to help them stay competitive. Twenty-first century organizations will need leader–entrepreneurs (John Chambers, JRD Tata, Bill Gates, Narayan Murthy, Sabeer Bhatia, Jorma Olila, Sanjeev Sidhu) who can tap new business opportunities and who could develop new core competencies.

The Organization: From Pyramid to Web

Organizations of the twentieth century were built in a tall pyramidal fashion. The origin of this shape lay in the Weberian bureaucratic model, combined with the Taylorian tenets of work specialization and Fordian semi-automatic assembly-line production. The basic mindset of these companies was that top management were the thinkers, planners and analyzers, whereas those at the lower levels were the doers and the imple-menters. This reflected the hierarchy embedded in the brahmanical social order differentiating between the thinkers and doers. Management layers were added between the thinkers and doers to monitor, coordinate and control functioning down the line. The lowest levels consisted of large numbers of people who produced and worked without much authority.

In such a set-up decision-making powers vested with top management who controlled the company. Those down the line—the doers—felt dis-empowered and experienced a lack of control over work leading to a sense of alienation, and helplessness.

Over time, people down the line actually began to behave as if they were incapable of thinking. It became a quid pro quo situation, with the management in turn assuming that people at the lower levels were incapable of thinking and decision-making. Thus, in the hierarchical organizational model, even people who had ideas, who could contribute to work improvements based on their direct experience with the work, stopped doing so, because no one really valued what a lower level employee had to say. Perhaps, gradually, they even stopped thinking. To manage feelings of powerlessness and lack of control many employees directed their energies to unionize, or sabotage, slow down and delay work. Since hierarchies were so tall, top management soon lost touch with the ground realities. They focused more on monitoring and chasing targets, paying scant attention either to quality or customer needs.

To thrive in the fast-shifting twenty-first century business realities, organizations must become flatter and mimic the network structure of the spider's web: in touch, flexible yet resilient. Being flatter will enable organizational members to be in greater contact with the ground realities. The key actors will also be highly accessible to both internal and external customers, decision-making will be faster and all ideas will have a fair chance of being shared and utilized. This will provide opportunities for the churning of ideas to build a roadmap to compete effectively. In the flat and networked organization, there will be a greater sense of empowerment, since all will have greater responsibility and every person will be valued. The nodal points of the flat web will typically be the leaders that hold the web of relationships together and collectively drive the company business. These nodal (leadership) points will have to work both independently and together.

The supporting architecture of the company will span continents, with nodes of the set-up being located in different parts of the world. Such a structure will render organizations boundary-less and geographical distances meaningless. This web-shaped corporation will behave like a living organism, totally sensitive to its environment, ready to respond to the environmental challenges and threats. People will experience control of all the tasks and activities especially since information will be readily available for timely decision-making. Further, with no division between thinkers and doers there will be a synthesis of thought and action. People will feel empowered to act effectively. The pace of decision-making in organizations will improve greatly because of the ready availability of information at all levels.

The move from the pyramidal to the web structure will help companies to respond more speedily to customer requirements; it will improve efficiency by facilitating greater outsourcing and easy online monitoring of the performance of suppliers, vendors and partners and enable integration of their activities into the organizational systems for cohesive action.

Style: Stability to Change

Three distinguishing features of twentieth century corporations were stability, structured mode of functioning and inward focus. These companies thrived by building stable organizations, characterized by predictability and control. Planning and forecasting were done using rational and linear approaches. There was preoccupation with developing elaborate systems to maintain, administer and monitor organizational activities.

Rules and systems were given greater weightage and, in due course of time, often became an end in themselves rather than a means to an end. Managements of many companies expected employees to work according to well-laid-out patterns and follow set reporting relationships. Conformity was approved of and deviance generally discouraged.

Such companies fulfilled market needs and wielded enormous power in terms of the money and resources at their command. As their power and reach increased, however, they developed a mindset of complacency to the extent that they took the customer for granted and did not pay attention to the emerging competition. The entry of companies like Toyota, Honda, Nissan in the American automobile markets, was not seen as a threat by incumbents like Ford and General Motors, such was their delusion of invincibility. Many mighty American and European corporations were beaten by Japanese companies like Cannon, Sharp, Sony, Panasonic, Toshiba. This happened because of their complacency and inward approach.

In the twenty-first century the rules of business are changing rapidly. The game will shift from firm ground to fluid ground.

Moving companies in the direction of change without being slowed down by the forces of stability will be critical. Technology will provide companies newer tools (this in turn will trigger dis-equilibrium within the industry) for improving speed, quality and efficiency. Although such dynamic shifts will be most evident in industries operating at the bleeding edge of technology—like computer chip making, software, telecom, mobile telephony, systems integration—no industry segment can remain untouched by the IT and web-enabled factors contributing to building speed and connectivity.

To compete on fluid ground, corporations will have to scan and sense the environment, the threats, the challenges and the competition, enhance capability, learn constantly, and reorient, reposition and respond. The outward orientation will help companies to read the signals from the market and the customer. Keeping your finger on the pulse of your customer will become a requirement. To thrive in such a scenario an entrepreneurial result-focused style, searching for newer and better ways to provide value to the customer will be needed. In the twenty-first century, those companies cultivating an outward orientation, change orientation and flexibility will be able to become the winners and the value creators.

Reach: Local to Global

Twentieth century corporations functioned as monopolies in domestic markets. They could thrive because there were virtually no challengers and because there was a strong home market. For decades they prospered by producing the same products with marginal improvements. With the onset change in the geo-political profile worldwide, adopted the capitalist model of growth increasing deregulation, reduction of tariff barriers and greater moves towards global integration.

The process of globalization has received an immense boost owing to the emergence of the IT-enabled networks which provide instant reach and real-time interaction.

The internet age has immensely boosted the reach and ability of giant companies like General Electric (GE), Sony, Toshiba, Omron, IBM, Coca Cola, Levi Strauss, Intel, Siemens AG, Compaq, Hewlett-Packard, Canon, Honda and Toyota Nissan to compete all over the world. Their ability to be truly global has been immensely boosted—they can monitor performance real time, they can conference across multi locations, they can access real time information from all over the world. Above all, they can do all these with great speed.

Globalization will benefit both customers and the companies. The customer will benefit through a wider variety to choose from; also, availability of information about prices and services of various companies (through the net) will enable selection based on price competitiveness. Prices will therefore move downward, as co-competitors as well as customers know competitors' pricing.

Companies will also benefit immensely as they will be able to reach out to multiple markets. They will not have to be big to get global reach— what they will need is a presence on the web and niche products that meet basic quality specifications and are competitively priced, combined with a lower time to market. Companies will also benefit by the ability to outsource work to various lower cost locations. For example, companies like IBM, Intel, TI, have been outsourcing some of their functions to Indian companies. In the future outsourcing will take a big leap as more and more companies strive to drive down costs.

Twenty-first century companies will have to build global operations and global alliances and managers will have to build global mindsets, both in terms of understanding and appreciating cross-cultural nuances as well as working with diversity.

Structure: From Thick Boundaries to Thin Boundaries

Twentieth-century organizations built thick boundaries between themselves and the environment as well as across departments within the organization. Weberian division of responsibility across functions encouraged the formulation of thick interdepartmental boundaries. In Indian companies, thick boundaries are typically seen not only across departments, but also across organizational hierarchy.

In thick boundary corporation, self-sufficiency and independence characterized the mindset. Reporting relationships were rigidly maintained across the hierarchy and functions. People were encouraged to restrict themselves to their job descriptions, roles and departments. Suggestions and feedback given across departments were viewed as interference. People developed a narrow focus and approach, and in fact often there were fierce turf battles across departments and divisions. Employees considered their job done when their particular activity was completed. Few bothered about outcomes and customers. Thus, managers became constrained and limited.

The twenty-first century corporation has to exist in a time-strapped era, where speed is of the essence to stay competitive. Most inputs are available, except time. There is no time to wait for problems to travel up the hierarchy and for the boss to give decisions. In addition to the obvious delays in decision-making, this style of functioning gets perverted when highly qualified knowledge workers operate at the lower levels and the inevitable ego clashes take place across the hierarchy.

With cogent and speedy responses to customer demands becoming increasingly essential in this century, organizations will not be effective if they continue to function by splitting into narrow bands and segments. Since the focus is on customer service, interdepartmental boundaries need to be really thin so that there is relevant information flow and people work together and sort out issues to meet customer requirements. The internal organizational mindset will have to be broad enough for people to identify with the larger organizational vision and respond to customer needs, rather than limiting their perspective merely to the task, job, role or department. This mindset will lead to cooperative and problem-solving behavior, a must to become a winner.

The external organizational boundaries will also have to be thin and porous to enable flexibility and outward orientation. More important, the ability to strike up alliances, and partnerships as well as develop vendors to enable reliable, predictable and efficient outsourcing will be critical.

Vertical Organization to Virtual Organization

Organizations of the twentieth century operated in the mode of self-sufficiency without depending on outside agencies. Whether in the coal, steel or manufacturing sectors, companies invested in infrastructure to build power plants, rail routes, roads, ports, etc. Engineering companies even had their own tool rooms from where they sourced their requirements. In large automobile and engineering companies, many divisions established which manufactured components and spares. Companies built business models where they got into upstream as well as downstream businesses in an effort to become more self-sufficient. Companies thus became vertically integrated and still made profits because of the less competitive and more stable business environment. As competition increased, hidden inefficiencies and unproductive practices of companies came to the fore.

In the twenty-first century, companies can no longer afford to be inefficient and costly—to survive they will have to become cost competitive and fit; they will have to vacate areas of non-core competence and focus exclusively on areas of their core competence and outsource all that they can get done cheaply and effectively. They will have to move to the virtual integration model of organization.

The shift to a virtual integration model will no doubt hinge on the development of dependable partners who are committed to the company goal. The mode of doing business will itself thus change dramatically. Again, technology will become a very powerful tool to accelerate communication across related business partners to mobilize the needed support services, and materials when they are needed. A major challenge to the success of the virtually integrated organization will be efficient supply chain management. Perhaps the truly virtual organization will be one in which the company has the option to choose across multiple suppliers/vendors based on their ability to provide better value for money. Such a company will be dynamic with immense flexibility to continuously improve efficiencies in every sphere of its business activities.

Products: Mass Production to Mass Customization

Mass production prevailed for a large part of the twentieth century. Companies produced in bulk to cater to booming markets, whether it was automobiles, personal care products or electronic goods. The general attitude of companies was that 'we know what the customer needs'. Operating on the principle of mass production companies paid scant attention to feedback from the market. For example, when computer companies were producing mainframe computers, Microsoft came up with the strategy of building desktop personal computers. On the other hand, Wang Labs, a highly successful mainframe company, did not sense the customer disposition towards PCs—their assumption was, 'we know what they need'. Thus, they quickly lost out to the competition as customer's switched en masse to desktop PCs.

The twentieth-century mindset of 'we know what they need' was so strong that many companies despite operating in markets with different needs and requirements stuck to the strategy of selling the same product worldwide. For example, for a long time Siemens India persisted in selling costly electrical products in India with features more useful in temperate climate and with not much utility in a tropical climate. The mindset here was, 'they don't know what a great product we are offering them; it is bound to be costly, customers should understand this'. Such companies managed to do well until the competitor emerged and provided better value for money to the customer. The latter part of the twentieth century witnessed the overwhelming competition in the electronics goods segments—from cameras, music systems, VCRs to VCPs, photocopiers, computers. The strategies and mindsets of the twentieth century will not provide the competitive edge in the twenty-first century. In fact in the twenty-first century, markets will be saturated the ease of access to information from multifarious sources via the web will create greater customer awareness, of options available worldwide. Call centres and Customer Relationship Management (CRM) systems will make customers used to instant service.

The twenty-first century customer will strive to establish a unique and differentiated identity and view products as an expression of self. However, the impulses for identity expression through product usage would be significantly heightened, given the scope and opportunity for expression.

Enhanced awareness, the plethora of information and higher educational levels will truly make the customer a king. In the twenty-first century, no company will therefore be able to say 'the customer is king' as a mere platitude: this will have to be practised in its fullest sense. The Gandhian concept of customer as God (Customer is God. We exist for the customer, he does not exist for us) will become acutely relevant, and companies that build their growth strategy around unique customer specifications and as per customer configuration will take the lead.

Financial Disclosure: Annual

For the better part of the century, the twentieth-century corporation operated on annual financial performance disclosure. In the last decade, however, there was a shift from annual to half-yearly and then to quarterly exercises. This was on account of stock market regulations and pressure from the investors to continuously gauge company performance. Companies were primarily operating on mindset of maximizing own wealth, and paying little attention to maximizing shareholder wealth. Companies have now also started focusing on maximizing shareholder wealth and have financial instruments like EVA for measuring the same.

The twenty-first century investor will be much more demanding, aware of rights and practise shareholder's democracy. The investor will thus expect performance information on a real-time basis.

Behavior at the stock market will be determined by this information, and investors will be able to load and unload shares wherever they can get better returns.

Thus organisations in this century will have to be highly transparent; they will have to share real-time performance data online. Companies using this approach will be highly valued, admired and trusted, and will attract investors. They will be in a position to mobilize financial resources and become attractive to all stakeholders.

Inventories: Months/Hours

The twentieth-century business scenario was characterized by a seller's market. Companies faced uncertainty regarding availability of materials. They were also limited by the lack of technology support and transportation bottlenecks and therefore had to perforce stock up. They thus built up inventories for months to ensure continuity of production. There were other kinds of inventories as well, for instance work-in-progress, finished goods inventory, which increased carrying costs and blocked capital. Companies also operated on a multi-supplier approach to ensure material availability. Towards the end of the twentieth century, companies built model of 'just-in-time' (JIT), kanban, vendor development, vendor rating and co-partnership with suppliers to minimize inventory-carrying costs. They began to develop a new mindset, of that inventory management in terms of months rather than the previously prevailing yearly, half yearly and quarterly.

In the twenty-first century corporation, the dynamics of cutting costs to increase competitiveness will make companies adopt the zero-inventory approach, by ensuring delivery of work/material based on requirement immediate. Systems like vendor satisfaction indices will become more and more relevant. Companies will have to outsource non-core company activities, like logistics, maintenance-related service, logistics, even manufacturing. Increasing IT-based support mechanisms—internet, intranet—will make it infinitely easier to outsource, monitor and place orders. This will presuppose efficient supply chain management.

In the twenty-first century, with all non-core activities getting outsourced, vendor development will become more crucial than ever before. Further, company perceptions mindsets regarding these agencies have to undergo a radical shift. They must be viewed as partners and treated as such. Vendors may have a greater commitment to company goals provided a relationship is built with them and trust is developed depending on how the company treats them. A win-win approach has to be followed in dealing with vendors. Perhaps what needs to be explored is the possibility of integrating vendors' goals with those of the organization to ensure vendor dependability. However, the growing dependence of more and more companies on vendors may result in a shift in the balance of power of the company vis-à-vis vendors/suppliers. The challenge here would be to manage this balance of power so as to mitigate dangers of dependence on outside agencies. In a situation of inter-dependence, both vendors and the company will work together for win-win.

Quality: Affordable Best—No Compromise

For much of the twentieth century the attitude to quality was 'this is best we can give', be it in electronics or automobiles or electric goods.

The Japanese brought in superior quality products to world markets at cheaper rates; for instance, Sony with its audio systems; Toyota and Honda with cars. It was only when competition peaked those attempts were made to understand the Japanese systems of quality improvement. By utilizing techniques such as outsourcing, JIT, teamworking, empowerment for problem solving to the shop-floor employee.

With the emergence of the borderless world as also the reduction of tariff barriers, twenty-first century customers will be much more conscious and aware of the options before them. They will not compromise on quality and will look for corporations that will provide the best quality product as also best value for money. Thus purchase preferences will be determined more by product quality and convenience than any other factors.

People: Employees to Nomads

In the twentieth-century corporation full-time jobs were highly valued for the security and status they provided, which used authority to get work done. While, this led to greater loyalty, concern for company interests and contribution focus; this type of psychological contract often also created management problems. Employees took companies for granted and developed many inefficient and wasteful practices. Organizations became the major playing ground for them to give vent to their competitive and aggressive instincts. In fact, organizations invariably got caught in the crossfire and company resources got misused.

In the twenty-first century the trend will shift quite dramatically. The massive restructuring exercises, technology-related developments, outsourcing models, will lead to greater job losses. Most large companies will have a smaller percentage of full-time jobs; the job market will have many part-time jobs and contract jobs, which will be handled by smaller companies and loose networks of people possessing complementary skills. In fact there will be greater scope for entrepreneurial efforts, self-employment, taking advantage of the opportunities thrown up by technological developments.

Part-time employment will fetch more returns to those with niche skills, as compared to those with the older or commonly available skills. Since job markets will be fragmented, its also likely that people will be paid much less for these skills. The issue gets complex because today's niche skills will become tomorrow's commonly available skills. People will thus wander from organization to organization. The consequences of this type of nomadic working will be felt at the individual, social as well as organizational levels. At the individual level, there will be greater uncertainty and anxiety to continuously learn and upgrade. People are likely to develop a short-term focus and have only a transient commitment and loyalty towards the company hiring their services. Further, there will be greater focus on self-advancement.

On the positive side, there will be greater work involvement, greater learning and a willingness to stretch. At the organizational level, there will be greater efficiency on routine jobs, less apparent costs and less redundancy. All this will translate into greater short-term efficiency.

To deal with medium- and long-term issues, however, companies will need highly specific competencies to build their competitiveness. In fact companies will be chasing talent by paying a premium. Retaining these people for a reasonable length of time will be the major challenge before companies. For long-term growth and sustainable competitive edge, companies will need people highly committed and able to concretize the company's vision and translate plans into action. The nomadic employees will contribute to the current company activities, not to creating the future.

Job Expectations: Job Security

In the twentieth century people joined companies for secure jobs. The mindset was to work hard and rebuild their lives. In Indian context, there was a scramble for government jobs since these provided job security and status. Authority of the company and management was accepted because in exchange people got secure jobs.

In the twenty-first century milieu, job security will be further threatened due to the constant changes in the mode of business transactions. There will be a constant demand for newer skills and competencies as these get more obsolete. There will be rapid technological obsolescence with the emergence of newer technologies. IT will play a much more powerful role in redefining work processes. Unless people keep pace with the rate of change they will be out of job. At the individual level there will be a need for continuous learning and development of new skills and competencies. Organizations will continually have to redraw their strategies for redeployment, building, learning and development of new skills and competencies, not only for achieving a competitive edge but to survive. A new work contract will emerge in this new scenario. According to researchers, under this psychological contract employees will exchange performance for continuous learning and marketability. The continued quest of both individuals and organizations will be building continued employability.

Job Expectations: Compensation—Self Actualization

In the twentieth century, the primary reason for working in corporations was adequate monetary compensation. A person's social status and acceptance were linked to the amount of money he had. Organizations leveraged on this and built their motivational strategies accordingly.

In the twenty-first century with its hi-tech and intelligent environment, people will be looking beyond the satisfaction of materialistic and hedonistic needs. With all the technological advancements and control over nature, a big challenge for people will be to understand themselves and develop their potential, talents and capacities. At the workplace, they will look not only for money, but also for values such as a sense of meaning, and personal, professional and spiritual growth. People will want to work in organizations where there is a sense of meaning.

Leadership: Transactional to Renaissance

In the twentieth century organization—characterized by structured, hierarchical centralized systems—the leader was the boss, the all in all, the key actor, the decision-maker, and he determined the destiny of the organization. The mindset of the organization was therefore to look up to the boss. 'The boss is always right' was the typical twentieth century organizational mindset.

In the twenty-first century, corporations will be flatter, decentralized, and loosely structured, and their operations globally dispersed. In addition they will be knowledge corporations, grappling with changes and increasing complexity, with innovation and experimentation being a way of life. Niche expertise will play a significant role in providing the winning edge. There will be the emergence of self-actualizing and eupsychian human beings; the number of knowledge workers will increase.

To provide effective leadership in the above context, a drastic shift in leadership style will be essential. Corporations will need leaders who can bring about a renaissance and a renewal. The key to this will lie in the ability of leaders to touch the consciousness of people, inspire, provide a unique sense of meaning, leadership through personal power rather than through old style authority. Teamwork will predominate over legitimate authority. Renaissance leaders will therefore need to create a work culture of tolerance of failure, openness to new ideas, and freedom for experimentation and exploration.

Renaissance leaders will need the capacity to collectivize and carry people along by inspiring them. This becomes especially important in the context of globally dispersed work units. To effectively deal with global operations, the leader will also have to build multiple leaders with a CEO mindset. They will have to empower, delegate, facilitate, support and play the role of coach and mentor.

The emergence of Eupsychian human beings will necessitate a leadership style, that can inspire, create a sense of identity, higher purpose and goal, as also provide opportunity for continued psychic and spiritual development.

Renaissance leaders will have to build the organizational spirit to deconstruct the present organization and reconstruct in line with future challenges.

What to deconstruct and how much to deconstruct will be the major renaissance challenge. With leadership requirements becoming more and more complex, the task of providing leadership is getting tough.

Conclusion

This chapter has highlighted the key shifts in the business environment as well as the contrasts on various organizational dimensions between companies of the twentieth century and those of the twenty-first centuries. On some dimensions, for example, emergence of the intelligent society, the shifts have already begun to. These shifts will in turn influence the changes on the organizational dimensions.

The contours of the business landscape indicate the presence of steep peaks of success as well as valleys of failure; there are opportunities to make big gains and fall down equally fast. Organizations have to beware what appears promising may not really be so, the deception may occur from the massive media based campaigns taken up by industry segments to drive growth of intangible products like ideas and software.

Though akin to computer-aided landscape painting, the only difference is that there is not one painter of this landscape; rather there are many painters who can simultaneously work on it. The confounding part is the speed at which such alterations can be made, which further compounds the complexity and uncertainty of the business scenario. The multiplicity of competitors only adds to the need for speed to ensure gains from the early mover advantage.

Organizations can navigate this treacherous business landscape through unusual and innovative means, which ultimately translate, into customer benefit in some way or the other. In this race, organizations will have to both recreate the environment as well as go along with environment-led priorities. Emerging organizations need to rethink and reposition in the context of intelligent society and accompanying dehumanization. They will have to become leaner, faster, open and change-oriented; develop an entrepreneurial attitude to take advantage of the opportunities thrown up by the need to create new products and services; they will have to work from a global perspective; redefine the meaning of quality and customer service; work with people in creative and new ways to involve, inspire and facilitate their functioning. Above all, they will need to build new mindsets on everything—strategy, technology, process, people and products.

The dimensions delineated above are more generic in nature, from the perspective of the broader scenario of business. While many of the challenges mentioned apply in the Indian business context, there are others that are specific and unique to it. This uniqueness stems from factors like culture and values, relatively late entry into world markets post-liberalization; the pace of technology absorption and larger role of government, which colour and intensify the nature of the challenges.

References

Gary, Hamel (2000). *Leading the Revolution*. Harvard Business School.
Heller, R. and Spenley, Paul (2000). *Riding the Revolution. How Businesses Can and Must Transform Themselves to Win the E-war*. London: Harper Collins.

3

Value-based Corporate Governance

M. RADHASWAMY • VINEET BASOTIA

Value-based corporate governance is essential in today's corporate scenario. It results when good governance becomes an important goal of the board of directors. Good governance is considered a combination of two aspects, namely, higher values and effective functioning. There are two views that can be adopted by corporates for good governance: business and spiritual views. The spiritual view is backed by dictums from the ancient Indian texts.

The term value-based governance necessitates a clear understanding of the two key words, values and governance. What are the implications when these two words are used together? 'Governance' in the context of the corporate scenario refers to 'governing the corporate', which is the collective responsibility of the board of directors.

The board can thus be understood as a body which acts as a steering mechanism for the corporate. Involvement in long-term decision-making, formulating strategies for growth, evolving corporate culture and an appropriate value system in dealings, building corporate image and framing the boundaries of corporate responsibility are among the important aspects of the functioning of the board.

The Value Foundation

The term value can be explained as the adherence to ideal behavior and expected norms, as not acting in a manner which adversely affects or is detrimental to people and environment.

When we speak of the term 'governance', which is built on the foundation of values, various aspects have to be addressed. An organization is a combination of individuals. Starting from workers at the assembly line, to lower, middle, top management, the CEO, and then the board of directors. The board is a group of individuals who make policy decisions not in isolation but with proper understanding and consensus among themselves and also with the management. If their decisions have to bear a stamp of values, then it will be incumbent on all board members to be individuals with high value standards and a clear understanding and acceptance of value-based norms.

A demarcation regarding individual and group values has to be made. Every individual functions and performs duties in adherence to the value norms of society to an acceptable degree. If the individual is part of a group or a body, as in the case of board of directors, individual values have to be transferred to, or evolved into acceptable group values, which can act as guideposts or directives of action for all the members of the group.

The board comprises individuals from various fields of knowledge and belonging to various organizations to form a cohesive mix of talent and thus constitutes a resource of the organization to successfully implement its vision and strategic objectives. Each individual in the board has his or her best to offer with regard to values, and a synergy of the combined values gives birth to a vision based on values for the organization. Thus higher value norms among the members of the board leads to higher value acceptability and value orientation in the organization. To illustrate this point, suppose nine members of the board are rated on a scale of ten for a concept called Value Quotient (VQ), the higher the rating of each member the higher is the average VQ of the whole board. Thus the VQ of the board as a whole is dependent on the individual VQ of its members.

For value-based governance, values should be part and parcel of the vision and mission of the organization. It is not enough for the board to take an idealistic decision in isolation; the management and employees at all levels must be able to understand and accept the decision in the true spirit. The board's function is not over with adopting high value standards or by just expressing them; till the decisions of the board percolate to the lowest level in the organization, the board will not have achieved its goals of value-based governance. Further, it is the duty of the board to see that the policies, strategies, goals and responsibilities laid down or defined by its directors fall under the umbrella of organizational values and are well disseminated at all levels.

The board should have a clear feedback mechanism to ascertain the extent to which value decisions have been communicated and implemented at all levels. The points that clearly emerge from the foregoing are:

- Every individual has his or her own value norms, which depend on the individual's family background, upbringing and society.
- When individuals get together for a common goal, acceptable group values should evolve.
- The board of directors comprises a group of people responsible for the governance of the corporate to which they belong.
- The directors are collectively responsible for following value-based governance and for formulating and effectively communicating the value framework at all levels of the organization.
- Managers and employees should be able to adopt in their daily working the values adopted at the highest level.
- The directors should design a feedback mechanism whereby implementation of values can be ascertained.

The Good Corporate Governance Equation

Another commonly used term is good governance. Good governance can have numerous meanings, with every author of management literature having his or her own connotations.

From the increasing attention given to good governance in recent times, among the questions that arise are: What does good governance exactly mean? What are the end results of good governance? Who are the beneficiaries of good governance?

The Birla Committee Report presents its view regarding good governance as 'a set of recommendations which distinguishes the responsibilities and obligations of the board and the management in instituting the systems of good corporate governance and restates the right of shareholders in demanding corporate governance,' albeit the report does not exactly define or explain what is meant by good governance. On the other hand the Confederation of Indian Industry (CII) code states: The key to good corporate governance is a well-functioning, informed board of directors. The board should have a core group of excellent, professionally acclaimed non-executive directors who understand their dual role of appreciating the issues put forward by the management and of honestly discharging their fiduciary responsibilities towards the companies 'shareholders as well as creditors.' This explanation somewhat bypasses the importance of the value perspective. Thus, the CII code and the Birla Committee recommendation both are not able to give a very clear picture of good governance.

Another view is the external view that good governance can be brought about effectively by external means. '... The failure of Indian corporates has made it clear that good corporate governance can only be brought about effectively by greater self-regulation and pressure of public opinion generated by large investor groups...' Here there is more stress on external pressure, which can result in greater sensitivity towards good governance. Value-based governance is more an internal, self-regulated process, distinct from good governance as a result of external pressures. The former is more long lasting than the latter.

The Importance of Effective Functioning

The literature highlights a number of constituents of corporate governance that are important and also pertinent for the effective functioning of the board. Mention can be made of a few such aspects:

- Frequency of board meetings
- Mix of executive and non-executive directors
- Role of non-executive directors
- Contribution of various committees such as audit and remuneration committee
- Role of nominee directors from financial institutions
- The CEO and chairman split

In addition to these, there are some other components of directors' responsibilities:

- Develop a basic understanding of the industry and company
- Stay informed about the major operating developments
- Confirm proposed strategy and monitor performance
- Communicate with the stakeholders

These aspects can be said to be necessary conditions of the board's functioning. The board has to address these aspects or else the organization can face competitive and functional disadvantage. However, though these are important, they are not adequate for good governance, for without a clear value perspective at the level of the board, good governance can turn out to be a superficial goal.

Two requirements need to be emphasized for good corporate governance:

- Need and importance of higher·values in the organization which have their genesis at the top level but are adopted at all levels of the organization.
- Need and importance of effective functioning of the board, for it to qualify as a professional body with the task of shaping and steering the organization.

This can be stated in the form of the following equation:

$$G.G = f(H.V + E.F)$$

where

    G.G = Good governance
    H.V = Higher values
    E.F = Effective functioning

Two Views on Good Governance

Various environments affect corporate governance. These are the societal, business and corporate environments (Figure 3.1).

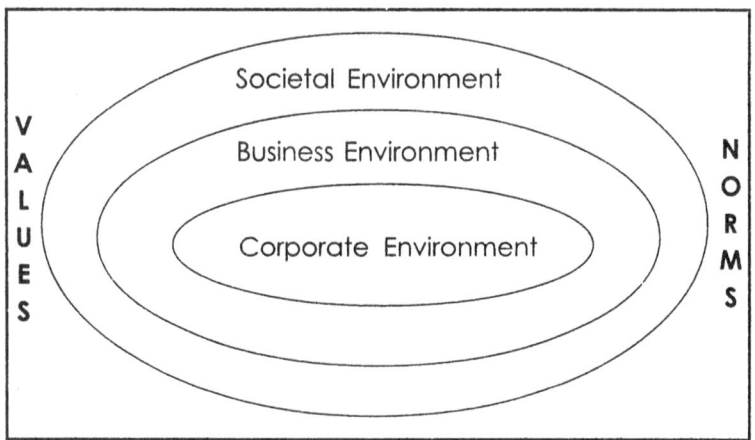

Fig. 3.1: Corporate Governance and Environment

Figure 3.1 clearly shows the innermost circle as the corporate environment, which falls under the overriding business environment, while the latter is subject to the societal environment; values and norms encompass all three. Here it may be noted that there are some values related to these environments, namely, corporate values, business values, societal values and, ultimately, the highest values, which can be termed spiritual values. The following are examples of values arising in different environments:

- The corporate environment may be dealing with, for instance, higher production at lower cost: the complementary corporate value associated with it can be 'No compromise on the quality of the product'.
- The business environment may cause the company to struggle in the face of competition for creating a niche for itself: here the value associated can be 'No use of unfair means to enhance brand image for grabbing a larger share of the market'.
- The societal environment may raise questions regarding pollution, etc.: the value associated can be 'Take care of society even in the face of possible losses, as business is a part of society.'

The values associated with these environments fall within the ambit of overall value norms. To properly understand and appreciate the good governance equation, two approaches that support two different views can be elucidated, namely, the business view and the spiritual view.

1. The Business View

The business view of corporate governance deals more with the second part of the good governance equation, that is, effective functioning. Here it takes an inside-out approach, that is, to start with, the business view has as its priority the corporate environment and the issues related thereto, such as higher profits, maximizing shareholders' value. It may be concerned with issues of the business and societal environments but not have them as top priority. In other words, it is not that the business view is insensitive to stakeholders' benefits; rather, running the business profitably in an effective manner is its prime concern.

Taking the business view, the board will not be willing to compromise everything for values. In theory, the board may state values but in practice short-term gains might take precedence. A mix of higher values with effective functioning may not be appreciated, and the board may go in for professional directors, without much hype about the value standing of the particular individual.

Most of the literature on corporate governance deals with the business view. While there is a lot of talk regarding the value approach, Western writers on management have not been able to do justice to this aspect as they ignore the spiritual aspects.

2. The Spiritual View

In the context of the totality of the value approach, the spiritual view of corporate governance becomes necessary and pertinent. This view deals with the first aspect of the good governance equation, that is, higher values. It can be stated to be an 'outside-in' approach. Spiritual values are the basis and foundation of this view, which adheres to and stands by these values and truth in all circumstances. It takes care of the highest values and then accordingly does justice to the societal, business and corporate environments.

Present-day literature may not adequately be able to support the spiritual view of good governance. In this view, if profits have to be sacrificed in the short run for adhering to value norms, it is worth doing so to maintain the corporate reputation. Good governance is like the dharma of the board of directors whereby if one adheres to good governance that will take care of the rest; as the ancient Indian dictum state *dharmo rakshathi rakshithaha* (one who protects dharma is protected by dharma) and *yato dharmah tato jayah* (wnere there is dharma there is victory).

Spirituality is often confused with religion. The best way to distinguish spirituality from religion is that spirituality is stems from the heart whereas religion is the thinking of the mind. The first and the most important principle of spirituality is universal love. This love is not confined to fellow human beings but extends to all creation. This is what is meant by seeing unity in diversity.

The next important principle of spirituality is sacrifice: the *Upanishads* say that *na karmana na prajaya dhanena tyaganaike amrutatvamaanasuhu* (Not by action, not by progeny nor by wealth, but it is by sacrifice alone that man can attain divinity).

The third principle of spirituality is unity in thought, word and deed. To understand this principle from the corporate context: religion is like group value whereas spirituality is like individual value. Love is a value each individual in a group should have. Religion can be misinterpreted but spirituality cannot be misinterpreted because great values like love uphold spirituality.

Another parallel can be drawn between the spiritual view and the concept of personality in Indian scriptures. The scriptures state that man's personality can be divided into three aspects: body, mind and soul. The spiritual view takes the organization as the body, the management as the mind and the board of directors with governance as their motive, as the soul. The soul is the subtlest and the most potent of the three, as are the directors in an organization, their decisions give a vision and a reason for survival to the organization. The spiritual view prioritizes the soul of the organization to provide a value perspective.

Points from the Scriptures Supporting the Spiritual View of Corporate Governance

Indian scriptures and holy texts (like the Vedas, Upanishads, *Gita* and the epics) have deliberated in depth on various points related to governance. Extracted from the vast store of wisdom contained in them are the following examples that emphasize the spiritual view in corporate governance:

- As far back as the second century A.D. Kautilya, author of the *Arthashastra*, stated, that '*In the happiness of the subjects lies the happiness of the king*'. The king can be considered the corporate governing authority and the subjects the stakeholders belonging to the various environments that affect corporate governance.
- *Enlightened collective interest or lokasangraha* (Gita 3–20 and 3–25). This implies that action should be performed keeping in view the interests of the whole society and not individual interest. Hence, the directors should strive for the welfare of society and not personal interest. This point supplements the view of Kautilya regarding the happiness of the subjects.
- Every act should be done with *shraddha*, that is, commitment, interest, due care and diligence. *Shraddha* is so important that according to the scriptures, anything done without *shraddha* amounts to sin.
- The *Gita* speaks in detail about the concept of *nishakama karma*, that is, duty without attachment. The tenth stanza of Chapter 5 in the *Gita* states:

> *brahmanay adhaya karmani*
> *sangam tyaktava karotu yah*
> *lipyate na sa papena*
> *padma-patram ivambhasa*

One who performs duty without attachment, surrendering the results unto the Supreme Lord, is unaffected by sinful action, as the lotus leaf is untouched by water.

The duty of the board thus is to govern justly, not compromise on values, and remain affected by the greed of the corporate world. Such organizations will exemplify good corporate governance.

- The last sloka of the *Gita* states:

> *yatra yogeesvarah krsno*
> *yatra partho dhanur-dhara*
> *tatra srir vijayo bhutir*
> *dhruva nitir matir mama*

Wherever there is Krishna the master of all mystics, and wherever there is Arjuna, the supreme archer, there will also certainly be opulence, victory, extraordinary power and morality. That is my opinion.

This preaching of the *Gita* is about what can be achieved by the combination of God and a perfect man. This is also stated as the duality of *nara* and *narayana*. Krishna stands for divine powers and values and Arjuna for human perfection and skills; the combination of the values of Krishna and the skills of Arjuna ensures victory. Importing this view into corporate governance: if Arjuna's skill is taken as effective functioning and Krishna's values as higher values then good governance is ensured.

- Another important concept in the texts is that of *trikarna suddhi*, or unity of thought, word and deed. The following Sanskrit verse illustrates this point:

> *manassekam vachassekam karmanyakem mahatmanam*
> *manas anyat vachasa anyat karmanyanyat duratmanam*

(He who has one mind, one word and one deed is a great soul. He who has a different mind, different word and a different deed is a bad soul.)

'The highest spiritual discipline is to bring about a unity in one's thoughts, words and deeds.' If corporate governance can ensure *'trikarana suddhi'* it will automatically ensure good governance.

References

Confederation of Indian Industry (2000). Desirable Corporate Governance: A Code. New Delhi, CII.

Felton, Robert F., Alec Hudnut and Valda Witt (1995). 'Building a Stronger Board'. *Mc Kinsey Quarterly* 2, 2.

Gopal K. (1998). Emerging trends in corporate governance. *Indian Management*. 37, 10–12.

Managalam Kumar (1999). Draft Report of the Kumar Mangalam Committee on Corporate Governance. Bombay, SEBI.

Prabhupada Swami (1995). 'Bhagavad-Gita as it is'. The Bhakti Vedanta Book Trust. 1995, p. 283, p. 863, Bombay.

Sathya Sal Baba (1999). Compilation of discourses by Bhagawan Sri Sathya Sai Baba. *Sathya Sai Speaks* (US Edition), vol. 10, p. 384, Sri Sathya Sai Institute of Higher Learning, *Prasanthinilayam*.

Sharma Subhash (1999). 'Corporate *Gita*: Lessons for Management, Administration and Leadership'. *Journal of Human Values*. 5(2), pp. 103–23, New Delhi, Sage.

4

Leadership Effectiveness on Organizational Climate and Burnout: A Path Analytic Approach

VAISHALI • MOHIT P. KUMAR

Successful organizations consistently differ from ineffective organizations in one respect: the former are characterized by a dynamic and effective leadership (Hershey and Blanchard, 1977: 83).

Leadership has been studied from different perspectives, depending on the researcher's conception of leadership and methodological preferences. Most of these studies are divided naturally along distinct lines of research on leaders' effectiveness, and can be classified into two categories: those that focus on type of leader or leadership and those that focus on the upward or downward exchange between leader and subordinates. The latter has been termed leader–member-exchange. Not disputing the importance and validity of the type of leadership (trait, behavior, situational, transformational and transactional leadership), this chapter tries to ascertain the possibility of leader–member-exchange as a major factor contributing to employees' perception of organizational climate which in turn leads to job burnout.

Leader–Member-Exchange

The superior–subordinate relationship, in the literature, has been conceived as a social exchange or negotiated transaction. This conception has led to a fully developed theory which explains the effect of leadership on the compliance of subordinates. Leader–member-exchange implies an informally developed role—one that is negotiated between each individual, group members and the leader (Graen, 1976).

TheLMX theory suggests that leaders differentiate among their subordinates within the work unit (Dansereau, Green and Hage, 1975). Rather than using the same style in dealing with all the subordinates, leaders develop a different type of relationship or exchange with each subordinate. These relationships range from those characterized by downward influences and role-defined relations (i.e., low LMX) to those characterized by mutual trust, respect, linking and reciprocal influence (that is, high LMX) (Dansereau, et al., 1975; Graen and Scandura, 1987). The key premise is that LMX has an influence on subordinates' perception of organizational climate, as, for most employees, their leader represents the organization.

Schneider (1973) stated that the concept of organizational climate may be described as personalistic, that is, it is an individual's perception of the organizational environment. Organizational climate represents the psychological environment consisting of individual opinions formed upon micro events, that happen to them, as well as to others around, over a period of time. It is a set of measurable properties of the work environment, perceived directly or indirectly by the members that influence their work and satisfaction. An organization differs from another not only in its physical structure but also in the attitude and behavior it elicits from people. Most organizations today have a highly formalized bureaucratic structure, with an inflexible and impersonal climate, which can lead to job burnout. Organizational climate represents the entire social system of a work group. The workplace itself and the treatment employees receive from the management are two important aspects of organizational climate.

Definition of Organizational Climate

Tagiuri and Litwin (1968) defined organizational climate as the 'internal environment of an organization that is experienced by its members, which influences their behavior'. Organizational climate arises from and is sustained by the systematized and customary practices of the organization deemed important by the organization and its members and it influences members' behaviors and attitudes.

Dimensions of Organizational Climate

Every organization has certain basic dimensions, the nature of which may or may not be similar to those of other organizations. How these dimensions operate depends on the atmosphere and employee perceptions. These dimensions interact and determine the totality of the physical climate. Litwin and Stringer (1968) and Meyer (1968) treated responsibility, standards, rewards and team spirit as independent dimensions. Similarly, Gilmer and Forehand (1964) identified leadership patterns and decision-making processes as independent dimensions.

Organizational climate appears to vary along the following basic dimensions:

- Conformity   This dimension is concerned with the perception of the extent of an organization's emphasis on strict adherence to rules and regulations.
- Standard   It is the extent to which employees feel they are assigned challenging and demanding goals. It is their perception of how much the emphasis is laid on quality and excellent work done by them.
- Responsibility   Every member in an organization is assigned some responsibility. This dimension relates to how much freedom the employee feels or experiences to take decisions without getting them checked.
- Rewards   This refers to an employee's perception about management's attitude towards the quality of his work and the extent to which, he feels, he is not being neglected.
- Leadership pattern   Leader's behavior or the pattern of leadership is a very important dimension of organization climate.
- Decision-making process   The perception along this dimension would largely depend on the extent to which decision-making is seen to involve various people.
- Communication network   Regarded as an important dimension of organizational climate, it can be one way or two way.
- Warmth and support   This dimension refers to the extent to which an employee feels that warmth and support exist in the organization. The relationship is perceived to be happy and employees feel secure if considerable warmth and support is experienced in the employee–management relationship. How far employees identify themselves with the organization, the extent to which they feel motivated, and their involvement can be another dimension.

Leader–Member–Exchange and Organizational Climate

Bavelas (1948) emphasized that in any organization of human beings, there accumulates over time a common fund of experience, out of which develop ways of behaving, ways of working, ways of cooperating and ways of resisting, and since every organization has its distinctive organizational climate, its subcomponents or dimensions tend to be pronounceable and differentially related to personal and work outcomes like job satisfaction, organization commitment, turnover, absenteeism, performance and job burnout.

Communication with superiors and co-workers has an important influence on employees' perceptions of psychologically important aspects of the work environment. Good communication with superiors, individual experiences of situations and their leaders are very important in influencing the perception regarding the psychologically important aspects of the work environment (Ashforth, 1985; Campbell, Dunnetle Lawler and Weick, 1970). James, et al., 1990; Poole and McPhee, 1983). Individuals' experiences of their situations, the objects around them, and even their own needs are dependent on their social environment (Salancik and Pfeffer, 1978) Such a workplace communication, as a form of perceptual control (McPhee, 1993), can have important implications for whether or not employees feel comfortable. Supervisor resistance is a key contributor to employees' leave-taking (Mercer, 1993; Scharlach and Grosswald, 1997). Warren and Johnson (1995) further concluded that employees who perceived their supervisors as supportive reported a higher level of comfort. Organizational leaders provide the primary impetus in defining, forming and shaping organizational climate. For most employees, leaders represent the organization; they perceive the organization mostly through the treatment given to them by their leader and the way he or she interacts with them. The amount of trust, respect and liking shown by the leader towards subordinates will determine their comfort level. LMX measures have been found to be positively related to climate perception (Kozlowski and Donerty, 1989). The leader plays an important role in shaping, forming and defining the above-mentioned dimensions of organizational climate. To test the validity of this statement, as leaders' relationship with their subordinates has a significant impact on subordinates' perception of organizational climate, it was hypothesized that:

Low Leader–member-exchange will lead to an unhealthy perception of organizational climate.

To validate this hypothesis, the research tried to develop the path from leader–member-exchange to organizational climate to job burnout.

Burnout

The climate at the workplace has a significant impact on how people feel and on how they perform. Subordinates' attitudes, perceptions and, dynamics effect their performance and most importantly, their behavior and reactions. How does one feel in the organization? Dynamic, energized, frantic, rushed or burnt out? An unhealthy perception of organizational climate may lead to individual job burnout. Research suggests that people's perception of climate influences their experience of stress and burnout. Banka and Augustyn (1991) found a negative relation between burnout and organizational climate.

The term burnout is a popular one, and many people confuse it with organizational stress. However, as noted by Pines and Aronson (1981), burnout occurs as a result of ongoing job stress. Thus, burnout is itself one of the most important consequences of uncorrected job stress. At first, burnout was considered a problem that was found primarily (or even exclusively) within the helping professions, and the major reason for this was the intense involvement with people that characterized these jobs. Burnout has now expanded beyond these original borders and is considered applicable to many other sorts of occupations and not just a problem exclusive to service providers. It now includes not only all forms of work stresses but also non-work spheres of life. The emotional strain of contact with people has been discussed in terms of people in one's personal life (spouse/child/friend/neighbor) and not just those people one works with on the job.

Assumptions of Burnout

- Since burnout is caused by prolonged exposure to stress and frustration, all the various personal and environmental factors that generate stress and frustration for humans must be considered as potential causes of burnout.
- Burnout is a holistic or psycho-bio-social concept. To construct it solely or even principally as a psycho-physiological stress management issue is to oversimplify it. How an individual fulfils or fails to fulfil his or her needs, especially those that are dependent on interpersonal relationships, deserves an equal status with the concept of stress management.
- Since the environment other than the work environment can generate stress and frustrate important needs, they must be considered as potential contributors to the experience of burnout on the job.

- To an outside observer, the behavioral manifestations and negative consequences associated with burnout may sometimes emerge suddenly, dramatically, with little or no warning. More typically, however, the signs of burnout occur slowly, over time with ever-increasing severity.
- Burnout may occur in varying degrees; in an individual, it varies from relatively mild distractions and energy loss to serious and debilitating illness that may result in death.
- Since the duration of burnout may vary considerably, the signs of burnout will also vary in duration.
- The same individual may experience burnout more than once.

Mashlash (1982) defined burnout with the help of its dimensions: emotional exhaustion, depersonalization and low personal accomplishment. He further defined the state of emotional exhaustion as that which is caused by excessive demand, both at the psychological and emotional levels, made by the job. The effective implementation of individual, managerial, and organizational practices to deal with work exhaustion hinges on a clear and accurate understanding of the concept (Cordes and Dougherty, 1993). The existing literature, heavily based on correlational studies and display-ing few attempts to provide theoretical frameworks for relationships (Kilpatrick, 1989), implies that individuals experiencing work exhaustion exhibit a slew of reactions, including reduced organizational commitment, diminished self-esteem and turnover.

The second dimension of this definitions is a negative shift in responses to others, that is, depersonalization, negative or inappropriate attitude towards clients, or colleagues, loss of idealism, and irritability. Deper-sonalization refers to treating people like objects and is often reflected in the use of object labels. Excessive depersonalization is found associated with the feeling of callousness and cynicism about people.

A third dimension is a negative response towards oneself and one's personal accomplishments, also described as depression, low morale, withdrawal, reduced productivity or capability and an inability to cope. In feeling of low personal accomplishment, an individual starts comparing himself/herself with others and believes he is less worthy, and that others have achieved more, and as a result the individual stops trying.

Organizational Climate and Burnout

As stated earlier, Bavelas (1948) emphasized the point that in any organization of human beings, there accumulates over time a common fund of experience, from which develop ways of behaving, ways of working, ways of cooperating and ways of resisting and since every organization has its distinctive organizational climate, its sub-components (dimensions) tend to be pronounceable and differentially related to personal and work outcomes like job satisfaction, organizational commitment, turnover, absenteeism, performance and burnout. The characteristics associated with an organization have been linked to occupational stress (Singh, 1980). The role organizational climate plays in job burnout is less investigated especially in India. Of the few researches conducted, some findings suggest a negative relationship between perceived healthy organizational climate, occupational stress and burnout. Banka and Augustyn (1991) studied occupational stress from two dimensions of organizational climate, that is, standards and warmth and support. The results indicated a negative relationship. Jayaratne, Nimle and David (1990) examined the relationship between organizational climate and burnout and they too found a strong association. Bennett, Lydia, Ross and Sunderland (1995) examined the relationship between stressors, rewards and burnout and found that rewards in the form of gratitude from clients and recognition and support from management positively influenced organizational climate (they perceive organizational climate to be high) and may reduce burnout and stress.

Organizational climate, being one of the largest constructs of the work environment, does have some bearing on the job stress experience of the organization's members. Not much research has, however, been undertaken to explore the relationship between job burnout and organizational climate. The current research projects organizational climate as a factor affecting the stress phenomenon and burnout as an important aspect of uncorrected job stress. Therefore, the second hypothesis formulated which stated that:

An unhealthy perception of climate will lead to job burnout, that is, emotional exhaustion, depersonalization and low personal accomplishment.

Grouped Hypothesis

Keeping in view the assumptions discussed earlier, a third, grouped, hypothesis was formulated:

Leader–member-exchange will predict organizational climate, which, in turn will predict job burnout.

Sampling

The research was conducted in an organization located in Mumbai, manufacturing engineering products. Data were collected from 150 full-time employees; however, missing data reduced the final sample to 139. The human resources department of the organization randomly selected the employees for the sample. These respondents were largely engineers and belonged to various functional areas like production, quality control, research and development and marketing. Executives were both male and female, ranging in age from 23 to 58 years. The tenure ranged from one to 37 years.

Scales Used

Leader–Member-Exchange

A six-item scale was used to measure the subordinate's perception of Leader–member-exchange. These items, adapted from Scandura and Graen (1984), used a five-point scale ranging from strongly disagree (1) to strongly agree (5) for the first six items.

Burnout

Burnout was measured by Maslach Burnout Inventory, which is designed to assess the three aspects of the burnout syndrome: emotional exhaustion, depersonalization, and lack of personal accomplishment. Each aspect is measured by a separate sub-scale.

ORGANIZATIONAL CLIMATE QUESTIONNAIRE

This questionnaire is a modified version of an organizational climate questionnaire developed by Litwin, et al. (1971). Perceived organizational climate is measured by this inventory along with the following seven dimensions: (1) conformity, (2) responsibility, (3) standards, (4) rewards, (5) organizational clarity, (6) warmth and support and (7) leadership.

Results and Discussion

Regression analyses were carried out to determine the causal path from leader–member-exchange to organizational climate to burnout. For this purpose leader–member-exchange was first regressed with organizational climate then organizational climate and leader–member-exchange were regressed with burnout. The research intended to develop the following path:

Leader–Member-Exchange → Organizational Climate → Burnout

The results of regression analyses tracing the path from leader–member-exchange to organizational climate to burnout in Table 4.1 demonstrate that the path was successfully formed. The present research which tried to ascertain the possibility of leader–member-exchange as a major factor contributing to employees' perception of organizational climate which in turn leads to job burnout was accepted by the results.

Leader–Member-Exchange and Organizational Climate

The results of these analyses indicate that the path coefficient from leader–member-exchange to organizational climate was 0.30. Leader–member-exchange refers to manager–employee dyadic transactions that have been found to affect employees' work attitudes and their reaction to the environment (Basu and Green, 1995; Dienesch and Liden, 1986; Mcclane, 1991). Table 4.1 shows the results of multiple regression, wherein leader–member-exchange is the independent variable and organizational climate is the dependent variable. It was observed that leader–member-exchange could predict organizational climate. Leader–member-exchange when regressed with organizational climate showed an explained variance of 9 per cent ($r^2 = 0.09$, f = 21.1*). Leader–member-exchange was found to be significant with beta=0.30 and t=4.1*. These results show that leader–member-exchange predicted organizational climate.

Leaders are in a unique position to create an impression about the environment in the minds of their subordinates, either willingly or unwillingly. If not healthy, leader–subordinate exchanges can be a source of tension for both, especially for the subordinate. The quality of relationship they have at work has consistently been linked to perceived climate. A number of behavioral scientists (Argyris, 1964; Cooper, 1973) have suggested that a good relationship between members of a work group is a central factor of organizational health.

Leader–member-exchange and climate dimensions have not been investigated earlier and very little research has been done in this area to support this hypothesis. Hence, this study is exploratory, and its

Table 4.1: Regression of the Independent Variable (Leader–Member-Exchange) with Organizational Climate

Variables	Multiple R	R square	F Sig.	Beta	T
Organizational Climate	0.30	0.09	21.3**	.30	4.1**

(**) = Significant at 0.01 level.

hypothesis was formed taking in view the strong relationship of leader–member-exchange with the attitude of the employees. The leader represents the organization for the subordinate; thus, the nature of relationship the subordinate shares with the leader has a direct impact on the attitude he or she forms about the environment. The results (Table 4.1) show that the hypothesis to understand the relationship of leader–member-exchange with organizational climate was accepted by the results.

Organizational Climate and Burnout

Burnout was the next dependent variable to be predicted by the independent variable, organizational climate. Burnout was measured with the help of Mashlash Burnout Inventory, which gives three different scores for it components: emotional exhaustion, depersonalization and low personal accomplishment (for this the statements are positively worded). Therefore, all three components were treated as dependent variables. From Table 4.2 it can be seen that the path significantly developed between organizational climate and the burnout components. The path coefficient was highest for emotional exhaustion, lowest and personal accomplishment. Organizational climate was regressed with emotional exhaustion. The analysis produced an explained variance of 20 per cent ($r^2 = 0.20$, $f = 51.8**$) and the beta values were found to be significant (beta = -0.45, $t = -8.3**$).

The next dependent variable regressed with organizational climate was the second component of burnout, namely, depersonalization. Results show that organizational climate was significantly causing depersonalization. The explained variance was 16 per cent ($r^2 = 0.16$, $f = 40.*1*$) and beta was found to be significant (beta = -0.40 and $t = -7.8**$). Organizational climate was then regressed with the third component of burnout, namely, personal accomplishment. The beta value was significant, which indicates that organizational climate predicted personal accomplishment. The

Table 4.2: Regression of the Independent Variable (Organizational Climate) with Burnout

Variables	Multiple R	R square	F Sig.	Beta	T
Burn.ee	0.45	.20	51.8**	−0.45	−8.3**
Burn.dp	0.40	0.16	41.1**	−0.40	−7.8**
Burn.lpa	0.27	0.06	17.3*	0.27	4.8*

(*) = Significant at 0.01 level; (**) = Significant at 0.01 level; ee is emotional exhaustions; dp is depersonalization and lpa is low personal accomplishment.

explained variance was 6 per cent ($r^2 = 0.06$, f = 17.3*) and the beta had a positive value as higher scores on this will indicate low burnout (the statements are positively worded for this component) (beta = 0.27, t = 4.8*).

Therefore, the hypothesis which stated that low organizational climate would predict high emotional exhaustion and depersonalization and low personal accomplishment was accepted by the results. Thus, subordinates perceiving an unhealthy organizational climate will experience greater emotional exhaustion and will also be more detached from their environment, that is, they will be impersonal with clients, customers and co-workers, and will perceive themselves less worthy as compared to others. Not many studies have been done to understand the relationship between burnout and organizational climate. Hence, this hypothesis too was exploratory in nature. Cooper and Marshall (1976) reported that a powerful source of organizational stress was simply being in the organization. A number of work characteristics are associated with organizational climate. Rajeshwari (1989) stated that the perception of a healthy organizational climate would reduce stress. Banka and Augustyn (1991) found a similar relationship and demonstrated that the workplace significantly influenced occupational stress. Though most of the research has been conducted with stress, burnout is a comparatively new research variable and is the outcome of uncorrected stress. Thus, the hypothesis which was formulated taking into account the strong association between burnout and organizational climate has been supported by the results. Results demonstrated that burnout could be predicted by organizational climate. (Table 4.3)

Path coefficients may be used to decompose correlations in the model into direct and indirect effects, corresponding, of course, to direct and

Table 4.3: Regression of the Independent Variable (Leader–Member-Exchange) with Burnout

Variables	Multiple R	R square	F Sig.	Beta	T
Burn.ee	0.21	0.04	10.19	–0.21	–3.1*
Burn.dp	0.22	0.05	11.25*	–0.22	–3.3*
Burn.lpa	0.11	0 .01	2.5	.11	1.5 (NS)

(*) = Significant at 0.01 level; (**) = Significant at 0.01 level; ee is emotional exhaustion; dp is depersonalization and lpa is low personal accomplishment.

indirect paths reflected by the arrows in the model. This is based on the rule that in a linear system, the total causal effect of variable a on variable b is the sum of the values of all the paths from a to b. Considering 'burnout' as the dependent variable in the model above, and considering 'Leader–member-exchange' as the independent variable, the indirect effects are calculated by multiplying the path coefficients for each path from Leader–member-exchange to burnout. The steps to be followed for the same are given below:

Leader–Member-Exchange → Organizational Commitment → Burnout = X
Leader–member-exchange → Burnout = Y
The total causal effect = (X + Y)
that is, for burnout emotional exhaustion
X = 0.30 * 0.45 = 0.14
Y = –0.21
(X + Y) = 0.35

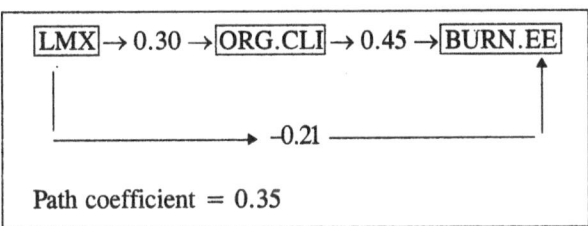

that is, for burnout depersonalization
X = 0.30 * 0.40 = 0.12

$Y = -0.22$
$(X + Y) = 0.34$

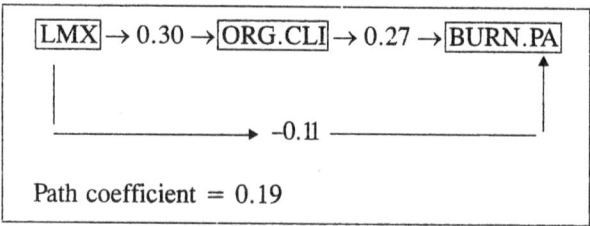

that is, for burnout low personal accomplishment
$X = 0.30 * 0.27 = 0.08$
$Y = -0.21$
$(X + Y) = 0.19$

LMX → 0.30 → ORG.CLI → 0.27 → BURN.PA

→ -0.11

Path coefficient = 0.19

The above results support the individual and the grouped hypotheses. The grouped hypothesis stated that the path will be traced from Leader-member-exchange to organizational climate to burnout. The results reveal that all three path coefficients were found to be significant. This means that leaders' interaction with the subordinates is a key factor contributing towards the latter's perception of organizational climate, which has bearing on job stress experience leading to job burnout among the members.

Conclusion

The twentieth-century leader tended to have strong but hard personal qualities, somebody who was arrogant but inspiring. However, twenty-first century leaders are going to be those who can demonstrate a greater empathy and concern for peoples' issues and those who do not rely on position or rank for their status. Geopolitical boundaries are increasingly being ignored as communication systems are evolving. With such market forces coming into play the business environment has become highly volatile and the attrition rate has shot up. In this scenario the only mantra for effective leadership, then, is to build stronger and lasting relationships.

The study demonstrates emphatically that a good quality Leader–member-exchange leads to a positive organizational climate, which, in turn reduces the behavioral impact of stress, that is, burnout. In today's business environment anything but human capital can be replicated. It is only this human capital that can define the market niche for any and every organization. To retain this asset, leaders need to refurbish their inter-personal skills, whereby a healthy work climate can develop, resulting in lesser negative effects of work stress. Further, it can also be assumed that whatever be the leadership style, if it is substantiated by transparent and positive exchanges between the leader and the led, it is likely to be successful. With this the main issues of importance that emerge and are the areas of concern for both academicians and researchers are: (1) the identification of the social skills required, which would facilitate the improvement of interpersonal skills, and (2) what can be the possible ways of developing them. One such attempt, which is gaining attention from all quarters, is the emergence of the concept of emotional intelligence, which can be expected to be addressing the need of the hour. The bottom line remains that a healthy leader–member-exchange would facilitate the organizational climate leading to reduced burnout among the corporate.

References

Argyris, Chris (1964). *Integrating the Individual and the Organization*. New York: Wiley.

Ashforth, B.E. (1985). 'Climate Formation: Issues and Extensions'. *Academy of Management Review*. 10(4): 837–47.

Bennet, L., Sunderland, R. (1995). *Burnout and Support: Impact for Professionals and Volunteers*. Amsterdam: Amsterdam University Press.

Campbell, J.P., M.D. Dunnette, E.E. Lawler and K.E. Weick (1970). *Managerial Behavior, Performance, and Effectiveness*. New York: McGraw-Hill.

Cooper, C.L. (1973). *Group Training for Organizational Development*. Basel, Switzerland: S Korger.

Cooper, C.L. and J. Marshall (1976). 'Occupational Sources of Stress: A Review of the Literature Relating to Coronary Heart Disease and Mental Ill-health'. *Journal of Occupational Psychology*. 49, 11–28.

Cordes, C.A., T.W. Dougherty and M. Blum (1997). 'Patterns of Burnout among Managers and Professionals: A Comparison of Models'. *Journal of Organizational Behavior*. 18, 685–701

Dansereau, F., J. Cashman and G.B. Graen (1973). 'Instrumentality Theory and Equity Theory as Complementary Approaches in Predicting the Relationship of Leadership and Turnover Among Managers'. *Organizational Behavior and Human Performance*. 10, 184–200.

Dansereau, F. (Jr.), G. Graen and W.J. Haga (1975). 'A Vertical Dyad Linkage Approach to Leadership within Formal Organization'. *Organizational Behavior and Human Performance*. 15, 276–96.

Dienesch, R.M. and R.C. Liden (1986). 'Leader–Member Exchange Model of Leadership: A Critique and Further Development'. *Academy of Management Review*. 11, 618–34.

Forehand, G. and B. Gilmer (1964). 'Environmental Variation in Studies of Organizational Behavior'. *Psychological Bulletin*. 62, 361–82.

Graen, G.B. (1976). 'Role Making Processes within Complex Organizations'. In M.D. Dunnette (ed.), *Handbook of Industrial and Organizational Psychology* (pp. 1201–45). Chicago: Rand McNally.

Graen, G.B. and T.A. Scandura (1980). *Leader Member Exchange*. Cincinnati: University of Cincinnati.

Graen, G.B. and T.A. Sz Scandura (1987). 'Toward a Psychology of Dyadic Organizing'. *Research in Organizational Behavior*. 9, 175–208.

Hersey, P. and K. Blanchard (1977). *Management of Organizational Behavior: Utilizing Human Resources*. Englewood Cliffs, NJ: Prentice-Hall.

Kozlowski, S.W.J. and M.L. Doherty (1989). 'Integration of Climate and Leadership: Examination of a Neglected Issue'. *Journal of Applied Psychology*. 74(4).

Maslach, C. (1982). *Burnout: The Cost of Caring*. Englewood Cliffs, NJ: Prentice-Hall.

Pines, A. and E. Aronson (1981). *Burnout from Tedium to Personal Growth*. New York: Free Press.

Poole, M.S. and R.D. McPhee (1983). 'A Structurational Theory of Organizational Climate'. In L. Putnam and M. Pacanowsky (eds.), *Organizational Communication: An Interpretive Approach* (pp. 195–219). Newbury Park, CA: Sage.

Scandura, T.A. and Graen, G.B. (1984). 'Moderating Effects of Initial Leader–Member Exchange Status on the Effects of a Leadership Intervention'. *Journal of Applied Psychology.* 69, 428–36.

Scharlach, A.E. and B. Grosswald (1997). 'The Family and Medical Leave Act of 1993: Analysis and Appraisal'. *Social Service Review* (in press).

Singh, S.P. (1980). 'Job Satisfaction, Participation and Alienation as Factors Influencing in Case of Blue-Collar Industrial Workers'. Unpublished doctoral dissertation, Varanasi: Banaras Hindu University.

Tagiuri, R. and G. Litwin (1968). *Organizational Climate: Explorations of a Concept.* Boston: Harvard University Press.

5

Transformational Leadership and Organizational Structure: The Role of Value-based Leadership

GARIMA GARG • VENKAT R. KRISHNAN

There has been a growing interest in the study of transformational leadership. However, the literature on transformational leadership in organizations has neglected the organizational context in which such leadership is embedded. In fact, the extant literature gives an impression that transformational leadership is equally applicable to all organizational situations. Shamir and Howell (1999) have presented a series of hypotheses linking contextual variables to the emergence and effectiveness of transformational leadership. One context that they consider is organizational structure. This chapter examines the relationship between organizational structure and transformational leadership. However, if transformational leadership is not coupled with value-based leadership it can lose its effectiveness. Therefore, we also look at the role of value-based leadership in the relationship between organizational structure and transformational leadership.

Theory and Hypotheses

Burns (1978) defined leadership as a relationship betweeen a leader and follower that seeks to address the goals of both. Such a relationship could take two forms—transactional and transformational. When leaders go by the current goals of followers, the relationship becomes nothing more than as exchange process, and is therefore, transactional leadership. The relationship becomes transformational when leaders try to bring about a charge in followers' motives and goals.

Transformational Leadership

Transformational leadership occurs when leaders and followers raise one another to higher levels of motivation and morality. Leaders address themselves to followers' wants, needs, and other motivations, as well as to their own, and thus may serve as an independent force in changing the makeup of the followers' motive base through gratifying their motives (Burns, 1978: 20). Transformational leadership comprises four interrelated dimensions: charisma, inspiration, individualized consideration, and intellectual stimulation (Bass, 1985). Transformational leaders attempt and succeed in raising colleagues, subordinates, followers, clients, or constituencies to a greater awareness about the issues of consequence. They bring about change, innovation and entrepreneurship. They focus on the process of corporate transformations that recognize the need for revitalization, create a new vision, and institutionalize change (Seltzer and Bass, 1990). Transformational leaders build confidence in followers, encouraging them to reframe the future and question the tried and true, and coaching them to develop their full capabilities (Avolio, Howell and Sosik, 1999). They integrate creative insight, persistence, energy, intuition and sensitivity with the needs of others to forge the strategy–culture alloy for their organizations (Bass and Avolio, 1993).

Transformational leaders adopt a long-term perspective. Rather than focusing solely on the current needs of their followers or themselves, they focus on their future needs as well; rather than being concerned only with the short-term problems and opportunities, they also concern themselves with the long-term issues of the organization; rather than viewing intra- and extra-organizational factors as discrete, they view them from a holistic orientation (Dubinsky, Yammarino, Jolson and Spangler, 1995). Behling and McFillen (1996) developed a model of transformational leadership that seeks to capture common threads running through many important works on charismatic leadership. They have identified six attributes of transformational leadership: (i) displaying empathy, (ii) dramatizing the mission, (iii) projecting self-assurance, (iv) enhancing the leader's image, (v) assuring followers of their competence, and (vi) providing followers with opportunities to experience success.

EFFECTS OF TRANSFORMATIONAL LEADERSHIP

A study by Howell and Frost (1989) concluded that individuals working under a charismatic leader had higher task performance (in terms of the number of courses of action they suggested and their quality of performance), higher task satisfaction and lower role conflict and ambiguity as compared to individuals working under considerate or structuring leaders. Thus transformational leadership may ultimately result in a higher level of satisfaction and effectiveness among the led (Bass, 1985). Transformational variables of charismatic leadership, individualized consideration, and intellectual stimulation add to the variations in subordinates' effectiveness, effort, and satisfaction explained by initiation and consideration (Seltzer and Bass, 1990). The leader's vision, which is a characteristic of the transformational process (Bass, 1985), plays an important role in motivating followers. It affects employee performance by inspiring them forwards specific goals and by raising their self-efficacy. Kirkpatrick and Locke (1996) found that the content of charismatic communication style (vision and task cues) led to higher performance quality and quantity. Leaders' articulation of vision emphasizing quality improved the attitudes and perception of followers and articulation of the task cues increased followers' task clarity and intellectual stimulation. Baum, Locke and Kirkpatrick (1998) found additional support for this finding in their study. They concluded that vision and vision communication have positive effects upon organization-level performances.

CONTEXT AND TRANSFORMATIONAL LEADERSHIP

While charismatic leadership is potentially applicable to most organizational situations, it is not equally applicable to all situations. Waldman, Ramirez, House and Puranam (2001) found that charisma predicts financial performance only under conditions of perceived environmental uncertainty. Organizations will be more receptive to transformational leadership during adaptation rather than during efficiency orientation (Pawar and Eastman, 1997). Shamir and Howell (1999) argue that charismatic leaders are more likely to emerge under conditions of turbulence and crisis than under conditions of stability and continuity. Charismatic leadership is more likely to emerge and be effective in dynamic organizational environments that require and enable the introduction of new strategies, markets, products and technologies. Charismatic leadership is more likely to emerge and be effective when the tasks

of organizational members are challenging and complex, and require individual and group initiative, responsibility, creativity and intense effort. Charismatic leadership is also more likely to emerge and be effective when performance goals are ambiguous and extrinsic rewards cannot be strongly linked to performance. Organizations with dominant boundary-spanning units will be more receptive to transformational leadership than will be organizations with dominant technical cores (Pawar and Eastman, 1997).

Organizational Structure

The primary structural variables are as follows:

1. Specialization   This is of two types: functional specialization, the extent to which official duties are divided between discrete, identifiable functional areas; and role specialization, the extent to which official duties are divided within discrete, identifiable positions (Child, 1972).
2. Standardization   The extent to which activities are subject to standard procedures and rules (Child, 1972), and the proportion of jobs that are codified, or range of variations allowed within jobs (Haga, 1965).
3. Formalization   The extent to which procedures, rules and instructions are written down (Haga, 1965).
4. Centralization   The extent to which the locus of authority to make decisions affecting the organization is confined to the higher levels of the hierarchy (Child, 1972) or the proportion of levels that participate in the decision-making (Haga, 1965).
5. Configuration   A composite concept embracing various dimensions of the shape of the organization. One such dimension, vertical span, concerns the number of levels in the organizational hierarchy (Child, 1972).
6. Stratification   Differences in income and prestige among jobs or the rate of mobility between low-and high-ranking jobs or status levels (Haga, 1965).
7. Span of control   A measure not just of direct supervision (total number of subordinates as a proportion of total number of superiors) but also of total supervision (i.e., taking into consideration the time spent by the supervisors and by the customer) (Ouchi and Dowing, 1974).

STRUCTURAL CONFIGURATIONS

Burns and Stalker (1961) outlined two kinds of organizational structures that represent two extremes in terms of their ability to adapt to environmental change. Mechanistic organizations are characterized by high complexity, formalization and centralization. They perform routine tasks, rely heavily on programmed behaviors, and are relatively slow in responding to the unfamiliar. Organic structures are relatively flexible and adaptive, with emphasis on lateral rather than on vertical communication, influence based on expertise and knowledge rather than on authority of position, loosely defined responsibilities rather than rigid job definitions, and emphasis on exchanging information rather than on giving instructions.

EFFECT OF ORGANIZATIONAL STRUCTURE

Ivancevich and Donnelly (1975) found that salespersons in flat organizations perceived more satisfaction and less anxiety and stress than salespersons in medium and tall organizations. It was found that salespersons in flat organizations were better performers than those in medium and tall organizations. Teachers in flat organizations had higher job satisfaction than their counterparts in tall and medium organizational types in three areas—community prestige, professional authority and participation in determining school goals (Carpenter, 1971). Organizational size has some effect on the relative effectiveness of flat versus tall structures. For smaller organizations, managerial satisfaction seems somewhat greater in flat rather than in tall organizations. For larger companies, this effect is reversed. The effects of organizational structure on satisfactions appear to vary with the type of psychological need being considered. A tall structure seems especially advantageous in producing security and social need satisfactions, whereas a flat structure seems more advantageous in influencing self-actualization satisfactions (Porter and Lawler, 1964).

TRANSFORMATIONAL LEADERSHIP AND ORGANIZATIONAL STRUCTURE

Burns and Stalker (1961) defined organic structure as the one appropriate to changing conditions that constantly present fresh problems and unforeseen requirements for action which cannot be broken down or distributed automatically arising from the functional roles defined within a

hierarchical structure. Organic structures are more loosely structured, more flexible and innovative and less specialized. They have decentralized decision-making processes, less formalization and standardization, lateral rather than vertical communication, fewer hierarchical distinctions and a less strict division of labor. Shamir and Howell (1999) propose that charismatic leadership is more likely to emerge and be effective in organic organizations than in mechanistic ones. According to them, organic organizations impose fewer constraints on members' activities, and offer fewer cues for appropriate behaviors. They enable and encourage both leaders and potential followers to express individual behavior. They thus provide a greater need as well as a greater scope for the emergence of charismatic leaders who influence behaviors by frame alignment, exemplary behavior, appeal to shared values and identities, and linking members' self-concepts to the organization and its mission. Mechanistic organizations, in contrast, are 'stronger' psychological situations for leaders and members since they provide fewer opportunities for organizational members to exercise discretion and also suppress the expression of individual differences by both leaders and followers. Exchange-based leadership, which relies on clear specification of duties and rewards, is more relevant in mechanistic organizations. Some linkages between transformational leadership and organizational structure can be understood in terms of their amenability to change. A transformational leader serves as an independent force in changing the makeup of the followers' motive base (Burns, 1978) and an organizational structure that is organic in nature is more appropriate for change (Burns and Stalker, 1961). Hence we had the following two hypotheses.

Hypothesis 1(a) Transformational leadership would be negatively related to the degree of formalization in an organization.
Hypothesis 1(b) Transformational leadership would be positively related to the degree of decentralization in an organization.

ETHICS AND TRANSFORMATIONAL LEADERSHIP

Those who argue that transformational leadership is unethical fail to distinguish between transformational and pseudo-transformational leadership. Rather than being immoral, transformational leadership has become a necessity in the post-industrial world of work. Self-aggrandizing pseudo-transformational leaders can be branded as immoral, but transformational leaders, who engage in the moral uplift of their followers, who move them to share in the mutually rewarding visions of success, who enable and empower them to convert the visions into realities, should be applauded, not chastised (Bass and Steidlmeier, 1999). Charismatic leadership is more likely to emerge and be effective when the organizational goals and primary tasks are consistent with the dominant social values, and offer both leaders and followers an opportunity for moral involvement (Shamir and Howell, 1999).

Value-based Leadership

Burns (1978) claimed that moral leadership emerges from, and always returns to, the fundamental wants and needs, aspirations and values, of the followers. It is a kind of leadership that can produce social change that will satisfy followers' authentic needs. Such leadership is not to be confused with the too-common political practice of promising the masses whatever they think they want, even if that is inherently bad. Instead, the leaders must discern the true interests of the public from their stated desires and learn to address the underlying needs that people as a body are unable to articulate. An effective democratic leader must refine public views in a way that transcends pettiness, contradiction and self-interest. Value-based and effective leaders illuminate their followers' better side, revealing what is good in them and thus ultimately giving them hope. In the end, the leader's vision becomes their vision because it is built on the foundation of their needs and aspirations (O'Toole, 1996: 9–10). Leaders appeal to the minds and hearts of their followers and the leadership goal is to change the beliefs and behavior of followers.

Leadership of change does not depend on the circumstances; rather, it depends on the attitudes, values and actions of the leaders. To be an effective leader, one must become a leader of leaders. In complex, democratic settings, effective leadership will call for vision, trust, listening, authenticity, integrity, hope and, especially, addressing the genuine needs of the followers. Without this, the likelihood of overcoming the ever-present resistance to change is minimal. If this is correct, what is required to guide effective change is not a contingency theory but, rather, a new philosophy of leadership that is always and at all times focused on enlisting the hearts and minds of followers through inclusion and participation. Such a philosophy must be rooted in the most fundamental of moral principles: respect for people. In this realm of morality, there are no contingencies. Value-based leadership, by definition, cannot be situational or contingent (O'Toole, 1996: 11–12).

Evidence indicates that leaders who understand why change is resisted and are willing to make the personal investment required to overcome the resistance are likely to achieve their goal. Leaders break this chronic and inevitable pattern of resistance in only one way—by buildiing an alternative system of belief and allowing others to adopt it as their own. That is the essence of value-based leadership. Value-based leadership is an attitude about people, philosophy, and process. To overcome the resistance to change, one must be willing, for starters, to change oneself. In essence, then, value-based leadership is unnatural (O'Toole, 1996).

The following are some characteristics of value-based leadership:

1. *Integrity*   Leadership requires integrity. Integrity has at least two meanings relevant to a discussion of leadership. It is synonymous with truth telling, honesty and moral behavior. A true leader must behave with integrity by being an honest and ethical individual, consistent in word and deed. In additon, the leader needs to have the type of integrity that has to do with selflessness, with the integration of one's personality. Integrity in this sense refers to the much-admired trait of wholeness or completeness that is achieved by people who have healthy self-confidence and self-esteem. People with integrity know who they are. Their self-esteem allows them to esteem and respect others. Such leaders' ease with themselves allows others to hold them in esteem and respect them. In spite of odds, they never lose sight of their goals or compromise on their principles. They are simultaneously principled and pragmatic: principled in that the long-term courses they adopt are based on what is morally right; and pragmatic in that they are willing to compromise or lose out on an immediate issue because they would not be distracted from the ultimate objective. Success in one's short-term mission is not the clearest sign of effective leadership, but lifelong consistency of high moral purpose is. Value-based leadership also manifests itself in its assertion of a natural right of all individuals to pursue happiness (O'Toole, 1996: 23–27).

2. *Vision*   Value-based leadership is based on an inspiring vision. The only course for the leader is to build a vision that the followers are able to adopts as their own because it is their own. Ultimately, the leader's vision becomes the vision of the followers because it is built on their needs and aspirations. Leadership is about teaching and finding ways to communicate a vision, and recognizing that no

one understands the need for change the first time it is presented (O'Toole, 1996).

3. *Trust*   Value-based leaders inspire trust and engender hope among their followers, who in turn feel encouraged to serve, sacrifice, persevere, and lead change. Leaders win the loyalty of the followers through their deeds and by example. Trust in leaders also grows out of their manifest integrity, their ability to lead emanating from their willingness to serve and their manifest respect for the followers (O'Toole, 1996: 27–29).

4. *Listening*   Value-based and effective leaders listen to their followers because they respect them and because they honestly believe that the welfare of followers is the goal of leadership. They encourage dissenting opinion among their closest advisers. While value-based leaders listen to the opinion of those they serve, they are not bound by public opinion (O'Toole, 1996: 29–31).

5. *Respect for followers*   The sine qua non of morality is respect for people. Effective leadership of change usually begins with leaders' commitment to the moral principle of respect for followers. Those who succeed in bringing about effective and moral change believe in and act on the inherent dignity of those they lead—in particular, in their natural, human capacity to reason. In bringing about change, these leaders of leaders include the people affected in the change process. All employees have certain inalienable rights, particularly that all are entitled to be treated with respect and as ends and not means (O'Toole, 1996: 31–34).

6. *Clear thinking*   Leaders must be clear about their own beliefs. They must have thought through their assumptions about human nature, the role of the organization, the measurement of performance, and so on. They listen to the needs, ideas and aspirations of their followers, and then, within the context of their well-developed systems of belief, they respond to these appropriately. That is why leaders must know their own minds. That is why leadership requires ideas (O'Toole, 1996).

7. *Inclusion*   Value-based leadership requires full inclusion of followers. Inclusive leaders enable others to lead by sharing information, by fostering a sense of community, and by creating a consistent system of rewards, structure, process and communication. They are committed to the principle of opportunity, giving all followers the chance to contribute to the organization (O'Toole, 1996).

O'Toole (1996; 34–36) argued that leaders need not be saint-like in order to be effective. While the leader's relationship with the follower is a value-based one, it is not essential for leaders to be Christ-like in their private lives. The morality of their leadership is rooted in the goals they pursue and the nature of their relationship with those they serve.

Value-based leaders grant ample authority to their subordinates, and lead by example rather than power, manipulation or coercion. They believe in the ideas of liberty, equality and natural justice. Such leaders are ambitious; but they are ambitious in the cause of idealism. They bring about change by pursuing moral ends that their followers would ultimately adopt as their own, ends that are derived from the real needs of the followers. Leaders must always keep the faith of their followers; they must never lie to their followers or break the laws they are charged with holding. In all dimensions, their public lives must meet the highest standards of morality. The standard of excellence for a value-based leader is the two-fold ability to lead change both morally and effectively. Promise keeping, service and faithfulness—these are moral principles.

TRANSFORMATIONAL LEADERSHIP AND VALUE-BASED LEADERSHIP

In transformational leadership one or more persons engage with others in such a way that leaders and followers raise one another to higher levels of motivation and morality (Burns, 1978: 20). Various names are used for such leadership: elevating, mobilizing, inspiring, exalting, uplifting. The leaders' relationship with the follower can be moralistic, of course. However, transformational leadership ultimately becomes moral in that it enhances level of human morality and ethical aspirations of both the leader and the led, and thus it has a transforming effect on both. Therefore:

Hypothesis 2. Transformational leadership would be positively related to value-based leadership.

VALUE-BASED LEADERSHIP AND ORGANIZATIONAL STRUCTURE

Value-based leadership can produce social change that will satisfy followers' authentic needs. This kind of leadership can effect a change in the beliefs and behavior of the followers. The leader needs to keep information flowing back and forth rather than to give decisive commands. In a practical, business sense, value-based leadership provides for internal strategic unity, while at the same time encouraging independent entrepreneurial initiative. The kind of organizational structure that is appropriate to changing conditions is the organic structure (Burns and Stalker, 1961). Such structures have decentralized decision-making processes and less formalization. Hence, we had the following two hypotheses:

Hypothesis 3(a). Value-based leadership would be negatively related to the degree of formalization in an organization.
Hypothesis 3(b). Value-based leadership would be positively related to the degree of decentralization in an organization.

TRANSFORMATIONAL LEADERSHIP, ORGANIZATIONAL STRUCTURE, AND VALUE-BASED LEADERSHIP

Various studies relate transformational leadership to their context. According to such views, charismatic leadership is not equally applicable to all situations.

Value-based leadership, by definition, cannot be situational or contingent. Thus, environmental factors being conducive have to first result in value-based leadership, which in turn could enhance transformational leadership. Therefore:

Hypothesis 4(a). Value-based leadership would mediate the relationship between the degree of formalization in an organization and transformational leadership.
Hypothesis 4(b). Value-based leadership would mediate the relationship between the degree of decentralization in an organization and transformational leadership.

Methods

The data for this study were collected from a leading software consulting firm in India involved in executing innovative projects for over 800 clients across fifty countries. It had around 60,000 person years of experience in providing end-to-end solutions in diverse business areas and technology domains. The organization had around 14,000 employees.

The sample size of the study was hundred: sixty-seven males and thirty-three females. The designations of the respondents were ASE Trainee, ASE, or Project leaders (PL). Their work experience ranged from one year to five years. The large majority, however, had work experience of between one and three years, with only a small number in the sample beyond this range.

Respondents answered questions on transformational leadership and value-based leadership of their leaders, and the degree of formalization and centralization in their organization. Transformational leadership was measured by twenty items taken from the Multifactor Leadership Questionnaire (Bass and Avolio, 1995). Four items were used to measure each of the five dimensions of transformational leadership—idealized influence (attributed), idealized influence (behavior), inspirational motivation, intellectual stimulation, and individualized consideration.

To measure the dimensions of organizational structure—formalization and decentralization—the method enumerated by Robbins (1990) was used. This method was chosen as it measures the two relevant dimensions of formalization and decentralization separately. Seven items were used to measure formalization. The response to the first item in this set of seven items was recorded on a 4-point scale, while a 5-point scale was used for the other items. Therefore, the response to the first item was converted into a 5-point scale by multiplying by 5/4. Similarly, seven items were used to measure decentralization.

A scale for value-based leadership was developed using the characteristics enumerated by O'Toole (1996). Seven dimensions of value-based leadership were identified and twenty items were developed for these dimensions (see Appendix). Respondents were asked to answer these items by judging the extent to which they agreed with each statement with respect to their manager (their immediate supervisor). Responses were recorded on a 5-point scale: 0=Not at all; 1=Slightly agree; 2=Somewhat agree; 3=Fairly agree; 4=Completely agree. The Cronbach alpha for the scale was 0.98. Therefore, the scale for value-based leadership was not broken down into dimensions and all the items were considered to constitute a single dimension.

Results

Table 5.1 presents the means, standard deviations, Cronbach alphas, and correlations between all variables in the study. All five dimensions of transformational leadership—idealized influence (attributed), idealized influence (behavior), inspirational motivation, intellectual stimulation and individualized consideration—were positively related to formalization. Hypothesis 1(a) was thus not supported. The four transformational leadership dimensions other than inspirational motivation were significantly

Table 5.1: Means, Standard Deviations, Cronbach Alphas, and Correlations among Variables Studied[a]

N = 100	M	SD	1	2	3	4	5	6	7	8
1. Idealized Influence (Attributed)	2.62	.83	(.87)							
2. Idealized Influence (Behavior)	2.44	.81	***.88	(.83)						
3. Inspirational Motivation	2.64	.81	***.87	***.86	(.88)					
4. Intellectual Stimulation	2.60	.79	***.87	***.84	***.88	(.86)				
5. Individualized Consideration	2.46	.81	***.86	***.80	***.81	***.86	(.82)			
6. Formalization	3.59	.44	*.24	†.19	*.23	*.20	*.20	(.61)		
7. Decentralization	3.38	.57	**.29	**.27	.16	*.21	**.26	**.32	(.76)	
8. Value-based Leadership	2.61	.81	***.88	***.87	***.88	***.84	***.80	**.32	***.33	(.98)

[a]Cronbach alpha is in parentheses along diagonal; † = $p < .10$. * = $p < .05$. ** = $p < .01$. *** = $p < .001$.

Table 5.2: Partial Correlations, Controlling for Value-based Leadership

N = 100	1	2	3	4	5	6
1. Idealized Influence (Attributed)						
2. Idealized Influence (Behavior)	***.50					
3. Inspirational Motivation	***.41	***.41				
4. Intellectual Stimulation	***.50	***.40	***.53			
5. Individualized Consideration	***.53	***.36	***.35	***.58		
6. Formalization	-.10	†-.19	-.11	-.13	-.10	
7. Decentralization	-.01	-.04	**-.29	-.12	-.01	*.24

† = $p < .10$. * = $p < .05$. ** = $p < .01$. *** = $p < .001$.

positively related to decentralization, thus supporting hypothesis 1(b). Value-based leadership was significantly positively related to all five transformational leadership dimensions thus supporting hypothesis 2. Value-based leadership was also significantly positively related to both dimensions of organizational structure. Thus hypothesis 3(b) was supported while hypothesis 3(a) not.

Partial correlations controlling for value-based leadership are given in Table 5.2. The positive and significant relationships that existed previously between transformational leadership and organizational structure ceased to exist. Thus, hypotheses 4(a) and 4(b) were supported.

Discussion

Transformational leadership is significantly positively related to decentralization. The implication of this finding is that transformational leadership is more likely to emerge within the context of decentralized organizational structures. Studies have shown the dependence of transformational leadership on contextual factors. According to Shamir and Howell (1999), charismatic leadership is more likely to emerge and be effective in organic organizations than in mechanistic organizations. Organic organizations are characterized by decentralized structures. Thus, this finding is in agreement with what Shamir and Howell proposed. A decentralized structure gives greater flexibility to member's activities, and enables and encourages the expression of individual behavior by both leaders and potential followers. Thus, it is more conducive to the emergence of transformational leadership.

Contrary to what was hypothesized, results suggest that transformational leadership is positively related to formalization. A possible explanation for this relationship is that the organization studied might have had a peculiar feature. The work of employees in the organization was centred on specific projects in which they were involved. They were made part of a certain project team and there onwards they worked for that project. These teams were usually small, depending on the size of the project. The employees who constituted the sample generally regarded the project leaders as their leaders. On the other hand, since the organization studied is a large organization, there are rules that are formed centrally and that govern the functioning of the employees. Thus, the followers may not attribute formalization in the organization to their leaders. In addition, these teams function like a unit and they have a lot of autonomy. Therefore, while they may perceive the organization to have a formalized structure, they may still regard their leader as transformational.

Another possible explanation for this comes from the nature of the software industry. A high level of abstractness characterizes the work in this industry. The task of developing software entails a lot of instructions and guidelines. These instructions and guidelines are generally codified in writing. Thus, the employees may associate formalization with these written instructions. Hence, more of these instructions would always be welcome for the employees. They may therefore associate a transformational leader with high level of formalization.

Value-based leadership is positively related to both decentralization and formalization. Since there is a high positive correlation between value-based leadership and transformational leadership, the relationship between value-based leadership and organizational structure variables shows the same pattern as that of transformational leadership and structure variables. The positive relationship between value-based leadership and transformational leadership opens another dimension of leadership for managers to consider. Working on some aspects that constitute value-based leadership can enhance the development of transformational leadership. Managers could increase their transformational leadership capabilities by being truthful and honest. Being value-based leaders requires that leaders to have a willingness to serve and do not lose sight of their goals or compromise on their principles.

Findings show that once the effect of value-based leadership is removed, transformational leadership is no longer related to either of the structure variables. The implication of the finding is that a decentralized structure would not directly enhance transformational leadership; decentralization would enhance value-based leadership, which in turn would enhance transformational leadership. This is a significant finding from the point of view of future research and highlights the importance of a value-based approach to transforming organizations and individuals.

Limitations and Suggestions for Future Research

The questionnaire for structure that was used in this study was possibly inadequate. The questions perhaps did not capture the two dimensions of formalization and decentralization comprehensively. A more comprehensive questionnaire for measuring formalization and decentralization could further our understanding of their relationship with leadership. Another limitation of the study is that the two dimensions of structure that were studied are probably not adequate to capture organizational structure comprehensively. Therefore, a better understanding of the relationship between structure and transformational leadership can be had by studying the entire range of organizational structure variables that define an organization to be mechanistic or organic.

A significant finding of the study is the one relating to the role played by value-based leadership in the relationship between transformational leadership and organizational structure. This finding is significant since most of the previous studies regarding transformational leadership ignored value-based leadership. According to this study, there is a high positive correlation between value-based leadership and transformational leadership, and the relationship between transformational leadership and structural variables might cease to exist if a value-based approach is missing. Thus, future studies can re-examine some of the findings about transformational leadership by studying the contribution of value-based leadership in those relationships.

Conclusion

In the new economy scenario of today, leadership is taking wider and newer dimensions. Leadership is no longer the province of the anointed few. In the digital organization, everyone is a leader, charged with creating an environment for collective gain and success, and the mark of a leader would be to create other leaders within the organization—disciples, of a sort, who are empowered to act. This is also the essence of transformational leadership. The significance of transformational leadership has increased manifold in the wake of these changes. E-organizations are also more organic in nature. Understanding the true nature of the relationship between organizational structure and transformational leadership would help organizations meet their needs of right structure and right leadership. This study was an attempt to empirically study how leadership is related to the nature of organizational structures. Earlier studies have emphasized that an organic structure is closer to the emergence and effectiveness of transformational leadership. This study took these ideas further by considering two dimensions of an organic structure and examining the previously mentioned relationships. While the environment in which the organizations operate today may have undergone rapid and significant changes, the importance of value-based leadership has only increased. True leadership cannot be said to exist if it is not value-based and ethical in character. Thus, organizations must understand that the effectiveness of transformational leadership exists only so long as it is also value-based.

References

Avolio, B.J., J.M. Howell and J.J. Sosik (1999). 'A Funny Thing Happened on the Way to the Bottom Line: Humor as a Moderator of Leadership Style Effects. *Academy of Management Journal*. 42(2), 219–27.

Bass, B.M. (1985). *Leadership and Performance Beyond Expectations*. New York: Free Press.

Bass, B.M., and B.J. Avolio (1993). 'Transformational Leadership and Organizational Culture'. *Public Administration Quarterly*. 17(1), 112–22.

—— (1995). *Multifactor Leadership Questionnaire*. Redwood City, CA: Mind Garden.

Bass, B.M. and P. Steidlmeier (1999). 'Ethics, Character, and Authentic Transformational Leadership Behavior. *Leadership Quarterly*. 10(2), 181–217.

Baum, J.R., E.A. Locke and S.A. Kirkpatrick (1998). 'A Longitudinal Study of the Relation of Vision and Vision Communication to Venture Growth in Entrepreneurial Firms. *Journal of Applied Psychology*. 83(1), 43–54.

Behling, O. and J.M. McFillen (1996). 'A Syncretical Model of Charismatic/Transformational Leadership'. *Group and Organization Management*. 21(2), 163–91.

Burns, J.M. (1978). *Leadership*. New York: Harper and Row.

Burns, T. and G.M. Stalker (1961). *The Management of Innovation*. London: Tavistock.

Carpenter, H.H. (1971). 'Formal Organizational Structures and Perceived Job Satisfaction of Classroom Teachers. *Administrative Science Quarterly*. 16, 460–65.

Child, J. (1972). 'Organizational Structure and Strategies of Control: A Replication of the Aston Study'. *Administrative Science Quarterly*. 17, 163–77.

Conger, J.A. and R.N. Kanungo (1987). 'Towards a Behavioral Theory of Charismatic Leadership in Organizational Settings'. *Academy of Management Review*. 12, 637–47.

—— (1988). 'The Empowerment Process: Integrating Theory and Practice'. *Academy of Management Review*. 13, 471–82.

Dubinsky, A.J., F.J. Yammarino, M.A. Jolson and W.D. Spangler (1995). 'Transformational Leadership: An Initial Investigation in Sales. *The Journal of Personal Selling and Sales Management*. 15(2), 17–34.

Haga, J. (1965). 'An Axiomatic Theory of Organizations'. *Administrative Science Quarterly*. 10, 289–320.

Howell, J.M. and P.J. Frost (1989). 'A Laboratory Study of Charismatic Leadership'. *Organizational Behavior and Human Decision Processes*. 43, 243–69.

Ivancevich, J.M. and J.H. Donnelly, Jr. (1975). 'Relation of Structure to Job Satisfaction, Anxiety, Stress, and Performance'. *Administrative Science Quarterly*. 20, 272–80.

Kirkpatrick, S.A. and E.A. Locke (1996). 'Direct and Indirect Effects of Three Core Charismatic Leadership Components on Performance and Attitudes'. *Journal of Applied Psychology* 8(1), 36–51.

O'Toole, J. (1996). *Leading Change: The Argument for Value-based Leadership*. San Francisco: Jossey-Bass.

Ouchi, W.G. and J.B. Dowing (1974). 'Defining the Span of Control'. *Administrative Science Quarterly*. 19, 357–65.

Pawar, B.S. and K.K. Eastman (1997). 'The Nature and Implications of Contextual Influences on Transformational Leadership: A Conceptual Examination'. *Academy of Management Review*. 22(1), 80–109.

Porter, L.W. and E.E. Lawler (1964). 'The Effects of "tall" vs. "flat" Organizational Structure on Managerial Job Satisfaction'. *Personnel Psychology*. 17, 135–48.

Robbins, S.P. (1990). *Organization Theory*. Englewood Cliffs, NJ: Prentice-Hall.

Seltzer, J. and B.M. Bass (1990). 'Transformational Leadership: Beyond Initiation and Consideration'. *Journal of Management*. 16(4), 693–703.

Shamir, B. and J.M. Howell (1999). 'Organizational and Contextual Influences on the Emergence and Effectiveness of Charismatic Leadership'. *Leadership Quarterly*. 10(2), 257–83.

Waldman, D.A., G.G. Ramirez, R.J. House and P. Puranam (2001). 'Does Leadership Matter? CEO Leadership Attributes and Profitability Under Conditions of Perceived Environmental Uncertainty. *Academy of Management Journal*. 44(1), 134–43.

Appendix

Items for Measuring Value-based Leadership

Your leader

1. Is truthful, honest, and displays moral behavior.
2. Has healthy self-confidence and self-esteem.
3. Does not lose sight of his or her goals or compromise on his or her principles.
4. Is pragmatic, i.e., willing to lose on this or that immediate issue because he or she would not be distracted from the ultimate objective.
5. Has an inspiring vision.
6. Finds ways to communicate his or her vision to his or her followers.
7. Inspires trust and hope in his or her followers.
8. Has the loyalty of the followers.
9. Has a willingness to serve.
10. Listens to his or her followers.
11. Encourages dissenting opinion among his or her closest advisers.
12. Is committed to the moral principle of respect for the followers.
13. Includes the people affected in the change process.
14. Is clear about his or her own beliefs, e.g., assumptions about human nature, the role of the organization, the measurement of performance, and so on.
15. Listens to the needs, ideas and aspirations of his or her followers and responds to them within the context of his or her well-developed systems of belief in the appropriate fashion.
16. Has ideas.
17. Shares information with his or her followers.
18. Fosters a sense of community.
19. Creates a consistent system of rewards, structure, process and communication.
20. Is committed to the principle of opportunity, giving all followers the chance to make a contribution to the organization.

6

An Emotionally Intelligent Leadership Style

MOHIT P. KUMAR • SHIVGANESH BHARGAVA

According to business and labor leaders, we are in the midst of a transformation to a knowledge society, a society in which knowledge will be the primary personal and economic resource. Virtual organizations are no more a far-fetched concept. Natural resources, labor and capital, long considered the only meaningful resources, are becoming secondary, 'they can be obtained easily, only if there is knowledge' (Drucker, 1993). In the changing business milieu, what is truly valuable is the ability to use knowledge effectively and creatively. Further, numerous studies suggest that it is emotions, properly managed, that drive the greatest productive gains, innovations, and accomplishments of individuals, teams and organizations (Cooper and Sawaf, 1997). Stafford (2000) called the ones who possess this ability as knowledge workers.

It is in this context that we can understand the role of emotions. Especially if we look at emotions in the Aristotelian notion of intellectual virtue, and the role of it in knowing well. Knowing well is essential to succeed in a the knowledge society; and by understanding the emotional aspects of intellectual virtue a winner knows what it is to know well and how to put that knowledge to work. The role of emotions in organizational life has only recently developed as a valid and pertinent area of interest among scholars and practitioners. A catalyst to this interest has been the concept of 'emotional intelligence' (EI), introduced by Mayer and Salovey (1990). Emotional intelligence has become the 'buzzword' of the present day, especially following the success of Goleman's (1995: 98) path-breaking works. The concept is not just another 'neo-psycho babble'; attempts have been made to explain the phenomenon by serious researches in the social sciences (Mayer and Salovey, 1997; Mayer, Caruso and Salovey, 2000; Ashkanasy and Jordan, 1997; Davis, Stankov and Roberts, 1998; Ashforth and Humphrey, 1995; Weisinger, 1998; Mehrabian, 1994, 1996). The most significant development in the direction has been the formation of the Consortium for Research on Emotional Intelligence, which has compiled research work on emotions done over 37 years and proposed a model for emotionally intelligent training in organizations.

Linking emotions to behavior in the modern-day work settings in general and leadership in particular, is relatively rare, but certainly not non-existent; it has been done, especially in conference papers (Ashkanasy, Hartel, Fisher and Ashforth, 1998, etc.). This chapter attempts to examine the application of EI and its components on transformational and trans-actional leadership styles.

Emotional Intelligence

Mayer and Salovey state that for defining something as intelligence break down the concept into a set of mental abilities. The abilities coming from the intelligence must form a related set; they should have a significant positive correlation to traditional intelligence, without being so highly correlated that they are just another indication of them; and these abilities should 'develop with age and experience'. Hence, they define it as 'the ability to perceive accurately, appraise, and express emotion; the ability to access and/or generate feelings when they facilitate thought; the ability to understand emotion and emotional knowledge; and the ability to regulate emotions to promote emotional and intellectual growth'.

Goleman (1995, 1998b) defined EI as 'a capacity for recognizing our own feelings and those of others, for motivating ourselves, for managing emotions well in ourselves and in our relationships. He further stated that its five elements—self-awareness, self-regulation, self-motivation, social awareness and social skills—determine our potential to learn practical skills. Cooper and Sawaf (1997) have explained EI as 'the ability to sense, understand and effectively apply our power and acumen of emotions as a source of human energy, information, connection and influence'. In the same league, Bar-On (1997) attempted a more operational definition, that is, while cognitive intelligence is more strategic (i.e., one's capacity to function), non-cognitive intelligence or EI is more tactical (i.e., one's ability for immediate functioning), thus suggesting that non-cognitive intelligence helps predict success because it reflects how a person applies knowledge to the immediate situation. In a way this suggests that to measure emotional, personal or social intelligence is to measure one's ability to cope with daily situations and to get along in the world.

The term 'emotional intelligence', then, implies the intersection of emotion and cognition. For the purpose here, we attempt to understand the relationship of leadership style and EI within the framework proposed by Goleman (1995).

Leadership Styles Defined

Most successful organizations or teams are managed by effective leaders. A leader may be the expert, the one in charge, the person most respected by her or his followers, the one who controls aversive power or the individual who has the ability to dispense rewards. In fact, a leader may possess any one, or a combination of the these sources of leadership powers (Wann, 1997). Yukl (1997) defined leadership broadly in terms of mobilizing human resources for attaining organizational goals. More specifically, it is 'an influence of processes affecting the interpretation of the events for followers, the choice of objectives for the group or organization, the organization of work activities to accomplish the objectives, the motivation of followers to achieve the objectives, the maintenance of cooperative relationships and teamwork, and the enlistment of support and cooperation from people outside the group or organization.'

To date, effective leadership has eluded many people and organizations, more so because no quantitative research has been able to demonstrate which leadership behavior would yield positive results. Most of the leadership experts proffer advice based on inference, experience and instinct, which is correct only at times (Goleman, 2000). Scholars have tried to categorize leadership styles mostly on the basis of the behavioral manifestations of the style (like coercive, authoritative, affiliative, democratic, pace-setting, coaching leadership styles). But in practice, no leader adopts just one of these styles. Thus, optimizing the mix of the different styles to attain the highest level of effectiveness for a leader, has been the bone of contention among the researchers.

Moreover, today's leaders (managers) have a highly developed sense of opportunity cost of time. They are aware, subconsciously if not consciously, that the time they devote to any one thing is taking away time and energy from the other things they could—or should—be doing (Cooper and Sawaf, 1997). Here the relevant research (Goleman, 2000) suggest that it is the power in one's emotions that can help decide about the right style at just the right time and in the right measure.

For the present study, we have considered Bass's (1985) classification of leadership styles—transformational and transactional. Bass viewed transformational leadership as being empathetic and attempting to increase the level of followers' awareness for the valued outcomes by expanding and evaluating their needs and encouraging them to transcend their self-interest. Three factors were regarded as being transformational:

(i)   charismatic leadership: the amount of faith, respect and inspiration engendered by the leader
(ii) individualized consideration: the degree of attention and support given to the followers
(iii) intellectual stimulation: the extent to which the leader enables followers to rethink the ways they do things.

Two factors were considered transactional:

(i) contingent reward: the degree to which the leader provides reinforcement in return for appropriate follower behavior
(ii) management-by-exception: the extent to which subordinates hear from the leader only when failures or problems occur.

Research has consistently demonstrated the superiority of the transformational over the transactional form of leadership, especially in the context of the present-day turbulent organizational environment (e.g., Dubinsky, et al., 1995; Yammarino, et al., 1993). But there might be situations where the transactional style would be more warranted. Ideal in an organization's life cycle is a smooth transition style of leadership from the transactional to transformational. In the light of these arguments, the attempt here is to identify which style (transactional or transformational) incorporates a higher level of EI and its sub-components. Thus, hypothesizing:

Hypothesis a: Emotional intelligence (EQT) will lead transformational leadership behavior
Subsequently, five sub-hypotheses were formulated:
Hypothesis a1: Effective handling of one's own emotions (EQ1) will lead to transformational leadership behavior.

Hypothesis a2: Good interpersonal skills (EQ2) will lead to transformational leadership behavior.

Hypothesis a3: Adaptability (EQ3) will lead to transformational leadership behavior.

Hypothesis a4: Effective stress management (EQ4) will lead to transformational leadership behavior.

Hypothesis a5: Positive work environment (EQ5) will lead to transformational leadership behavior.

It was also hypothesized that

Hypothesis *b*: Emotional intelligence (EQT) and its factors (EQ1, EQ2, EQ3, EQ4, EQ5) will predict transactional leadership behavior.

These hypotheses were formulated with the assumption that transformational leaders will transform organizations by persuading their followers to join them in achieving positive and visionary goals. In so doing they will also motivate followers to behave in a way that contributes to the overall direction of their plans, while carrying out the necessary transactions of the business. They will challenge the status quo, stimulate intellectual thinking and pay extra attention to their individual needs and provide feedback to their subordinates. Thus, by applying an emotion perspective we will try and understand what makes a better leader.

Sample

Data were collected from 190 executives from four different privately owned organizations—two engaged in manufacturing consumer goods, one IT company and one manufacturing engineering goods—located in Mumbai. Of the sample, 187 was the valid data; of these, 52 were leaders with supervisory span ranging from 1 to 7. There was no female leader but the sample included 19 women and 168 men. The average age of the respondents was 40 years, with the range being 22 to 64 years. The average term of service was 19 years, with the range being one to 43 years.

Procedure

People of relevant influence were contacted and a research proposal was given to them. They in turn arranged a meeting with the HR head of their respective organizations. With the help of the HR team, the forms were distributed to executives at all the levels—from assistant manager to the general manager/vice presidents. The forms were subsequently collected by the respective HR departments. The response rate was close to 75 per cent.

SCALES USED

(A) MEASUREMENT OF EI

For the purpose, 133 item BarOn emotional intelligence inventory [EQ-I] was used. EQ-I has been developed over 19 years of research and tested on more than 48,000 individuals. It measures five mega-factors, that is, intrapersonal (EQ1), interpersonal (EQ2), adaptability (EQ3), stress management (EQ4) and general moods (EQ5), and fifteen specific factors that form the core of EI. It takes approximately thirty minutes to complete. The reliability studies focused on internal consistency and test–retest reliability. The average Cronbach's alpha coefficients are high for all the subscales, ranging from 0.69 (social responsibility) to 0.86 (self-regard) with an overall average internal consistency coefficient of 0.76. The test–retest reliability refers to stability of scale over time. The average stability coefficient is 0.85 after one month and 0.75 after four months (BarOn, 1997).

(B) ASSESSMENT OF LEADERSHIP STYLE

For the purpose, 40 items of Bass's 73 item multi-factor leadership questionnaire [MLQ] consisting of 5 factors—two facets of transactional leadership (TSC) (contingent reward and management-by-exception) and three facets of transformational (TRF) leadership (charismatic leadership, individualized consideration and intellectual stimulation)—were used. Bycio, Hackett and Allan (1995) took a subset of forty items to further conceptualize Bass's concepts.

Results and Discussion

EI as a phenomenon is still in very nascent stage of formalization. The focus of research continues to be on defining and explaining the concept by the processes of inclusion and exclusion. The attempt is primarily to demonstrate how EI is different from cognitive intelligence, social abilities, etc. especially by Mayer and Salovey (2000). Goleman (1997), Cooper and Sawaf (1997), Weisinger (1998), Rayback (1999) and others have been trying to identify the relevance of EI in work. In the process, the first aspect that they focus on is the emotional intelligence of the leader. This has been observed closely by Ashkanasy et al. (2000).

Ashkanasy et al. have tried to demonstrate the link between the transformational style of leadership and the leader's emotional intelligence. Their work yet is more theoretical than empirical, as they have proposed a likely logical hypotheses. Developing upon their work and hypotheses, the study was designed to demonstrate the difference in the leadership style and its causal relationship with the leader's EI quotient. Table 6.1 provides the descriptive details of the scales used. Correlation, regression and t-test analyses were performed on the data. The data on EI obtained from the leaders was analyzed for their correlation with the subordinates' aggregate assessment of the leadership style of their respective leaders. Further, the leaders with their respective aggregate leadership styles (transformational or transactional) were compared using the t-test, for normative scores on each subscale and the total EQ.

Table 6.1: Descriptive Statistics

	Minimum	Maximum	Mean	Std. deviation
Intrapersonal	116.00	189.00	157.78	15.04
Interpersonal	87.00	135.00	112.20	10.04
Adaptability	77.00	121.00	100.35	9.90
Stress management	42.00	89.00	67.06	10.17
General mood	53.00	84.00	69.46	6.76
EQ Total	410.88	600.00	506.87	42.00
TRF	13.00	108.00	71.62	21.28
TSC	14.00	48.00	29.90	7.17

The results revealed that the leadership style adopted by leaders in Indian organizations does not consider the transactional and transformational styles to be on a continuum. The leadership scale contained 40 items of which 27 represented components of transformational and 13 of transactional. The leaders' aggregate assessments of the leadership style they adopted was found to be a combination of both styles, being somewhere close to the average (2.5) on both. This can be considered a unique aspect about the leadership style adopted by the leaders.

Table 6.2: Correlation between EQ and Transformational Leadership

	EQ 1	EQ 2	EQ 3	EQ 4	EQ 5	EQ T
TRF	0.33**	0.38**	0.29**	0.10	0.31**	0.37**

Table 6.3: Correlation between EQ and Transactional Leadership

	EQ 1	EQ 2	EQ 3	EQ 4	EQ 5	EQ T
TRF	0.07	0.20	−0.03	−0.15	0.14	0.25*

The above finding can be viewed in the light of the fact that, mostly, in Indian work organizations even if the leader is transformational, followers are not characteristically equipped for taking on responsibilities. Often they prefer to receive orders and instructions from the leader, rather than take decisions on their own. This makes it necessary for the leader to create a balance of the two styles.

Table 6.2 shows the correlations between transformational leadership behavior and emotional intelligence and its five components. The correlation coefficients of EQ1, EQ2, EQ3, EQ5 with the transformational leadership style were 0.33, 0.38, 0.29, 0.31 respectively, they were all significant at 0.01 level. The EQ total was also found to be significant at 0.01 level with a coefficient value of 0.37. EQ4 failed to show any association with transformational leadership. Thus, except for stress management (EQ4), there is a strong positive correlation between transformational leadership and EQ (see Table 6.2). Further, an important result that emerged was that none of the components of EI could correlate significantly with the transactional leadership style. But the EQ total was found to correlate with transactional leadership at 0.05 level (see Table 6.3).

To further explore the relationship between leadership style and EI the sample was divided into two groups, that, high and low on EI (see Table 6.4). The two groups were then compared for the difference of their means on the transformational and transactional scores. The results demonstrated that the t-value for the transformational scores was significant at the 0.05 level, while it was not significant for the transactional scores. This facilitates us to assume that although both styles correlated significantly

Table 6.4: t-test of Leadership Styles with High and Low Emotional Intelligence (N_{high} = 33, N_{low} = 19)

	$Mean_{high}$	$Mean_{low}$	SD_{high}	SD_{low}	t-value	Sig.
TRF	79.27	70.93	12.52	22.46	2.37	0.02
TSC	30.80	29.38	5.70	7.34	1.06	0.29

with the total EQ, high EI is a better predictor of the transformational style than of the transactional style of leadership.

Table 6.5 demonstrated that the transformational style regressed highly with the total EQ as well as its components. The explained variance for EQ total was 13 per cent. The beta was found to be significant at 0.0.1 level (beta = 0.37, t = 3.48, p > 0.01) supporting hypothesis *a*, according to which EQT will lead to transformational leadership behavior. Intrapersonal skill (EQ1) could predict 11 per cent of the variance in the transformational style (beta = 0.33, t = 3.48, p > 0.01), thus supporting Hypothesis *a1*, according to which the ability to effectively handle one's own emotions (EQ1) will lead to transformational leadership behavior. Hypothesis *a2* was also supported by the results, which stated that good interpersonal skills (EQ2) will lead to transformational leadership behavior. The explained variance for EQ2 was found to be 14 per cent, the positive beta value was found to be significant (beta = 0.38, t = 4.17, p > 0.01). The results of the test of the causal effect of one's adaptability (EQ3) on transformational leadership behavior, also supported, Hypothesis *a3* as EQ3 could predict up to 10 per cent of variance in transformational leadership. The positive beta value was found to be significant (beta = 0.34, t = 3.74, p > 0.01). Stress management (EQ4) was the only component that could not predict the transformational leadership, as the beta weight was not found to be significant. Thus the hypothesis which stated that the ability to manage stress would lead to transformational leadership was not supported by the results. The last component of EQ could also predict transformational leadership. The explained variance for this relation was found to be 10 per cent (beta = 0.31, t = 3.38, p > 0.01), thus supporting the sub-hypothesis *a5,* which stated that the ability to create a positive work environment will lead to transformational leadership.

Table 6.5: Regression of EQ on Transformational Leadership

	Multiple R	R Square	Std. Beta	T	Sig. T
EQ total	0.37	0.13	0.37	3.48	.00
EQ 1	0.32	0.11	0.33	3.49	.00
EQ 2	0.38	0.14	0.38	4.17	.00
EQ 3	0.29	0.10	0.34	3.74	.00
EQ 4	0.31	0.10	−0.31	−2.16	.03
EQ 5	0.31	0.10	0.31	3.38	.00

Computation of the simple regression analysis for transactional with EI revealed that the EQ total could regress transactional leadership, but none of the components of EQ could regress transactional leadership (see Table 6.6). Therefore, *Hypothesis b* could only partially be supported by the results.

Table 6.6: Regression of EQ on Transactional Leadership

	Multiple R	R Square	Std. Beta	T	Sig. T
EQ total	0.25	0.10	0.25	2.05	.03
EQ 1	0.07	0.01	0.07	0.23	.81
EQ 2	0.20	0.25	0.20	1.87	.08
EQ 3	−0.03	0.11	−0.03	0.27	.82
EQ 4	−0.15	0.00	−0.15	−1.02	.15
EQ 5	0.14	0.25	0.14	1.31	.10

The findings of the study thus, support most of the hypotheses formulated in the context of transformational leadership. The transformational leadership style is likely to emerge among leaders who are emotionally more intelligent. This is so because EI involves handling relationships and managing the discharge of emotions within and between the relations. Thus leaders who are more capable of handling their emotions, manage their relationships with others effectively, are more flexible and have substantial control over their stresses, and are generally happy and optimistic, adopt more of the transformational style in the long run. One of the significant findings that the ability to manage stress does not relate with transformational leadership can be viewed in the light of the fact that well-managed emotions provide no reason for stress to generate, and hence the leader is not burdened with managing stress.

Further, with regard to the transactional leadership style, there is more of a give-and-take kind of relationship between the leader and his followers, which allows minimal formal and informal interaction within the dyads; as a result, the opportunities for emotions to surface are likely to be less. Thus, a transactional leader focuses less on the kind of relationships that he builds with followers. A significant aspect of the finding that none of the factors of EI could regress with transactional leadership but that the EQ total could relate with it can be understood in the light of the finding of Table 6.1, that leaders in Indian organization tend to create a balance between the two styles, as part of the situational necessity. Hence, although the components of EQ do not relate individually with the transactional style, the total EQ finds a significant positive relationship with the style.

Conclusion

The relevance of EI at work is undeniable in the current business environment. This is more so, because it is only human capital that can be a unique possession of an organization. It becomes highly critical to identify this uniqueness and to pamper, develop and facilitate its growth if the organization wants to remain lean, yet effective. To remain lean the organization needs to retain only those who really add to its net worth and effectiveness. At the same time it also needs to pamper the ones of value, as the net worth of an effective employee is always higher outside than within the organization, which might take him away from the organization. This can lead to loss in the net effectiveness of the organization as also entail the cost of hiring and training the replacement.

This study demonstrates that EI is a significant predictor of the leadership style. Transformational leadership has a strong bearing on EI and its constituents. Although, the study does not have any support from literature, it is logical that a transformational leader is likely to be in better control of his or her owner and others' emotions. But at the same time the result demonstrates a mix of both the transformational and transactional styles among Indian leaders (managers).

Thus, as is evident from the results, transformational leadership is more warranted in a mature organization and its leaders need to have a high level of EI. Further, for the sake of succession planning and to have effective leaders in the future, the organization needs to emphasize the EI development of and training among its prospective leaders. Hence, the study strongly recommends for organizations a comprehensive focus and development of the emotional intelligence of their workforce, not just for the sake of achieving excellence, but perhaps for survival in years to come.

References

Ashforth, B.E. and R.H. Humphery (1995). 'Emotions in the Work Place'. *Human Relations*. 48, 2.

Ashkanasy N.M. and P.J. Jordan (1997). 'Emotional intelligence: Is this the key to understanding the job insecurity behavior link in organizational restructuring?' Interactive paper presented at the Annual Meeting of the Academy of Management, Boston.

Ashkanasy, N.M. and B. Tse (2000). 'Transformational Leadership as Management of Emotions: A Conceptual Review'. In N.M. Ashkanasy, C.E.J. Hartel and W.J. Zerbe (eds.). *Emotions in the Workplace: Research, Theory and Practice*. Westport, Connecticut: Quorum Books, 221–304.

Bar-On, R. (1997). *EQ-i: A Measure of Emotional Intelligence: Technical Manual*. New York: Multi-Health Systems Inc.

Bass, B.M. (1985). *Leadership and Performance Beyond Expectations*. New York: Free Press.

Bycio, P., J.S. Allen, and R.D. Hackett (1995). 'Further Assessments of Bass's (1985) Conceptualization of Transactional and Transformational Leadership'. *Journal of Applied Psychology*. 80, 468–478.

Cooper, R.K. and A. Sawaf (1997). *Executive EQ: Emotional Intelligence in Leadership and Organizations*. New York: Grosset/Putnam.

Davis, M., L. Stankov and R.D. Roberts (1998). 'Emotional Intelligence: In Search of an Elusive Construct'. *Journal of Personality and Social Psychology*. 75(4) 989–1015.

Drucker, P.F. (1993). *Post-Capitalist Society*. New York: Harper Collins.

Dubinsky, Alan J., Francis J. Yammarino, Marvin A. Jolson and William D. Spangler (1995). 'Transformational Leadership: An Initial Investigation in Sales Management'. *Journal of Personal Selling and Sales Management*. 15 (Spring), 17–31.

Goleman, D. (1995). *Emotional Intelligence: Why it Can Matter More than IQ*. New York: Bantam Books.

——— (1998). *Working With Emotional Intelligence*. New York: Bantam Books.

——— (2000). 'Leadership that Gets Results'. *Harvard Business Review*. 2, 78–90.

Mayer, J. and P. Salovey (1993). 'The Intelligence of Emotional Intelligence'. *Intelligence*. 17, 433–42.

——— (1997). 'What is Emotional intelligence'. In P. Salovey and J.D. Sluyter (eds.). *Emotional Development and Emotional Intelligence*. New York: Basic Books.

Mayer, J., D.R. Caruso and P. Salovey (2000). 'Emotional Intelligence Meets Traditional Standards for an Intelligence'. *Intelligence*. 27(4), 267–98.

Mehrabian, A. (1998). 'Personality Tests Bearing on Emotional Intelligence'. Unpublished.

Rayback, D. (1998). *Putting Emotional Intelligence to Work: Successful Leadership is More than IQ*. Boston: Butterworth-Heinemann.

Stafford, S.P. (2000). 'The Role of Emotions in Knowing Well'. Unpublished. Simmons College, Mass.

Wann, D.L. (1997). *Sport Psychology*. Upper Saddle River, NJ: Prentice Hall.

Weisinger, H. (1998), *Emotional Intelligence at Work*. San Francisco: Jossey-Bass.

Yammarino, F.J., W.D. Spangler and B.J. Bass (1993). 'Transformational Leadership and Performance: A Longitudinal Investigation'. *Leadership Quarterly*. 4(1), 81–102.

Yukl, G. (1981). *Leadership in Organizations*. Englewood Cliffs, NJ: Prentice Hall.

7

Leadership in High Performing Organizations

SHAILENDRA SINGH

We all are interested in high performance, be it at the individual, team or organizational level. At the individual level it could be achieving results or surpassing targets/responsibilities. Similarly, timely project completion by a team can be an indicator of team-level performance. At the organization level, performance can be assessed through sales turnover, market leadership/market share, consistency in profits, increased or constant profitability over a period of time, consistency in growth, reputation in the industry—among peers, customers, etc.

Kaplan and Norton (1997) used a four-component model comprising customer perspective, internal business processes, learning and growth, and financial performance to assess organizational performance. It was found that a high-performing organization does well on financial goals, employee learning and growth, customer service and satisfaction, and internal business processes. As the law of equifinality suggests that the same objectives can be attained by an organization with a variety of inputs and through a number of paths (Katz and Kahn, 1978), this chapter argues that organizations can follow many routes to attain high performance.

Organization-wide leadership plays a crucial role in creating a conducive climate and in attaining high performance (Schein, 1987; Sinha, 1980). A number of studies have clearly pointed out that the single most important factor that differentiates winning companies from losing ones is that winning companies possess leadership engine—a proven system for creating dynamic leaders at every level (Tichy, 1999). Recently, emotional intelligent leadership has also seen to be linked with high performance and positive organizational culture (Goleman, 2000). Therefore, this chapter proposes that high-performing organizations have enabling leadership and organizational culture. And at the core of enabling leadership is emotional intelligence. By implication, emotional intelligence of personal, team and organizational systems needs to be enhanced for high performance.

Specifically, here a case is made for emotional intelligence among leaders of high-performing organizations in India and abroad. To this end, evidence has been cited from experiences of the World's Most Admired Companies as well as from those of the top ten employers of India. How emotional intelligence can be enhanced is also discussed.

Emotional Intelligent Leadership and Organizational Culture

Emotional Intelligence

Emotional intelligence relates primarily to the softer skills of the leader. While describing emotional intelligence, Goleman (1998) states that one thing common among effective leaders is what is known as 'emotional intelligence'. He emphasizes that IQ and technical skills are important but serve only as entry-level requirements for executive positions. Without emotional intelligence a leader can not be a great leader despite having the best training and possessing a great mind.

Mayers, Dipaolo and Salovey (1990) were the first to use the term 'emotional intelligence'. They defined emotional intelligence in terms of being able to monitor and regulate one's own and others' feelings, and to use feelings to guide thought and action. They suggested five components of emotional intelligence: (i) knowing one's emotions, (ii) managing emotions, (iii) motivating oneself, (iv) recognizing emotion in others, and (v) handling relationships. Goleman (1995) broadly followed the same conceptualization but rephrased some of the components. Goleman termed these dimensions as: (a) self-awareness, (b) self-regulation, (c) motivation, (d) empathy, and (e) social skills (Figure 7.1).

(a) *Self-awareness* This relates to understanding and recognition of one's emotions, mood, drives, strengths and weakness as well as their effects on others.

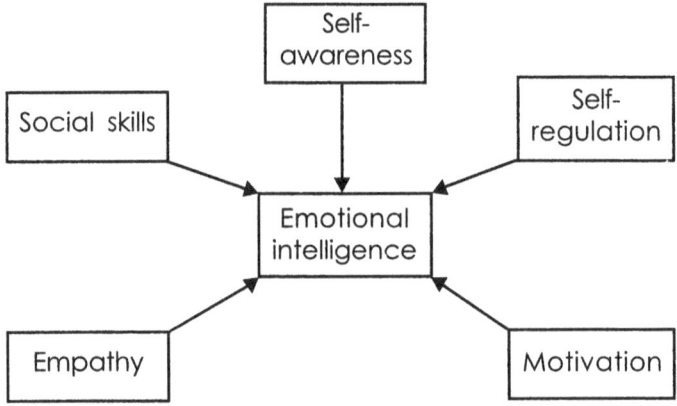

Figure 7.1: Dimensions of Emotional Intelligence

(b) *Self-regulation* This is the ability to control or redirect negative impulses and moods. It protects people from becoming passion slaves.

(c) *Motivation* This includes the tendency to set high goals and find meaning in work, and to persist beyond the call of duty.

(d) *Empathy* This refers to sensitivity to the needs of person and environment and the ability to respond to people according to their emotional needs.

(e) *Social skills* This includes the ability to manage relationship and to establish networks.

In a subsequent modification Goleman (2000) defined emotional intelligence as the ability to manage ourselves and our relationships effectively and as containing four fundamental capabilities: self-awareness, self-management, social awareness, and social skills. In the revised conceptualization, motivation has become part of self-management while the scope of empathy has been enlarged and renamed social-awareness. Each capability consists of a specific set of competencies along with corresponding traits (Table 7.1).

Leaders

All leaders, in any organization, face the same challenge. They are given a set of human, technological, financial resources to manage, with the

Table 7.1: Dimensions of Emotional Intelligence

Self-awareness	Self-management	Social Awareness	Social Skills
Emotional self-awareness: The ability to read and understand one's emotions as well as recognize their impact on work performance, relationships, and so on.	*Self-control:* The ability to keep disruptive emotions and impulses under control.	*Empathy:* Skill at sensing people's emotions, understanding their perspective, and taking an active interest in their concerns.	*Visionary leadership:* The ability to take charge and inspire with a compelling vision.
Accurate self-assessment: A realistic evaluation of your strengths and limitations.	*Trustworthiness:* A consistent display of honesty and integrity.	*Organizational awareness:* The ability to read the currents of organizational life, build decision networks, and navigate politics.	*Influence others:* The ability to wield a range of persuasive tactics.
Self-confidence: A strong and positive sense of self-worth.	*Conscientiousness:* The ability to manage oneself and one's responsibilities.	*Service orientation:* The ability to recognize and meet customers' needs.	*Developing others:* The propensity to bolster the ability of others through feedback and guidance.
	Adaptability: Skill at adjusting to changing situations and overcoming obstacles.		*Communication:* Skill at listening and at sending clear, convincing messages.
	Achievement orientation: The drive to meet an internal standard of excellence.		*Change catalyst:* Proficiency in initiating new ideas and leading people in a new direction.
	Initiative: A readiness to seize opportunities.		*Conflict management:* The ability to de-escalate disagreements and orchestrate resolutions.
			Building bonds: Proficiency at cultivating and maintaining a web of relationships.
			Teamwork and collaboration: Competence at promoting cooperation and building bonds.

goal of making these resources more valuable in tomorrow's world. That means a leader's job is to add value. The leader does this through people. Skandia's (1998) *Intellectual Capital Prototype Report* mentions that the leadership's task is to break down all barriers—perceived or actual—to human capital development in an organization.

What are the qualities of leaders that instill confidence in their subordinates? Research suggests seven essential qualities of leaders to succeed in leading knowledge workers (Bennis, 1999):

> *Technical competence*   Understanding of business and mastery of one's field of work.
> *Conceptual skills*   Ability to deal with abstracts and foresee, relate and think strategically.
> *Track record*   A history of achievements.
> *People skill*   Ability to communicate, motivate, influence, and delegate.
> *Taste*   Ability to identify and cultivate talent.
> *Judgement*   Making difficult decisions in a short time-frame with imperfect data.
> *Character*   The qualities that define an individual.

Skills if reinforced by supportive traits lead to superior performance. Yukl and Van Fleet (1992) identified four traits that have the potential to render a leader effective:

> *Emotional maturity*   Consisting of stable emotions, strong self-control, less of self-centredness, and less of defensiveness.
> *Integrity*   Signifying that the leader's behavior is consistent with his espoused values, that he is trustworthy and dependable.
> *Self-confidence*   Expressing perseverance and optimism.
> *Socialized power*   Enabling a leader to build subordinates' commitment, and empower and inspire others to realize the vision and mission of the organization, which indicates that the leader has been able to transcend his personal need to control these working around him.

What do Subordinates Expect from the Leadership of their Organization?

Knowledge workers have more power than owners and managers, thus meeting their expectations has become a new leadership requirement.

Bennis (1999) reports that subordinates seek four things from their leader: meaning or direction, trust in or from the leader, a sense of hope and optimism, and results. While fulfilling these expectations leaders provide four supporting conditions, which ultimately lead to four outcomes (Table 7.2).

Table 7.2: Leader's Response to Followers' Expectations and Outcome

Expectation	Leaders Provide	To Achieve
Meaning and direction	Sense of purpose	Goals and objectives
Trust	Authentic relationships	Reliability and consistency
Hope and optimism	Hardiness; confidence that things will work out	Energy and commitment
Results	Bias towards action, risk, curiosity and courage	Confidence and creativity

Emotional maturity, integrity, self-confidence, socialized power, goal orientation, breaking down barriers real or imagined, performance orientation, supportiveness, high expectations, trust, hope, etc. are an integral part of emotional intelligence. They can thus be addressed in leadership development programmes and developing emotional intelligence competencies.

Organizational Culture

Organizational culture is defined as the sum of individual opinions, shared mindsets, values and norms (Skandia, 1998). Culture is created and transmitted mainly through employees sharing their interpretations of events or through storytelling. The cultural features attributed to the organization actually come to characterize when employees share their beliefs about leadership. The more employees discuss leadership qualities, the more the qualities become organizational characteristics.

Leadership, Organizational Climate and Emotional Intelligence Relationship

In a recent study Goleman (2000) examines the relationship between climate and leadership styles. The leadership styles included are coercive, authoritative, affiliative, democratic, pace-setting, and coaching, while the climate dimensions included are flexibility, responsibility, standards, rewards, clarity, and commitment. An overall climate score was also derived. On the basis of his analysis, Goleman has concluded that the authoritative leadership style has the most positive impact on climate, but the styles affiliative, democratic, and coaching styles follow closely. He says that no style should be relied on exclusively and that all have at least short-term uses. In order to link leadership styles with emotional intelligence, he goes on to examine what actually comes within the label of each leadership style (Table 7.3).

Two dimensions of leadership, namely, coercive and pace-setting, had a negative relationship with overall climate.

Table 7.3: Emotional Intelligence Base of Leadership Style

Leadership Style	Emotional intelligence base
Coercive	Desire to achieve; initiative; self-control
Authoritative	Self-confidence; empathy; change catalyst
Affiliative	Empathy; building relationships; communication
Democratic	Collaboration; team leadership; communication
Pace-setting	Conscientiousness; drive to achieve; initiative
Coaching	Developing others; empathy; self-awareness

World's Most Admired Companies

Fortune and the Hay Group (Kahn, 1999) examined the world's most admired companies, on the basis of the following attributes: overall management quality, product or service quality, innovativeness, value as a long-term investment, financial strength, ability to attract and develop talent, commitment to community and to the environment, use of corporate assets, and global business acumen. The study rated General Electric as number one and Microsoft as number two, followed by Coca-Cola, Intel, and Berkshire Hathway.

Effective leadership differentiated the most admired organizations from their peers. To further explore what distinguished the top-rated companies from the rest, the Hay Group (1999) studied the leadership approach of these companies. The CEOs and heads of human resources of the top three companies answered a series of questions regarding the quality of their leadership and their development programs. Other global Fortune 500 companies answered the same set of questions. The results showed that the top-rated organizations differed from their peers on certain key factors. Most of these companies accorded top priority to the role of leaders in driving performance in the list of 'must haves'; disciplined leadership identification and selection; intensive leadership development programmes that address individual needs and the organization's strategic goals; values that emphasize people as well as financial results; and leadership models that include such characteristics as self-confidence and self-control, achievement orientation, empathy and teamwork. Specifically, the study revealed that the most admired companies have a larger proportion of executives with the emotional intelligence competencies (Table 7.4).

Table 7.4: Proportion of Executives Who Effectively Demonstrate Each Competency

(in percentage)

Dimensions Emotional Intelligence	Almost None/Few		About Half		Most/All	
	Most Admired	Peers (%)	Most Admired	Peers (%)	Most Admired	Peers (%)
Self-awareness	9	24	35	35	56	41
Self-management	4	14	13	30	83	57
Social-awareness	9	19	30	46	61	35
Social skills	0	11	9	27	91	62

Source: The Hay Group Report, 1999.

Evidence from Indian Companies

The BT-Hewlitt Associates' (2001) study on India's Best Employers to Work For identified the top ten organizations which really charged the 'the emotional and intellectual energy' of their managerial employees. The companies were identified and ranked on the basis of data gathered through: (*a*) Employee Engagement Survey and written comments; (*b*) Hewlitt People Practices Inventory and materials submitted by the company; (*c*) CEO's Employee Orientation; and (*d*) site visits. The top 10 companies thus identified are in order of their rank: (1) Infosys, (2) Procter and Gamble, (3) Hewlett-Packard, (4) ICICI, (5) Hughes Software Systems, (6) LG Electronics, (7) Hindustan Lever, (8) Compaq, (9) Asian Paints, (10) Bharat Petroleum.

On an average the best employers also perform better financially than other companies in the same industry. Based on the report and the homepage of these companies, it was examined how these top 10 employers of India respond to leadership and the work environment/culture to attract and nurture talent (Table 7.5).

The leadership across the best employer organizations shares the value that people are great assets and provides a supportive, empowering, open, and enabling environment. Emotional maturity, self-confidence, integrity, empathy, trust, learning, experimenting, performance orientation are the hallmarks of leadership in these organizations. The Fortune–Hay Group study also emphasizes leadership characteristic such as self-confidence and self-control, achievement orientation, empathy and teamwork.

Goleman's (2000) dimensions of emotional intelligence can be compared with the findings of the BT–Associates' study as well as the Fortune–Hay Group study. Both reveal the presence of several themes of emotional intelligence:

Self-awareness   Self-confidence, pride.
Self-management   Trust, transparency, initiative, challenging and engaging work, motivation, commitment, result oriented and performance as part of achievement orientation, innovation and experimentation as part of adaptability.
Social awareness   Relationship orientation, people orientation, caring attitude, and social and environmental concern as a part of service orientation, and empathy.
Social skills   Leadership, empowerment, freedom, flexibility, recognition, value orientation, learning and feedback, providing nurturance as part of developing others, innovation and experimenting with new ideas as a part change catalyst, relationship orientation as a part of building bonds; openness, informal communication as a part of communication, cooperation, fellow feeling teamwork as part of teamwork and collaboration.

Table 7.5: Leadership and Work Environment in Most Admired Companies of India

Company	Leadership	Work Environment
Infosys	To make people believe in themselves, the organization, the value system, in aggressive targets the organization sets. Belief comes from trust: the trust that this organization is not about making one set of stakeholders better off; it is about making everyone of us better off. Leadership has to be by example, and Infosys has done this in its small way. Practise fairness in every decision.	Exceptional place to work. People are key assets. High involvement of senior management. Hiring decisions depend on (in order of priority) the degree of learnability, fit with organizational culture and values and educational qualifications. Communicate and share information on a regular basis. Everyone is equal. Stock options for every category of employees. Work life of Infosys is tailored around personal lives of employees. Builds personal rapport with employees. Continuous upgradation of skills. Regular value workshops. Contribution to society through the Infosys foundation.
P&G	Interests of the company and of the employees go hand in hand.	The culture of the organization is informal, flexible and transparent.

(Table 7.5 continued)

(Table 7.5 continued)

Company	Leadership	Work Environment
	Provides global opportunities and early responsibilities, thus gives a feeling of empowerment. While enhancing shareholders' value, employee interests are kept in the forefront.	People are enthusiastic, willing to experiment with new ideas; and motivated and exuberant. Employees describe it as 'a great place to work', 'has a strong caring for its people' 'has trust in us' and 'is a people company'. The company follows the principle-based approach, thus practices are aligned to the needs of each employee not on his role or level in the organization. Takes care of the health of its employees and family members. The company matches people with P&G's business needs. Has open communication. Believes in introducing change through the people who are going to stay with it. All initiatives at P&G are executed by the taskforce, with HR serving as facilitator's role. Employees are committed and strive to make work at P&G a great experience.

h-p	Founder-CEO of h-p India considers employee satisfaction as the first goal on the business agenda.	This industry is hi-tech and dynamic and therefore requires a free flow of fresh ideas, perspectives and mindsets, thus, an h-p employee is an individual with honesty, integrity, commitment to the customer and a belief in professional excellence.
	Since h-p is a knowledge-driven company, people who possess and disseminate knowledge become primary assets; thus focus on people and development becomes a critical success factor.	Openness, respect for individuals, team-work, integrity, trust and flexibility are the keywords that describe the organizational culture of h-p.
	Leader's job is to create enabling environment. He should be essentially a coach and not a commander with a constant focus on performance.	Free flow of information is a way of life.
		Employees enjoy enormous freedom; the company follows the practice that once the strategy, structure and processes are defined, employees have the flexibility to achieve their objectives within the frame-work of h-p.
		What matters is performance and not hierarchy.
		Offers flexibility through flexitime, tele-commuting, and reduced hours of employment.

(Table 7.5 continued)

(Table 7.5 continued)

Company	Leadership	Work Environment
		HR policies are driven to cater to employees' personal needs.
		Compensation package is performance based, and all employees are eligible for stock.
		Employees are encouraged to learn and update continuously and company reimburses the fee of various learning programmes.
ICICI	Employee-centric focus. Of the three types of capital—finance, human, technology—human capital is at the centre of ICICI's strategy. The fourth capital is speed which ICICI has made the central point along with human capital, around which technology and finance revolve. Learning and teaching is emphasized.	ICICI leverages technology to serve its internal customers.
		It has an automated recruitment process.
		Believes that quality of life enhances performance, thus the company takes care of all employees' needs and, in turn, they focus better on their work.
		Work facility is state of the art. All conceivable facilities are provided onsite. The office is open 24 hours and employees have flexible hours.
		Imparting and managing knowledge is a priority area.

	ICICI's knowledge management portal ('WiseGuy') stores a wealth of information, which is accessible to all employees.
	Employees are encouraged to acquire higher competencies through various learning programmes and are facilitated by reimbursement of fee and by provision of sabbaticals.
	Employees are recognized for their performance in innovative ways, including gifts, paid holidays with family, featured on intranet.
Hughes Software	People hold the key. We provide the type of work and overall package. HSS is a cutting edge technology company that pays its employees well.
	Company environment can be described as open, friendly, warm, non-hierarchical, and flexible.
	Relationships are cultivated 'virtually' through HSS website.
	Recruitment through employee referrals is encouraged.
	Flexibility to change roles within the company, thus there is no need to look outside.

(Table 7.5 continued)

(Table 7.5 continued)

Company	Leadership	Work Environment
		All employees are offered stock in the company.
		Incentive programmes for managers include a component on leadership which includes variables like retention, development of employees, employee relations, performance management and career planning.
		Recognition programmes include e-greetings, formal awards for sense of humor, outstanding performance, adherence to company culture.
		Employees meet with senior management to have open communication on any issue and evolve action plans to change the situation.
		Company is sensitive to environmental and societal needs and does its bit by recycling papers and encourages employees to contribute to charitable causes and has charity boxes in the campus.

| LG Electronics | It is time to change mindset and be more innovative. Each employee of LG must be equal to four of rivals' employees. Top leadership states 'We don't need geniuses, we need normal people with strong legs and good hearts. The strong legs help in numerous trips to the field and a good heart is important in view of community programmes that LG undertakes and in creating fellow feeling among employees.' | The most frequently used words in LG are empowerment, freedom, transparency and performance. Everyone has a target and a budget apart from a key performance index. LG tries to maintain the highest level of motivation; performance-linked bonuses are paid every six months; uses congratulatory notices to motivate people. LG uses visuals to constantly inform its people about current status and targets. Openness is practised by the company; the MD has lunch with different teams every week. Everybody has lunch together in the canteen. There is frequent attitudinal training. HR interacts with employees' families' and employees' family members are treated as members of the LG parivar. Picnics and family get-togethers are common. LG's culture is result oriented. |

(Table 7.5 continued)

(Table 7.5 continued)

Company	Leadership	Work Environment
		Feedback is used for improvement and learning. Internal competition is encouraged. People are given operative freedom.
HLL	Our common goal is to 'meet the everyday needs of people every where' and the company's key strength is its people: 'HLL is a people's company'. 'In the ultimate analysis a company is nothing but a collective intellect. The dynamism we wish to inculcate in our organization is directly proportional to the dynamism we unlock in the minds of our employees. Businesses are ultimately built by the spirit of the women and men behind them, fired with capability and desire to succeed. We must transform our people into sustained winners, accentuating their strengths and bridging their gaps' (Dadiseth, 2001).	Employees need to do just their job; the rest of the things are taken care of by HLL. An ideal employer believes in looking after every aspect of employees' life needs. Women managers can take leave up to two years. Company helps employees to get admission for their children in good schools. Employees are provided with club membership. There is constant emphasis on developing talents internally. Various kinds of training, like the five-month management trainee program, the compulsory rural stint, and outbound programs ensure business growth through people's growth.

Compaq	Leader provides human touch.	Compaq is sensitive to employee needs. Ownership and empowerment are a way of life.
		All employees have stock option.
		Employees have the flexibility and freedom to chalk out their action plan.
		Health and fitness needs of employees are taken care of.
		The HR portal provides feedback. Learning is encouraged: self-paced learning, knowledge-enriched Fridays, reimbursement of fee of technical courses. There is flexibility to address development needs.
Asian Paints	Asian Paints provides a lot of freedom to people: they are given a fixed context but are free to devise there own way of working.	Support system is very good and leaders provide nurturance to initiative.
		While in hiring decisions the most important criterion is a fit with the company's values.
		Mentors and colleagues coach and socialize new recruits.
		The company follows a no-lay-off policy.

(Table 7.5 continued)

(Table 7.5 continued)

Company	Leadership	Work Environment
		The company believes in developing talents from within; hence there is a strong learning culture in Asian Paints. Employees are encouraged to upgrade their skills by participating in various development programs. Employees are satisfied with company's emphasis on learning culture, its performance orientation and freedom to work.
BPCL	What differentiates BPCL from others is the commitment of its employees. The company's vision is to make it a great place to work. The company focuses on people as it believes that the only competitive advantage is people.	The CEO starts his morning with sending birthday greetings to employees—a small gesture but employees appreciate it. The company practises openness, informality and close relationships. People are accessible. Empowerment has made it attractive to managers. Performance expectations and feedback are openly discussed.

The company rewards employee input and performance in the form of variable pay.

The company has set up the Foundation of Organizational Learning—a forum sharing concepts on being a learning organization. Similarly, visionary leadership and planning process and transition labs are used to inculcate desirable behavior.

BPCL takes care of employees' basic and social needs.

This classification suggests that issues of leadership and organizational culture can be addressed simultaneously with the issue of emotional intelligence. The data presented here strongly suggest that leadership and organizational climate are positively related with emotional intelligence.

A Model of High Performance: Leaders Need to Develop their Own Emotional Intelligence and Coach Others

In an era of uncertainty and constant change, it is futile to suggest any prototype of high-performing organizations which can be replicated to go from average performance to high performance, or from poor performance to average performance because every organization transacts in a unique ecology. Nevertheless, it is tempting to suggest that if the proposed processes are followed there is a high probability of attaining high performance, and that if these processes are not followed there is a high likelihood that organizations may not do well.

Intrinsic Rewards

Extrinsic rewards are taken for granted. The challenge lies in creating motivational intrinsic rewards, which can address the higher-order needs of employees. These rewards are recognition, empowerment, freedom, autonomy, feedback, encouragement, opportunity to grow as a person, opportunity to utilize one's abilities, opportunity to network and collaborate, opportunity to experiment with new ideas, opportunity to help others, being respected and trusted, etc. Here is where emotional intelligence comes handy. Leaders high on emotional intelligence are better at creating an empowering and motivational climate. The four dimensions of emotional intelligence, namely, self-awareness, self-control, social awareness, and social skills subsume almost all the necessary competencies required for motivating people intrinsically. The emotional intelligence framework also provides enough flexibility to leaders to choose styles appropriate to the culture/climate they want to create. Goleman (2000) gives a very apt analogy: 'Imagine the style, then, as the array of clubs in a golf pro's bag. Over the course of a game, the pro picks and chooses clubs based on the demand of the shot. Sometimes he has to ponder his selection, but usually it is automatic. The pro senses the challenge ahead and swiftly pulls out the right tool, and elegantly puts it to work. That 's how high impact leaders operate too.'

Following Noel Tichy (1997), the framework also suggests that there is a need for many leaders at various levels without which an organization would not be able to sustain its success, thus leaders need to multiply themselves. They should develop their own emotional intelligence and leadership styles, and eventually become coaches and mentors.

How Emotional Intelligence Can be Enhanced

Unlike IQ, emotional intelligence is not static: it can be learnt and developed. The competence framework (McKnight, 1991), (Figure 7.2) suggests that competence is a function of the training, education and skills a person develops over time. It also depends on some innate qualities, which can be developed, and which help the person acquire knowledge and skills faster. Some amount of knowledge is however, a must for a person to become emotionally intelligent. Knowledge also directly influences skills. Thus, competence is a composite of knowledge, skill and aptitude.

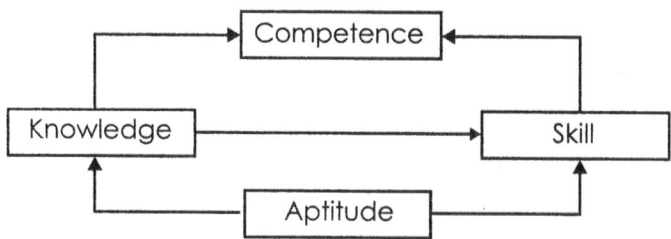

Figure 7.2: Competence Framework

In order to develop emotional intelligence, one has to first unlearn old dysfunctional habits through creative destruction and acquire a new set of behavior. For this, Lewin's (1951) model of change—de-freezing, developing and experimenting with new behavior and refreezing the newly found behavior and experimenting with new behavior with the highest proficiency levels—can be followed. T-Group or learning group method-ology can be used for acquiring emotional intelligence. In addition, instrumentation, behavior modeling and coaching and mentoring may also be useful for developing emotional intelligence and interpersonal skills. Since an elaboration of each technique is beyond the scope of this chapter, a graphic illustration of the process through which learning can be integrated has been presented in Figure 7.3.

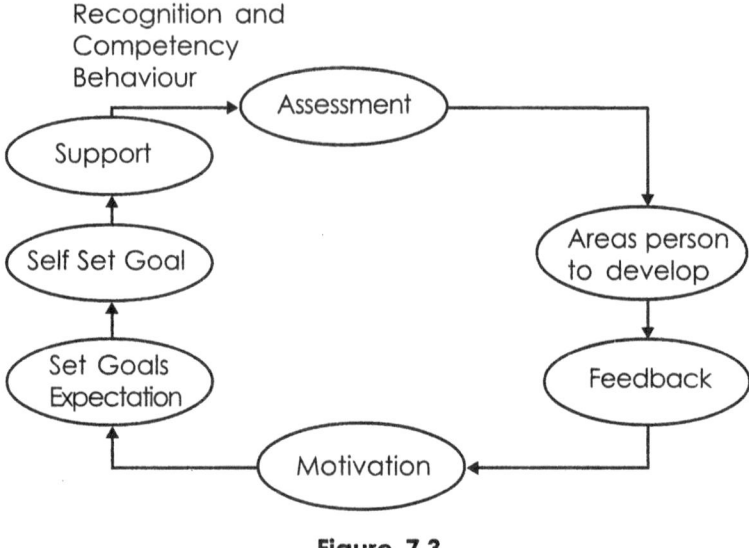

Figure 7.3

Conclusions

A high-performing organization does well on financial goals, employee learning and growth, customer service and satisfaction and internal business processes. This chapter makes the point that there are routes to attaining high performance among them leadership and organizational culture. On the basis of the culture and leadership in the world's most admired companies as also the ten Indian employers, a proposition is made that a positive motivational work culture can be treated by enhancing emotional intelligence. The emotional intelligence framework also suggests that leaders have a broad range of competencies and styles that they can leverage according to the need of situation. Moreover, since leaders are required at all levels of an organization, it is proposed that in order to sustain high performance, leaders need to hone their emotional competencies and subsequently become coaches and mentors to multiply leadership across the organization. Ways to enhance emotional competencies have also been suggested. The conclusions may be accepted with caution in the light of limitations of the data.

References

Bennis, W. (1999). 'The Leadership Advantage'. *Leader to Leader*. Spring, No. 12, Online Journal.

B.T.-Hewitt Associates (2001). 'The Best Employers in India'. *Business Today*. 10(1), 21 January.

Dadiseth, K. (2001). Cited at Homepage www.hll.com.

Goleman, D. (1995). *Emotional Intelligence*. New York: Bantam Books.

—— (1998). 'What Makes a Leader'. *Harvard Business Review*. November–December 93–12.

—— (2000). 'Leadership That Gets Results'. *Harvard Business Review*. March–April, 78–90.

Hay Group (1999). 'What Makes Great Leaders: Rethinking the Route of Effective Leadership'. www.HayGroup.com.

Henry, J.W., M.J. Martinko and M.A. Pierce (1993). 'Attributional Style as a Predictor of Success in a First Computer Course'. *Computers in Human Behaviour*. 9(4), 341–52.

Kahn, J. (1999). 'World's Most Admired Companies'. *Fortune*. October 11.

Kaplan, R. and R. Norton (1996). *The Balance Score Card*. Boston: Harvard Business School Press.

Katz, D. and R.L. Kahn (1978). *The Social Psychology of Organizations* (2nd edn). New York: Wiley.

Lewin, K. (1951). *Field Theory in Social Science*. New York: Harper and Row.

McKnight, M.R. (1991). 'Management Skill Development'. In J.D. Bigelow (ed.). *Management Skills*. Newbury Park, CA: Sage

Meyers, J.D., M.T. DiPaolo and P. Salovey (1990). 'Perceiving Affective Content in Ambiguous Visual Stimuli: A Component of Emotional Intelligence'. *Journal of Personality Assessment*. 54, 772–81.

Skandia (1998). 'Human Capital in Transformation. Intellectual Capital Prototype Report'. At http://www.skandia.se.

Stein, N. (2000). 'The World's Most Admired Companies'. *Fortune*. 2 October.

Tichy, N.M. (1999). 'The Growth Imperative'. *Leader to Leader*. Fall, No. 14, Online Journal.

Tichy, N.M. and E. Cohen (1997). 'The Leadership Engine'. New York: HarperBusiness.

Yukl, G. and D.D. Van Fleet (1992). 'Theory and Research on Leadership in Organizations'. In M.D. Dunnette and Leatta M. Hough (eds.). *Handbook of Industrial and Organizational Psychology* (2nd edn., vol. 3, 147–98). Paulo Alto, CA: Consulting Psychology Press.

8

Transformational Leadership, Values and Effectiveness: Towards Creating a Context for Value-based Leadership

SUMITA RAI • ARVIND K. SINHA

Organizations that truly belong to the twenty-first century are going to be vastly different from those that only barely managed to get up to modern times somehow. Most social organizations in the twentieth century were more linear, with structures that were hierarchical and bureaucratic. The old mindset may be summarized in just three words: control, order and predict (Bennis and Goldsmith, 1997). By contrast, in the twenty-first century, the scenario is going to be rather different, marked by rapid changes. In order to deal with change, organizations are going to have to become hinged. They are going to be confusing, chaotic places to work in, and they will be full of surprises.

Leading in Twenty-first Century Organizations

One of the challenges of modern times is how to develop the organization's social structure or the architecture that might help generate and develop the intellectual capital. In other words, the major challenge for twenty-first century leaders would be how to release the brainpower of their organizations. With the advent of e-business, the rules of the game will be rewritten every day, and the information age will witness the emergence of new business models. Even the most efficient companies may be made redundant by superior business models that emerge, seemingly from nowhere (Mariwala, 2000).

Need to Match the Pace of the Changing Scenario

As we are going through a period of the most rapid acceleration of 'creative destruction' in history, can one think of recreating a company at a similar pace? In the changing nature of organizations there is a need to change the nature of CEOs as well as leaders, who in turn, have to reinvent and redesign their roles too. Once they do this they should make sure that they redesign and reinvent their organizations also. Harish Mariwala (2000), CEO of Marico Industries Limited, observes, 'Leadership paradigms are bound to change in this environment, as the new world will require "integrative" and holistic thinking. The hierarchical leadership model will disappear, and the leadership will reside less at the top. Instead, it will be shared and distributed throughout the organization in order to make companies much more responsive—and fast'.

Is there a Way of Leading that Might Help Achieve this End?

In a world where things are changing daily we need leaders who can recreate the organization according to the changing scenario and at a matching pace. But, does behavioral science offer any model of leadership that might fit the bill? Perhaps yes. Leadership has been exhaustively examined, studied, dissected and discussed, but much of the focus has been on how American businesses define leadership. What works in the US-based businesses may or may not work in business environments in other parts of the world. The general description of a leader, in the modern context, might be someone who is charismatic and seeks to develop a transformational style of leadership. Charismatic and transformational leadership is thought to broaden and elevate the interests of followers, generate among them an awareness and acceptance of the purpose and mission of the group, and motivate them to go beyond their self-interests for the good of the organization. But different cultural groups may vary in their conceptions of the most important characteristics of charismatic and transformational leadership. In some cultures, one might need to take strong, decisive action in order to be seen as a leader, while in other cultures consultation and a democratic approach may be the preferred one. Leaders are expected to have vision, but how this is displayed differs from culture to culture. In China, the influence of Confucian values makes people wary of leaders who talk without taking specific action. Indian managers, on the other hand, care less about visionaries, preferring bold, assertive styles of leadership.

A leadership style that has received considerable amount of attention for its desirability in the past few years is transformational leadership. It is assumed that an individual's attributes such as values, and systemic forces such as transformational leadership style of the superior ultimately have to be evaluated in terms of some criteria. One relevant criterion is personal effectiveness. Thus the present research incorporated the variables of transformational leadership, values and personal effectiveness. The underlying assumption was that some specific value realization combined with transformational leadership might result in heightened effectiveness. Effectiveness was measured in terms of personal effectiveness. Personal effectiveness may be considered a combination of some other constructs as well. Some variables associated with personal effectiveness were considered: These included self-esteem, internal work motivation, and increased awareness of self-pattern of behavior.

Transformational Leadership

A significant amount of attention has been given to the theories related to transformational leadership in the recent years (e.g., Barling, Weber and Kelloway 1996; Bass, 1985, 1990; Conger and Kanungo, 1987). The concept of transformational leadership was first highlighted in a comprehensive manner by Burns (1978). Burns (1978: 3) noted a qualitative distinction between transactional and transformational political leaders. In transactional leadership, leader–follower relationships are based on a series of exchanges or bargains between leaders and followers. Thus transactional leaders approach followers with an eye to exchanging one thing for the other such as jobs for votes, or subsidies for campaign contributions. According to Burns, transformational leaders also recognize the need for a potential follower, but they go further, seeking to satisfy higher needs, in terms of Maslow's (1954) need hierarchy, to engage the full person of the follower. Transformational leadership results in mutual stimulation and elevation that converts followers into leaders and may convert leaders into moral agents (Bass, 1990: 23). Bass (1985, 1990, 1997,

1998) has contributed a great deal to the evolution of the theory and ramifications of transformational leadership. Transformational leadership includes charisma (providing a vision and a sense of mission, and raising followers' self-expectations), intellectual stimulation (helping employees emphasize rational solutions, and challenge old assumptions), and individualized consideration (developing employees and coaching). Howell and Avolio (1993) note that *transformational* leaders concentrate their efforts on longer term goals; place value and emphasis on developing a vision; change or align systems to accommodate their vision rather than work within existing systems; and *coach followers to take on greater responsibility for their own development, as well as the development of others. These leaders are often described by the followers as inspirational* (emphasis added). Such leaders frequently display transactional leadership behavior as well (pp. 891–92). Apparently, transformational leadership has been found to be an important variety of leadership functions. Bass (1997) maintains that transformational leadership is more effective and satisfying than just constructive transactions and constructive transactions are more effective and satisfying than corrective ones.

Values

Constructs that are believed to play significant roles in people's lives in modern times include an important construct called values. Values may be defined as 'an enduring belief that a specific mode of conduct or end-state of existence is personally or socially preferable to an opposite or converse mode of conduct or end-state of existence' (Rokeach, 1973: 5). A related concept called value system is 'an enduring organization of beliefs concerning preferable modes of conduct or end-states of existence along a continuum of relative importance' (Rokeach, 1973: 5). According to Rokeach (1973), values may be of two kinds, terminal and instrumental. Super (1970) defined values as the objectives that one seeks to attain to satisfy a need (p. 190). This approach to understanding values indicates the existence of some relationship between needs and values. A related concept is that of value expectancies, which means the chance to realize an important value with the help or anticipated help of work. It is thus the product of the importance attached to a value and the probability of the value being realized through work experience. Super and Nevill (1986) consider it a component of work salience. Conceptually the importance or salience of work has to be distinguished from the instrumentality of work. In the Indian setting, Sinha (1990) uses the eighteen values identified in the Work Importance Study (WIS), plus three more values typical to Indian culture. The three Indian values are: peace of mind, comforts of life, and dependency (Sinha, 1990: 55). Sinha (1990) argued that values are important building blocks of culture, and that the values that contribute to what he termed as synergetic (as against 'soft') work culture, may be important in organization building.

Several scholars and practising managers have identified some kind of value that, they believe, has been the driving force behind the organizations that are admired on some count or the other. Chakraborty (1995: 3–6) compiled the transformation from several contributors with first-hand experience in or about major organizations in India. They identified the dominant values of the relevant organizations. It was pointed out that the Tatas put strong emphasis on *complete trust in the people chosen*. The Bhilwara group emphasized *human and spiritual value combined with dedication*. Indian Petro Chemicals Limited emphasized *discipline of the senses and self-control, and a blend of rationality with morality*. The Tata Engineering and Locomotive Company's (TELCO) Jamshedpur unit puts great premium on the dictum that *to be a good manager one has to be a good man*.

The foregoing emphases point to the fact that (a) values are perceived as of importance in work settings, (b) different organizations emphasize different values, that become their respective hallmarks, and (c) the values may have the quality of a driving force. In the present work, the authors have used a concept called value realization, which represents the extent to which a particular value or value dimension a person has been able to achieve or realize during the course of his or her organizational experience. Values form the central core of human existence in organized societies. It may be important to distinguish between the desirable and the desired values. Of the two, desired values are closer to actual behavior. Thus, they may be a little more important. Not much work is yet available in terms of *value realization*. Based on our research experience (Rai, 2000), we have reasons to believe that the realization may act as a kind of reinforcer for the values one holds and maintains. Hence, apart from (a) desirable and (b) desired values, it may be useful to think also in terms of (c) *realized values*, as a concept that has ramifications for organizational dynamics.

Personal Effectiveness

Effectiveness may be defined in many ways. One of the important things to consider is how 'well' a person does his or her job, whatever the job or role is. In other words, if a person does his or her job or role effectively and/or attains the goals he or she had set for himself/herself, the person may be considered effective. Findings show that there is little correlation between a person's effectiveness and his or her intelligence, knowledge and imagination. Such people who may otherwise have reasonable or even high intelligence, knowledge and imagination are often ineffectual because they fail to realize that insights become effective only through hard and systematic work. Hence, it may be said that intelligence, imagination and knowledge are essential inputs, which set limits to what can be attained, but only effectiveness converts them into results. The effectiveness of a person may derive added strength from some other individual-related constructs. For instance, Rao (1985) contends that self-efficacy or personal efficacy is one of the important factors that contributes to managerial effectiveness. Self-efficacy is found to be strongly related to past performance (Bandura, 1982). Some other variables could be self-esteem, internal work motivation, and an increased awareness of self-pattern of behavior; all these may add to the effectiveness of the person in an organizational setting.

Self-esteem

People differ in the degree to which they like or dislike themselves. This trait is called self-esteem. According to Hill and Ritchie (1977), 'Self-esteem is a subjective evaluation of how a person feels about himself, a composite measure of one's perception of competence and feelings of security and confidence, and a recognition of one's strengths and weaknesses' (p. 493). People who score high on self-esteem are those who attend to, and emphasize their abilities, strengths, and good qualities whereas persons who score low on self-esteem are those who focus on, and emphasize their deficiencies, weaknesses, and bad qualities (Baumeister and Tice, 1985: 451). In organizational behavior research, low self-esteem has generally been considered dysfunctional (Dipboye, 1977; Korman, 1976). Therefore it may be important to learn how positive self-esteem develops.

Internal Work Motivation

The concept of motivation is invariably linked with a notion of reinforcement or reward. It has been noted in the literature that rewards can come from sources external to the organization as well as from within. Variables like autonomy, satisfaction, a feeling of being in control and making meaningful contributions, can all come from within, and may serve as a powerful reinforcement or reward for making an individual sustain the motivated work performance. This phenomenon is known as internal or intrinsic work motivation, that is, the individual is primarily motivated to work due to the reward value of reinforcements coming from within and not for the sake of rewards coming from external sources. Additionally, there is evidence to show that very high intrinsic motivation levels have strong tendencies to resist the negative impacts of extrinsic rewards (Arnold, 1976).

Increased Awareness of Self-Pattern of Behavior

Since the focus of the present work is on the individual, one may note an important point of view that emerged rather early within the framework of mainstream psychology. More specifically, the reference here is to what has been labelled as the *self*, though with varying connotations in the writings of different authors. The focus shifts from a mechanistic notion of human being to the humanistic one. The person *as the doer* is the focus of attention when one talks about the self, and it is the adaptive efficacy of this self with the environmental forces that may ultimately get reflected in the personal and systemic effectiveness, of which the individual is considered a fundamental ingredient. Kelly (1969) asserted the need for human beings to mitigate confusion by striving to improve through learning. Rogers (1951) too who emphasized the need to be aware of and to monitor the self. According to Rogers, 'The organism has one basic tendency and striving—to actualize, maintain, and enhance the experiencing organism' (1951: 487). These viewpoints clearly presage what has now received some attention in the area of organizational behavior, namely, the construct of self-awareness.

Self-awareness refers to the extent to which individuals focus on their own attitudes and actions—a state that can be induced even by such simple actions as looking into a mirror. It has been argued that self-focus (such as looking into a mirror, which could presumably induce a state of private self-consciousness) can make significant improvements in one's relevant values or attitudes (Hutton and Baumeister, 1992: 69). Additionally, several leadership executive and management development efforts have been initiated in the past based on the belief that enhanced self-awareness leads to increased performance (e.g., Bernardin, 1986; Burke, Richley and De'Angelis, 1985; Shipper and Neck, 1990). However, it is only now that researchers seem to be beginning to build evidence in support of such views (Church, 1997).

Method

Participants and Setting

The study was conducted in two states of north India. Two hundred and sixty-one middle-management level officers from sixty-three branches of five major nationalized (public sector) banks responded to the questionnaires. The respondents were all male, graduates and above in terms of educational qualification.

Measures

Data were collected on three main variables, namely, transformational leadership, value realization and effectiveness. It was decided to use instruments that have been used in some form at least once before in the Indian setting in a documented study.

The transformational leadership questionnaire was taken from Singh and Bhandarkar (1990: 22) consisting of thirty-one items. This was adapted to generate scores on a five-point scale. The one used by Singh and Bhandarkar requires respondents to choose seven dominant qualities out of thirty-one. For an assessment of transformational leadership, the respondents gave ratings of their immediate superior in the hierarchy. Their own ratings were obtained on the measures of value realization, and aspects of effectiveness, namely (a) personal effectiveness, (b) self-esteem, (c) internal motivation and (d) increased awareness of self-pattern of behavior.

The values-related measure was a culmination of a larger study (Rai, 2000). The original measure consisted of fifty-one items. Apart from newly constructed items, the items used in this questionnaire were based on the writings of J.B.P. Sinha (1990). Rai (2000) found that six major dimensions (consisting of thirty-one items) of value realization could be identified that show good predictive properties with regard to organizationally relevant outcome variables. These dimensions were:

(a) Serenity and social contribution
(b) Ability utilization, authority and personal development

(c) Altruism and physical activity
(d) Individualized lifestyle, and physical activity
(e) Truthfulness, honesty, and cordiality
(f) One-upmanship, security, integrity, making a difference, economic rewards, and effectiveness.

Effectiveness at the individual level was purported to be mapped in terms of the following constructs:

Personal effectiveness
Self-esteem
Internal motivation
Increased awareness of self-pattern of behavior.

The personal effectiveness questionnaire had fourteen items, constructed by Sinha (1992). This instrument has been used by *associates of the second author* in earlier studies, and shown good results (e.g., Srivastava, 1996). The self-esteem questionnaire was a twenty-item questionnaire adapted from Robinson and Shaver (1973). The internal motivation questionnaire was adapted from Hackman and Oldham (1975); it consisted of six items. The increased awareness of self-pattern of behavior questionnaire had fourteen items. This questionnaire was also developed by Sinha (1992) and associates, and has been used earlier in the Indian setting with satisfactory results.

Results

The study used six measures: transformational leadership, value realization, personal effectiveness, self-esteem, internal work motivation, and increased awareness of self-pattern of behavior.

Box 1

Factor analysis: Factor analysis is a statistical method that may be used for more than one purpose. In most behavioral science research it is used to identify the underlying dimensions or factors of a complex phenomenon that is usually perceived as a whole by most laypersons. It groups the concepts reflected in individual items of a questionnaire in such a way that a common theme running across items can be identified and accorded a meaning. More than one such concept may underlie a single complex phenomenon. There is greater homogeneity within a factor or group of such items. The loading of an item on a factor reflects the strength with which the content of an item is associated with the common theme of the concept represented in the respective factors or one of the dimensions of a complex phenomenon.

Forced factor analysis: Due to conceptual or methodological requirements of the researcher, at times it is useful to treat the underlying dimensions as forming a unitary concept. Using statistical manipulations the researcher 'forces' the items or dimensions into the desired number of categories. The number of categories of forced factors cannot exceed the number of the total items through which the phenomenon is aspired to be mapped.

Responses on all the scales were subjected to factor analysis using PA2 option with oblimin (oblique) rotation of the SPSS-X (1988) release 3.0 for HP-UX computing system. It was decided to retain and include only those items in a factor that had a loading of ≥ 0.30 and not use single item factors. Having identified the meaningful underlying dimensions comprising each scale, it was further decided to do a 'second order' forced factor analysis seeking to reduce all the derived dimensions of a particular scale into a single dimension. This was done mainly for conceptual ease and brevity in presentation. It is possible to argue that the use of forced factor analysis to merge the underlying dimensions obtained through factor analysis is not the most desirable. After all, why merge dimensions after having segregated them? The answer lies in the following. First, while factor analyzing a scale the first time, one of the aims is to identify only those robust items having a good enough loading that forms a particular underlying dimension of the overall construct. So, by merging again the dimensions into a single forced factor, one strives to get a purer unidimensional measure of the overall construct, by excluding the items that are relatively superfluous to the construct and dimensions thereof. Second, when looking at the moderating effects, it is much more parsimonious and elegant to use one independent, one dependent, and one moderator variable, rather than using all the permutations and combinations of all the factors of all three components in a moderator regression equation—especially, when the immediate interest is to check the moderating effect not the individual underlying dimensions of the constructs being used. Forced factor analysis is still used for specific purposes (e.g., King, Leskin, King and Weathers, 1998; Ng, 1998; Ng, 2000).

In the description below, two types of coefficients appear after each of the factor names. The first coefficient (in parentheses) denotes the number of items comprising each factor. The four dimensions of transformational leadership that turned out to be the significant predictors were capable and participative leadership; formal objective leadership; empowering attitude; and learning oriented and participative leadership.

The transformational leadership measure yielded eight factors, the value realization measure six, the personal effectiveness measure five, the self-esteem measure five, the internal work motivation measure two, and the increased awareness of self-pattern of behavior measure only one.

The eight factors of the transformational leadership measure were named as follows:

1. Formal–objective Leadership (3), ffl= .82.
2. Protective and supportive (care and concern), (3), ffl= .42.
3. Capable and participative leadership (5), ffl= .65.
4. Effective boundary management (4), ffl= .38.
5. Work appreciation, confidence and trust (4), ffl= .70.
6. Empowering attitude (3), ffl= .71.
7. Learning-oriented and participative leadership (4), ffl= .56.
8. Composed, risk-taking, and efficient leadership (3), ffl= .78.

The six factors of the value realization dimension were as follows:

1. Serenity and social contribution (7), ffl= .75.
2. Ability utilization, authority and personal development (7), ffl= .85.
3. Altruism and physical activity (3), ffl= .53.
4. Individualized lifestyle and physical activity (5), ffl= .62.
5. Truthfulness, honesty and cordiality (3), ffl= .71.
6. One-upmanship, security, integrity, making a difference, economic rewards, and effectiveness (6), ffl= .82.

The three factors of the personal effectiveness measure were as follows:

1. Effective dealing with individuals (5), ffl= .88.
2. Effective dealing with group (4), ffl= .62.
3. Effective dealing with environment (3), ffl= .68.

The five factors of the self-esteem measure were as follows:

1. Self-esteem (7), ffl = .87.
2. Self-confidence (4), ffl = .12.
3. Abilities and skills confidence (3), ffl = .06.
4. Overall general confidence (2), ffl = .43.
5. Self-assured (2), ffl = .70.

The two factors of the internal work motivation measure were named as follows:

1. Personal internal work motivation (2), ffl = .30.
2. Internal work motivation belief (2), ffl = .30.

The measure of the increased awareness of self-pattern of behavior yielded only one significant factor, namely,

1. Awareness of self-pattern of behavior (2), ffl = not available, as only one factor was retained.

Further analyses and the report of the results are based on multiple regression analysis (MRA) and follow two main lines. First, the strength of association of the dimensions of transformational leadership (as predictors) with the various indicators of personal effectiveness (as the criterion) will be evaluated. Next, the results of the 'moderator' regression analysis with value realization as the moderator of the relationship between transformational leadership and aspects of personal effectiveness would be reported. The latter would be based primarily on the second-order single-factor solutions of the variables in the study.

Box 2

Multiple regression analysis: MRA is another statistical method that may be used for examining the strength of association between two variables, such as between transformational leadership and personal effectiveness, in the present case. *Multiple moderator regression analysis*: MMRA is a variant of MRA that shows if there is any modification, i.e., increase or decrease of the 'effect' of one variable (e.g., transformational leadership) on the other variable (e.g., personal effectiveness),

---

if a third variable (e.g., value realization) is considered an ingredient of the conceptual scheme, as in the present case. *Beta weights*: Beta weights are statistical coefficients that show the relative strength of association of 'independent' variables (e.g., different factors or dimensions of transformational leadership) with a 'dependent' variable (e.g., a dimension of personal effectiveness). Greater the beta weight associated with a variable, the greater is the strength of association of that variable with the 'dependent' variable.

Table 8.1 shows the results of the step-wise multiple regression analysis with the dimensions of transformational leadership predicting the different variables pertaining to personal effectiveness. As mentioned earlier, the variables pertaining to personal effectiveness include personal effectiveness, self-esteem, internal motivation, and increased awareness of self-pattern of behavior.

The first set of MRA results showed that the overall regression was significant ($F_{(4,256)} = 18.14, p = .01; R^2 = .23$), and the four dimensions of transformational leadership explained 23 per cent of variance in the criterion (personal effectiveness). The significant predictors turned out to be Capable and Participative Leadership; Formal–Objective Leadership; Empowering Attitude; and Learning-oriented and Participative Leadership.

In the second set of MRA results also the overall regression was significant ($F_{(4,256)} = 6.15, p = .01; R^2 = .27$), and the four dimensions of transformational leadership explained 27 per cent of variance in the criterion (self-esteem). The significant predictor dimensions were Empowering Attitude; Learning-oriented and Participative Leadership; Protective and Supportive Leadership; Work Appreciation, Confidence, and Trust.

The results for the third set again showed that the overall regression was significant ($F_{(4,256)} = 28.42, p = .01; R^2 = .27$), and the four dimensions of transformational leadership explained 27 per cent of variance in the criterion (internal motivation). The four predictor dimensions that turned out to be significant were Empowering Attitude; Work Appreciation, Confidence and Trust; Capable and Participative Leadership; Protective and Supportive Leadership.

The result for the fourth set showed that the overall regression was significant ($F_{(3,257)} = 24.35, p = .01; R^2 = .25$), and the four dimensions of transformational leadership explained 25 per cent of variance in the

Table 8.1: Summary of Regression Analysis for Dimensions of Transformational Leadership Predicting the Variables Pertaining to Effectiveness (N = 261)

For personal effectiveness as criterion				
Predictor variable	B	SE B	β	Adjusted R^2
Capable and Participative Leadership	3.07	0.34	0.36**	
Formal Objective Leadership	2.12	0.14	0.32**	
Empowering Attitude	1.54	0.19	0.25**	
Learning-oriented and Participative Leadership	0.77	0.20	0.19**	.23

For self-esteem as criterion				
Predictor variable	B	SE B	β	Adjusted R^2
Empowering Attitude	1.07	0.36	0.41**	
Learning-oriented and Participative Leadership	2.19	0.17	.31**	
Protective and Supportive Leadership	0.73	0.17	0.28**	
Work Appreciation Confidence and Trust	0.73	0.12	.49**	.27

For internal motivation as criterion				
Predictor variable	B	SE B	β	Adjusted R^2
Empowering Attitude Work Appreciation	2.12	0.06	.35**	
Confidence and Trust	2.10	0.02	0.31**	
Capable and Participative Leadership	0.16	0.03	0.31**	
Protective and Supportive Leadership	0.10	0.02	0.23**	.27

For increased awareness of self-pattern of behavior as criterion				
Predictor variable	B	SE B	β	Adjusted R^2
Formal Objective Leadership	0.36	0.10	0.24**	
Learning-oriented and Participative Leadership	0.20	0.03	0.28**	
Composed, Risk-taking and Efficient Leadership	0.21	0.03	0.29**	.25

Note: ** p = .01

criterion (increased awareness of self-pattern of behavior). Three of the six predictor dimensions turned out to be significant. They were Formal Objective Leadership; Learning-oriented and Participative Leadership; and Composed, Risk-taking and Efficient Leadership. Based on MRA results, one may conclude that the above-mentioned dimensions of transformational leadership are useful predictors of the relevant aspects of personal effectiveness.

The next step in the analysis was to examine the moderating effect of the value realization on the relationship between transformational leadership and the relevant aspects of personal effectiveness. A 'moderator' regression analysis was done with transformational leadership as the predictor of the relevant aspects of personal effectiveness, namely, that included personal effectiveness, self-esteem, internal motivation, and increased awareness of self-pattern of behavior. In the interest of brevity of presentation and ease of understanding, the dimensions of the variables in the study were sought to be reduced to a single dimension using a single-factor solution, 'second' order forced factor analysis. The respective factor loadings for the forced factor solutions have already been given earlier, together with the names of the factors pertaining to various dimensions. The results of the moderator factor analysis appear in Table 8.2.

The first set of the moderator regression analysis showed that the overall regression was significant ($F_{(3,257)} = 197.27, p = .01; R^2 = .70$). It also showed that all the β weights pertaining to the main effects as well as the interaction effect turned out to be significant. This meant that the value realization had a significant positive moderating effect on the relationship between transformational leadership and personal effectiveness.

The overall regression was again significant ($F_{(3,257)} = 112.79, p = .01; R^2 = .32$) for the second set of results. This meant that for self-esteem as the variable, both transformational leadership and value realization, as well as the interaction effect of the two had significant contributions to make.

Similar was the case with the third set of results, pertaining to internal motivation as the criterion, which showed that the overall regression was significant ($F_{(3,257)} = 28.45, p = .01; R^2 = .22$). In the fourth set of results, pertaining to increased awareness of self-pattern of behavior also the overall regression was significant ($F_{(3,257)} = 58.56, p = .01; R^2 = .40$). The general pattern of the results showed that value realization does play a role of significant positive moderator for the relationship between the transformational leadership style and effectiveness criteria.

Table 8.2: Summary of Moderator Regression Analysis for Value Realization as a Moderator of the Relationship between Transformational Leadership and the Variables Pertaining to Effectiveness (N = 261)

For personal effectiveness as criterion				
Variable	B	SE B	β	Adjusted R^2
Transformational Leadership	5.87	0.96	1.80**	.12
Value Realization	0.22	0.07	0.35**	.65
Transformational Leadership X Value Realization	0.19	0.03	1.86**	.70
Constant	5.43	3.12		

For self-esteem as criterion				
Variable	B	SE B	β	Adjusted R^2
Transformational Leadership	1.18	0.38	1.46**	0.21
Value Realization	0.51	0.10	0.58**	0.29
Transformational Leadership X Value Realization	0.21	0.03	0.24**	.32
Constant	22.65	6.20		

For internal motivation as criterion				
Variable	B	SE B	β	Adjusted R^2
Transformational Leadership	0.52	0.20	1.36**	.06
Value Realization	0.41	0.01	1.20**	.18
Transformational Leadership X Value Realization	0.03	0.01	1.22**	.22
Constant	4.72	.71		

For increased awareness of self-pattern of behavior as criterion				
Variable	B	SE B	β	Adjusted R^2
Transformational Leadership	0.17	0.02	0.39**	.19
Value Realization	0.12	0.03	0.48**	.38
Transformational Leadership X Value Realization	4.06	0.02	0.40**	.40
Constant	3.81	2.10		

Note: ** p = .01

Discussion

The study   The study was based on the assumption that the collectivity of individuals makes the body of the human resource of organizations. Further, the objectives of quality human resource could be facilitated by (a) transformational leadership of the superiors under whom the role incumbents work and (b) the extent of value realization of some specific nature. It was also argued that the quality of the human resource would be indexed and reflected in the personal effectiveness measures of the individuals.

The objective   The main objectives of the study were to investigate the strength of association of the construct of transformational leadership with the aspects pertaining to the constructs of personal effectiveness and to explore the hypothesized 'moderating' effect of value realization on the relationship between transformational leadership and the aspects pertaining to the construct of personal effectiveness. Apart from the personal effectiveness itself, the other aspects related to the construct that were used in the study included self-esteem, internal motivation, and increased awareness of self-pattern of behavior.

The research questions   The main research questions raised in the study were two-fold: first, whether transformational leadership is associated with personal effectiveness, and second, whether value realization 'moderates' this relationship. For the purpose, it was decided to use MRA, and moderator multiple regression analysis. The research and analytical strategy included (*i*) factor analyzing all the variables (that is, the scales measuring the variables) to identify the underlying dimensions pertaining to each of the variables, (*ii*) forming a composite unified (unidimensional) scale by doing a 'second order' forced factor analysis for a single factor solution for each variable in the study, and then, (*iii*) using the unified value realization scale as a moderator variable, examining the moderating 'effect' of value realization, on the relationship between transformational leadership and the variables pertaining to personal effectiveness.

The findings   The findings suggest that transformational leadership has a meaningful relationship with the aspects of personal effectiveness of the human resource in a service organization. Further, there is some indication that the relationship between transformational leadership and the aspects of personal effectiveness may be moderated by the value realization of the individual.

The results showed that by and large the dimensions of transformational leadership emerged as the significant predictors of aspects of personal effectiveness. For personal effectiveness (in a general sense), the relevant dimensions of transformational leadership seemed to be the following. Capable and Participative Leadership; Formal–Objective Leadership; Empowering Attitude; and Learning-oriented and Participative Leadership.

For self-esteem as an aspect of personal effectiveness, the relevant dimensions of transformational leadership were Empowering Attitude; Learning-oriented and Participative Leadership; Protective and Supportive Leadership; and Work Appreciation, Confidence and Trust. Since self-esteem by itself can be regarded as an important component of human existence, it may be is worthwhile to emphasize upon these attributes while exercising the leadership role.

For internal motivation, another highly valued attribute in an organizational set-up, the following transformational leadership dimensions turned out to be significant predictors: Empowering Attitude; Work Appreciation, Confidence and Trust; Capable and Participative Leadership; and Protective and Supportive Leadership. It was rather surprising that even for something so internal to an individual as internal motivation, transformational leadership can make a positive difference. Maybe in the presence of a conducive leadership one can have greater opportunities of maximizing internal rewards too. How exactly this relationship takes place is not very clear from the present study and needs to be further tested. However, this indication is worth noting, as internal motivation has some important ramifications for organizational dynamics.

It has been noted in the literature that (an increase in) awareness of self-pattern of behavior may add to the effectiveness of the person. The results showed three of the dimensions of transformational leadership to be the significant predictors of increased awareness of self-pattern of behavior. These dimensions were Formal Objective Leadership; Learning-oriented and Participative Leadership; and Composed, Risk-taking and Efficient Leadership. These are apparently the important dimensions of leadership as they are related to increased self-awareness, a variable highly crucial for self-empowerment of role incumbents in the organizational setting.

The other objective of the study was to explore the hypothesized 'moderating' effect of value realization on the relationship between transformational leadership and the aspects pertaining to the construct of personal effectiveness. The results based on 'moderator' regression analysis showed that value realization was a significant moderator of the relationship between transformational leadership and personal effectiveness. Based on this, an important pointer could be to identify the relevant important values and to arrange for design of the workplace so that the role incumbents may realize their personally relevant values. The idea needs further testing though.

The study enhances our understanding of two important variables, namely, transformational leadership and value realization, in several ways. First, it finds the heretofore relatively unconfirmed but likely potential of the construct of transformational leadership in contributing to aspects of personal effectiveness. Second, it offers evidence that value realization may enhance the relationship between transformational leadership and some aspects of personal effectiveness. An additional feature of the study was the use of the factor analytically derived dimensions of the measures. This, compared to the commonly adhered to uni-dimensional approach, has pointed to the possibility that selected dimensions of a composite construct, in particular transformational leadership, may be more meaningful than some of the other dimensions of the construct with reference to specific criterion. This may hold true especially when it comes to exploring their relationship with several aspects that may be related to a composite construct like personal effectiveness. Finally, the study provides an indication that the concept of transformational leadership may have some relevance across cultures (e.g., in the Indian setting, as in the present case) also.

The Insights   Based on an empirical study, this chapter brings out the importance of transformational leadership. Several contemporary experts on leadership phenomenon would agree. According to Oakley and Kruy (1991), transformational leaders have not only the vision, but also the ability to get their employees to accept ownership of that vision as their own, thus developing the commitment to carry it through to completion. They actually do not have so much need to have the vision themselves; what they need more is to possess the willingness and ability to inspire and empower their employees them to do what it takes to translate the vision into reality. Only when a critical mass of its employees has taken ownership and responsibility for the needed changes, can an organization gain competitive advantage in today's challenging global marketplace. It is in this manner that successful transformational leaders play a significant role in developing and maintaining the culture of their organization. Among that the most important traits of great leaders are their quest for learning, and an ability to take risk when there is no obvious reason for them to do so. Trichy and Cohen (1997) point out that leaders are the winning individual with ideas and values, full of energy and the edge to do what needs to be done. Winning organizations are so because they have good leaders, people who understand the importance of selecting the right things to do and who are able to manage the complex forces required to get them done. So such organizations are leader driven. 'Finally, winners win because of their ability to continually and consistently create more leaders at all levels of their organizations. (Trichy and Cohen, 1997: 40).

The study also points to the importance of value realization, which might work towards reinforcing to the desirable values, and such value realization may be facilitated under transformational leadership. Once value realization is facilitated it might in turn positively impact the relationship between transformational leadership and aspects of personal effectiveness. Hence, there may be a kind of 'feedback' loop relationship between values and transformational leadership when it comes to impacting the magnitude of the personal effectiveness aspects of individuals in organizations.

Towards conclusion   In conclusion, transformational leadership may have significant positive ramifications for certain aspects of personal effectiveness wherein the facilitating role of the impact of value realization of individuals may not be overlooked. However, further studies are doubtless required with larger samples, different outcome criteria, different contexts, different data collection (e.g., longitudinal, experimental, field experimental), and analytical strategies to extend the idea of importance of transformational leadership and value realization for effective human resource.

References

Arnold, H.J. (1976). 'Effects of Performance Feedback and Extrinsic Reward upon High Intrinsic Motivation'. *Organizational Behavior and Human Performance*. 17, 275–88.

Bandura A. (1982). 'Self-efficacy Mechanism in Human Agency'. *American Psychologist*. 37, 122–47.

Barling, J., T. Weber, and E.K. Kelloway (1996). 'Effects of Transformational Leadership Training on Attitudinal and Financial Outcomes: A Field Experiment'. *Journal of Applied Psychology*. 81(6), 827–32.

Bass, B.M. (1985). *Leadership and Performance Beyond Expectations*. New York: Basic Books.

—— (1990). 'From Transactional to Transformational Leadership: Learning to Share the Vision. *Organizational Dynamics*. 18(3), 19-36.

—— (1997). Does the Transactional–Transformational Leadership Paradigm Transcend Organizational and National Boundaries? *American Psychologist*. 52(2), 130–39.

—— (1998). *Transformational Leadership: Industrial, Military and Educational Impacts*. Mahwah, NJ, USA: Lawrence Erlbaum Associates, Inc., Publishers.

Baumeister, R.F., and D.M. Tice (1985). 'Self-esteem and Responses to Success and Failure: Subsequent Performance and Intrinsic Motivation'. *Journal of Personality*. 53, 450–67.

Bennis, W., and J. Goldsmith (1997). *Learning to Lead*. London: Nicholas Brealey Publishing.

Burke, W.W., E.A. Richley and L. DeAngelis (1985). 'Changing Leadership and Planning Processes at The Lewis Research Center, National Aeronautics and Space Administration'. *Human Resource Management*. 24, 81–90.

Burns, J.M. (1978). *Leadership*. New York: Harper and Row.

Church, A.H. (1997). 'Managerial Self-awareness in High-Performing Individuals in Organizations'. *Journal of Applied Psychology*. 82(2), 281–92.

Conger. J.A., and R.N. Kanungo (1987). 'Toward a Behavioral Theory of Charismatic Leadership in Organizational Settings'. *Academy of Management Review*. 12, 637–47.

Dipboye, R.L. (1977). 'A Critical Review of Korman's Self-Consistency Theory of Work Motivation and Occupational Choice'. *Organizational Behavior and Human Performance*. 18, 108–26.

Hackman, J.R., and G.R. Oldham (1975). 'Development of the Job Diagnostic Survey'. *Journal of Applied Psychology*. 60(1), 159–70.

Hill, N.C. and J.B. Ritchie (1977). 'The Effects of Self-Esteem on Leadership Achievement: A Paradigm and a Review'. *Group and Organization Studies*. 2, 491–503.

Howell, J.M. and B.J. Avolio (1993). 'Transformational Leadership, Transactional Leadership, Locus of Control, and Support for Innovation: Key Predictors of Consolidated-Business-Unit Performance'. *Journal of Applied Psychology*. 78(6), 891–902.

Hutton, D.C., and R.F. Baumeister (1992). 'Self-awareness and Attitude Change: Seeing Oneself on the Central Route to Persuasion. *Personality and Social Psychology Bulletin*. 18, 68–75.

Kelly, G.A. (1969). The Language of Hypothesis. In B. Maher (ed.). *Clinical Psychology and Personality: The Selected Papers of George Kelly* (147–62). New York: Wiley (original work published 1964).

King, D.W., G.A. Leskin, L.A. King and F.W. Weathers (1998). 'Confirmatory Factor Analysis of the Clinician-Administered PTSD Scale:

Evidence for the Dimensionality of Post-traumatic Stress Disorder. *Psychological Assessment*. 10(2), 90–96

Korman, A.K. (1976). 'Hypotheses of Work Behavior Revisited and an Extension'. *Academy of Management Review*. 1, 56–63.

Mariwala, H. (2000). 'Leadership in the New Age'. *Business Today*. 9(7), April 7–21.

Maslow, A.H. (1954). 'Motivation and Personality'. New York: Harper.

Ng, C. (1998). 'I'm motivated because of who I am: The effects of domain specific self-schemas in students' learning engagement patterns'. Paper presented at the Annual Conference of Australian Association for Research in Education, November/December 1998, Adelaide.

—— (2000). 'A Cross-Cultural Comparison of the Effects of Self-schema on Learning Engagement'. Paper presented at the Annual Conference of Australian Association for Research in Education, (4–7 December 2000), Sydney.

Oakley, E. and D. Krug (1991). *Enlightened Leadership*. Fireside, New York: Simon and Schuster.

Rai, S. (2000). 'Organizational Worth: A Social Equity Perspective'. Unpublished doctoral dissertation, Department of Humanities and Social Sciences, Indian Institute of Technology, Kanpur, India.

Robinson, J.R. and P.R. Shaver (1973). *Measures of Social Psychological Attitudes* (pp. 79–80). Ann Arbor, MI: Institute of Social Research.

Rogers, C.R. (1951). *Client-Centered Therapy: Its Current Practice, Implications, and Theory*. Boston: Houghton Mifflin.

Rokeach, M. (1973). *The Nature of Human Values*. New York: Free Press.

Shipper, F. and C.P. Nick (1990). 'Subordinates' Observations: Feedback for Management Development'. *Human Resource Development Quarterly*. 1, 371–85.

Singh, P. and A. Bhandarker (1990). *Corporate Success and Transformational Leadership*. New Delhi: Wiley Eastern Limited.

Sinha, A.K. (1992). 'Measures of Some Organizational Variables'. Unpublished manuscript. Indian Institute of Technology, Department of Humanities and Social Sciences, Kanpur, India.

Sinha, J.B.P. (1990). *Work Culture in Indian Context*. New Delhi: Sage Publications.

SPSS Inc. (1988). *SPSS - X Users guide (3rd ed.)*. Chicago, IL: SPSS Inc.

Srivastava, M. (1996). 'Effectiveness: Considerations Appertaining to Individuals, Groups, and Organizations'. Unpublished doctoral dissertation, Indian Institute of Technology, Kanpur, India.

Super, D.E. and D.D. Nevill (1986). *The Salience Inventory: Theory, Application, and Research*. Palo Alto, California: Consulting Psychologist Press.

Trichy, N.M. and E. Cohen (1997). *The Leadership Engine: How Winning Companies Build Leaders at Every Level*. New York: HarperCollins Publishers Inc.

Appendix

The Measures Used in the Study

Transformational Leadership Questionnaire

Formal–Objective Leadership

1. I am interested in the welfare and well-being of people working in the organization.
2. I am totally logical and data based and do not believe in relating on the level of feelings and emotions.
3. I generally adhere to organizational rules, procedures and regulations.

Protective and Supportive (care and concern)

4. I not only tolerate mistakes while achieving results but also protect people if necessary.
5. I protect and support people when needed.
6. I treat organizational members like the brothers.

Capable and Participative Leadership

7. I am quite open and receptive to new ideas.
8. I encourage the total development and growth of people.
9. I am technically very sound and knowledgeable.
10. I believe in consensus building before taking a decision.
11. I am intellectually of a high calibre.

Effective Boundary Management

12. I have care and concern for the individual's work as well as his personal problems.

13. I consider genuine mistakes at work to be part of the learning process but do not tolerate repeated mistakes due to carelessness.
14. I am a good boundary manager of the relevant environment, such as the government, politicians, and heads of other departments.
15. I am a good planner.

Work Appreciation, Confidence, and Trust

16. I evoke a sense of confidence and trust by my behavior.
17. I value and appreciate good work.
18. I provide clear instructions of what to do and what not to do.
19. I not only tolerate mistakes while achieving results, but also protect people if necessary.

Empowering Attitude

20. I demonstrate an empowering attitude, i.e., make people feel that they are worthwhile and important for the organization.
21. I give people complete freedom to decide, and evolve plans and strategies at work.
22. I am accessible to anyone who wants to see me.

Learning-oriented and Participative Leadership

23. I consult relevant people before taking decisions concerning them and their departments.
24. I give adequate responsibility for job performance.
25. I believe that real learning and growth takes place when people explore and in the process also make mistakes.
26. I am innovative and creative.

Composed, Risk-taking and Efficient Leadership

27. I do not lose my balance in the face of calamities.
28. I am not afraid of taking risks to achieve results.
29. I am very particular about the speed and quality of work.

Unclassified Items

30. I am a good team builder capable of generating positive group feeling among the members.
31. I am clear about the mission, purpose and goal of the organization.

Selected Value Realization Dimensions and Respective Items

Serenity and Social Contribution

- Have a comfortable life at workplace.
- Live a righteous life.
- Strive for and attain perfection in whatever I do, and/or in life.
- Have an existence with marked self-effacement.
- Give positive strokes to others.
- Live by truth and truth alone.
- Give my very best to society at large in general or at least to those who are professionally connected to me.

Ability Utilization, Authority and Personal Development

- Use all my skills and knowledge in work.
- Reach a high standard in my work.
- Tell others what to do.
- Develop as a person through my work.
- Work at a place where I can have peace of mind.
- Do hard work (not necessarily physical).
- Live a professionally dedicated life.

Altruism and Physical Activity

- Get a lot of exercise in my work itself.
- Excellent physical health.
- Undergo self-sacrifice for the good of others and humankind in general.

Individualized Lifestyle, and Physical Activity

- Tell others what to do.
- Work in my own style.
- Develop as a person through my work.
- Get a lot of exercise in my work itself.
- Get the things done the way I want them to be done.

Truthfulness, Honesty, and Cordiality

- Entertain friends and relations during working hours.
- Oblige those who work around me.
- Live by truth and truth alone.

One-upmanship, Security, Integrity, Making a Difference, Economic Rewards, and Effectiveness

- Have a high standard of living by my earning.
- Be where employment is regular and secure.
- Make a positive difference in other people's lives.
- Effectively meet challenges of life.
- Establish my one-upmanship over others.
- Be recognized and remembered as someone who never unduly favored people from his own caste, race, religion or region.

Personal Effectiveness Questionnaire

Effective Dealing with Individuals

1. I am able to deal with problems related to individuals who work with me.
2. I am quite effective in taking care of the problems that arise due to my own way of doing things.
3. I can take care of two individuals simultaneously even if they approach me with mutually conflicting proposals.
4. It is very rare that an individual can create problems that I cannot handle.
5. During my stay I have focused on learning and growth of people by giving them individual attention and support.

Effective Dealing with Group

6. As a member of my work group I have almost constantly been learning and growing.
7. Most often I have contributed to my work group towards task accomplishment.

8. Most often I have contributed to my group in terms of providing them social and emotional support.
9. I have reasons to believe that my group members look up to me for ideas and motivational strength.

Effective Dealing with Environment

10. I am quite capable of dealing with the demands of the changing environment.
11. I have enough expertise to change myself to meet environmental requirements.
12. Even if my organization ventures into a totally new area of operation, I am confident I will be one of the last ones to be laid off.

Unclassified Items

13. I have been able to discover my potential for greater effectiveness in the organization.
14. I have been able to attain the goals of my life.

Self-esteem Questionnaire

Self-esteem

1. How often do you have the feeling that there is nothing that you can do well?
2. When you talk in front of a class or group of people your own age, how often do you feel worried or afraid?
3. How often are you troubled with shyness?
4. How often do you feel inferior to most people you know?
5. How often do you feel that you are a worthless individual?
6. How often do you worry about how well you get along with other people?
7. How often do you feel that you dislike yourself?

Self-confidence

8. How often do you feel that you are a successful person?
9. How often do you feel confident that your success in your future job or career is assured?

10. How often do you feel sure of yourself when among strangers?
11. How often do you feel confident that some day people will look up to you and respect you?

Confidence about Abilities and Skills

12. How often do you feel that you have handled yourself well at a social gathering?
13. How often do you feel self-conscious?
14. In general, how often do you feel confident about your abilities?

Overall General Confidence

15. How often do you have the feeling that you can do everything well?
16. How often do you worry about whether you can finish what you started?

Self-assuredness

17. How often do you feel so discouraged with yourself that you wonder whether anything is worthwhile?
18. How often are you comfortable when starting a conversation with people you don't know?

Internal Work Motivation Questionnaire

Personal Internal Work Motivation

1. I feel a great sense of personal satisfaction when I do this job well.
2. I feel bad and unhappy when I discover that I have performed poorly on this job.

Work Motivation Belief

3. Most people on this job feel a great sense of personal satisfaction when they do the job well.
4. Most people on this job feel bad or unhappy when they find they have performed the work poorly.

Unclassified Items

5. My opinion of myself goes up when I do this job well.
6. My own feelings are generally not affected much one way or the other by how well I do this job.

Increased Awareness of the Self-Pattern of Behavior Questionnaire

People in organization are known to have attained maturity as a result of the experience that they get on work Such experience, over a period of time, gives an increase to the person on several dimensions relevant to the personal quality of life. *Please tell us, the extent of increase that you feel as a result of past five years or of your experience on the job.*

1. Awareness of the self-pattern of behavior on my own
2. Awareness of the self-pattern of behavior as a result of feedback received from others during intense interactions

Unclassified Items

3. Awareness of dilemmas (in the context of perceived relations) of life
4. Capacity to work on those dilemmas of life
5. Capacity to control myself
6. Capacity for self-direction
7. Confidence in ambiguous situations
8. Capacity to deal with apparently threatening situations involving issues, authority, etc.
9. Capacity to deal with personal conflict (such as whether to do this or that, or whether or not to do it) quickly and without any remainder or residual, uncertainty, guilt or dissatisfaction
10. Ability to deal with internal conflicts (such as choosing between mutually incompatible thoughts, impulses and feelings) effectively
11. Capacity to act on the environment
12. Capacity of being able to initiate action whenever needed otherwise things would have moved differently
13. Discover my potentialities for greater effectiveness in the organization
14. Life goal realization.

9

*Knowledge Management for Sustainable Innovation**

ARCHANA SHUKLA • R. SRINIVASAN

'In an economy where the only certainty is uncertainty, the one sure source of competitive advantage is knowledge. When markets shift, technologies proliferate, competitors multiply, and products become obsolete almost overnight, successful companies are those that consistently create new knowledge, disseminate it widely throughout the organization, and quickly embody it in new technologies and products' (Nonaka, 1991).

Introduction

Successful implementation of a knowledge management (KM) programme should result in the ability of the organization to create new knowledge and to replicate this knowledge to its advantage. Knowledge management begins with acquiring new knowledge, documenting existing knowledge, processing this knowledge within the organization, and applying it for generating competitive advantage. This application results in an identification of new knowledge sources and develops experience within the

* An earlier version of this paper was presented in the 4th World Congress on Intellectual Capital, Hamilton, Ontario, Canada held at the McMaster University, 17–19 January, 2001.

organization. In following this process, organizations learn as they complete the cycle.

There are two major obstacles in organizational learning (Morath and Schmidt, 1999). The first is the existence of defensive routines in organizations. These routines are a product of organizational processes like micro politics, power games, or groupthink. 'Defensive routines result in "skilled incompetence" in dealing with new insights, leading to organizational inertia ... (Morath and Schmidt, 1999: 196). Another source of this inertia can be the existence of strong organizational culture and identity (Van den Bosch, Volberda, and de Boer, 1999). The second obstacle occurs due to the fact that learning is fundamentally a self-organizing process. Even though organizations can create and promote an open learning environment, people have to be motivated enough to learn on their own (Morath and Schmidt, 1999). More than this, individual tacit knowledge has to be shared within the organization to create organizational knowledge. Individuals and organizations are also known to be bounded by their ability to understand and process complete information available to them. They act primarily on the basis of their cognitive schema (Simon, 1991). These obstacles force organizations to limit their learning to what they have seen and been through in the past, that is, there is a heavy dependence on prior experience, and therefore lead to adaptation—'the ability to make incremental adjustments as a result of environmental changes, goal structure changes or other changes—and not learning—'the development of insights, knowledge, and associations between past actions, the effectiveness of those actions, and future actions' (Fiol and Lyles, 1985: 811).

The focus of any KM programme should be on innovation and not having incremental adjustments in the organization. Beckman (1999), in an attempt to review the literature on the field of knowledge management, identifies six perspectives of knowledge management: conceptual, process, technology, organizational, management, and implementation perspectives. These perspectives of understanding KM as a concept have stood in isolation, and their integration into an implementation plan is required. Before an elucidation of the implementation process, let us understand the six perspectives individually as described by Beckman (1999).

The conceptual perspective deals with defining and describing the foundations and frameworks of managing knowledge. There are variety of definitions of KM in the literature: KM as a field, characterization of the field of KM into dimensions like storage media, accessibility, typology, and hierarchy, and development of principles and frameworks for managing knowledge.

The process perspective of knowledge management is concerned with the specific steps involved in generating, formalizing, distributing, sharing and applying organizational knowledge. These steps might be concurrent, or linear, or include supporting activities.

The technological perspective focuses on the use of information technology for implementing a KM programme in the organization. Creation of IT infrastructure, representation of knowledge objects within the system, formation of knowledge repositories and databases and integrating these repositories into integrated performance support systems (IPSS), and knowledge transformation (using techniques like data mining, metadocuments, etc.).

The organizational perspective is concerned with the internal organization that is created for spearheading, evangelizing and implementing knowledge management. The variety of forms include KM task forces, chief knowledge officer, KM specialists, knowledge project managers. This perspective also deals with creating a culture of sharing, trustworthiness, and collaboration and cooperation.

The management perspective deals with the measurement and evaluation of the benefits of implementing a KM program, and the emergent reward/incentive/motivational systems.

The implementation perspective focuses on the specific issues encountered in the implementation process—the building of IT infrastructure, identification of the critical success factors for implementing KM, understanding the prerequisites and challenges, and the integration of KM with the business and corporate strategies.

These perspectives, make clear that it is not sufficient for an organization to restrict its KM implementation to just one or a few of these perspectives, but a complete understanding of all these perspectives and their integration into the organization's strategy is necessary.

Most KM implementation programs tend to focus on documentation and dissemination of the knowledge embedded either within the system (in employees, systems, documents, etc.) or outside the system (in customers, markets, competitors, alliance partners, etc.). Cohen and Levinthal (1990) describe a firm's 'absorptive capacity' as the firm's 'ability to identify, assimilate, and exploit knowledge from the environment.' They maintain that the absorptive capacity of the firm is largely dependent on the stock of existing knowledge. Van den Bosch, Volberda and de Boer (1999) introduce organizational form and combinative capabilities as two building blocks of a firm's absorptive capacity. But, even here, the determinant of the firm's absorptive capacity is the level of prior related knowledge. The main problem with this approach of managing knowledge is that these perspectives lead to managing only 'existing' knowledge, rather than focusing on innovation and creativity.

The genesis of a KM program should form part of the organization's strategic intent. An explicit and formal KM strategy should be formulated and clearly articulated for determining the scale and scope of KM implementation. As per the firm's strategic intent, the KM objectives would need to be realigned either to exploit existing knowledge, explore external knowledge, or vie for industry/environment leadership. At these three levels, we call them first-, second-, and third-generation KM programs. Innovation is fostered when an organization graduates to implementing third-generation KM programs.

The effectiveness of a KM program in generating innovation depends on the continuous generation of new knowledge, in the application of this knowledge, and in questioning the basic assumptions of this knowledge creation, that is, the business realities.

In this chapter, we discuss the problems in learning from experience, build the concepts of second-and third-generation KM programs, and then elucidate the formulation and implementation of a KM strategy for innovation.

Learning from Experience

The main issue with typical KM programs is that organizations tend to capture and manage existing knowledge very efficiently. As stated earlier, these systems of managing organizational knowledge do not explicitly foster innovation and creativity; rather they inhibit creation of new knowledge within the organization. Emphasis is laid on acquisition and creation of new knowledge through sharing of current practices, rather than creation of new practices, products or services. As Feldman (1986: 275) observed, 'a prerequisite to learning is awareness of errors.' In the absence of feedback on the effectiveness of the learning, a suboptimal but efficient system might be generated out of current practices. It is important that new information from within and outside the system interact with experience for new knowledge to be generated. 'Pre-existing category systems and schemas, in interaction with environmental factors, influence what is learned,' (Feldman, 1986: 278). In order to overcome biases that arise out of experience, he provides the following suggestions (Feldman, 1986):

Increase the amount and immediacy of feedback.
Create a social environment that requires learning.
Hire or train employees to be experts in both substance and process.
Don't expect infallibility.

Therefore, we need to change the focus from the 'solution' to the 'seriousness of the problem.' In doing so, we will be able to concentrate equally on the outcome of the KM program and the process of implementation. In other words, we need to move from single-loop to double-loop learning (Argyris and Schon, 1978).

Individuals enact and create their own world (Weick, 1995). Also, organizations are socially constructed mental models residing in the minds of the individuals (Weick and Bougon, 1986). For learning to prosper, it is required that we focus on interaction and collaboration within organizations, apart from prior related experience.

Second-generation KM

McElroy's (1999) concepts of first-generation and second-generation knowledge management correspond to single-loop and double-loop learning (Argyris and Schon, 1978). First-generation KM schemes are technology-centric. 'Only first generation KM schemes, for example, begin, and end, with the assumption that current knowledge in practice is valid! Their goal, then, is to optimize the delivery of currently held organizational rules, or knowledge, to workers so that they can function in their normal, operating environments.' He therefore concludes that, 'conventional knowledge management practice, then, boils down to little more than getting the *right information to the right people at the right time*. Think *single-loop learning*.' (McElroy, 1999: 3, italics in original).

The purpose of first-generation KM programs is to improve the operational efficiency of employees by enhancing access to organizational rule sets. The wider the access, the more the chances of first-generation KM programs being implemented. The objective of KM programs is restricted to answering the following questions: 'What knowledge do people need to do their work?' and 'How can we help them get it?' These questions demonstrate a clear obsession with operational efficiency rather than knowledge creation. This is probably why first-generation KM programs have focused heavily on creating technological solutions that promote knowledge sharing and transfer within the organization.

In contrast, second-generation KM programs focus on both the 'know-how' and 'know-what' of knowledge. While 'know-how' includes procedural knowledge of doing the business, 'know-what' emphasizes the declarative knowledge of doing the business, that is, it is concerned with the business realities, and therefore lays high stress on how the knowledge is generated. The organizational knowledge-production process then becomes the beginning of implementation a second-generation KM program.

McElroy (2000) defines the revised knowledge life-cycle that includes three phases: knowledge production, knowledge diffusion, and knowledge use (Figure 9.1).

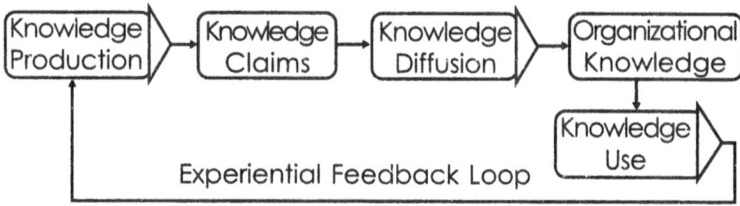

Figure 9.1: Revised Knowledge Cycle

The production phase includes integration of self-managed individual learning into organizational learning through the formation of communities, generation of knowledge claims, peer review, validation and reformulation by communities of interest and practice. The outcome of this phase is a 'knowledge claim'. This knowledge claim then enters the diffusion phase. The diffusion phase deals with knowledge sharing and transfer, teaching and training, broadcasting, storytelling, and production of knowledge artefacts (codification). This results in generation of 'organizational knowledge'. This knowledge then enters the third and final phase of the knowledge life-cycle, namely, the knowledge-use phase. The knowledge-use phase emphasizes on practising knowledge, in terms of application in business strategies, business processes, policies and procedures, products and services, organizational models, market analyses, beliefs and values, and culture. This application gives rise to a feedback loop, to the first phase (knowledge production), on the effectiveness of the knowledge produced. This is how the organization identifies the 'know-what' of managing knowledge. The questions asked as organizations move through the life cycle are 'What do I know, and why?' and 'What is the application of the knowledge that is generated, developed, produced, diffused, and used?' (McElroy, 2000).

Another way of characterizing the differences between first-generation and second-generation KM programs is through *supply-side* and *demand-side* interventions. Whereas first-generation (or single-loop) KM focuses on managing the supply of existing knowledge, second generation (or double-loop) KM emphasizes the demand for new knowledge. Whereas first-generation KM programs are more prone to redesigning existing systems for imitation across the whole organization, second-generation KM programs create a conducive environment for generation of new knowledge and, therefore, foster innovation.

From Second-generation to Third-generation KM

Organizational knowledge is increasingly being treated as a strategic resource. A knowledge-based competitive advantage is more sustainable if and when an organization develops the ability to acquire, generate and use more knowledge. When a KM program is implemented with this objective, we graduate from second-generation KM to third-generation (or triple loop) KM. In this graduation, we question the 'governing values' of KM implementation. That is, we ask the question 'Why do we need KM?' and thereby, we not only rationalize the application of organizational knowledge, but also devise new applications. In contrast to second-generation KM, where the focus is on meeting the needs of the environment (understanding the business imperatives as a function of the environment), third-generation KM leads to shaping the environment itself. This is done through the ability of the organization to continuously renew itself, and innovate.

Zack (1999) classifies knowledge into three levels, namely, core knowledge, advanced knowledge, and innovative knowledge. Core knowledge 'is that minimum scope and level of knowledge required to "just play the game". Having that level of knowledge and capability will not assure the long term competitive viability of a firm, but does present basic industry knowledge barrier to entry.' Advanced knowledge makes the firm competitively viable. This level of knowledge makes a firm better than its competitors. The firm begins to differentiate itself from the competitors in terms of some unique knowledge that it possesses, and the competition does not. This knowledge differentiation provides the firm with sufficient competitive advantage to 'win the game'.

Innovative knowledge is that knowledge which enables a firm to lead its industry and competitors, more than significantly differentiating itself from the competition. Possession of innovative knowledge often 'changes the rules of the game'.

When an organization focuses on innovative knowledge, rather than on core and advanced knowledge, we see third-generation KM in practice. First-generation KM programs make organizations 'exploit' existing knowledge with an 'internal' focus, second-generation programs make them 'explore' new knowledge with an 'external' focus, and third-generation programs make them 'innovate' beyond organizational boundaries (Figure 9.2).

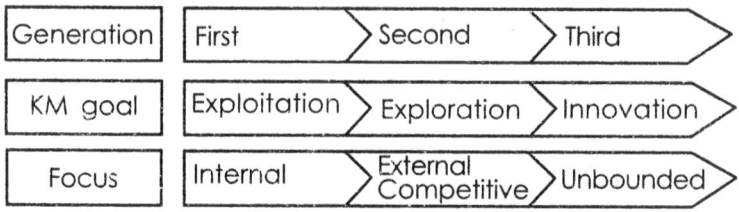

Figure 9.2: Three Generations of KM

An organization has to begin with implementing a first-generation KM system to exploit the internal knowledge already available within the organization, graduate to the second-generation KM program to acquire and generate new knowledge demanded by the competitive environment, and finally aspire to lead the industry and shape the environment through a third-generation KM program.

The KM program is either in the first, second or third generation depending on the organization's strategic intent. As the organization integrates knowledge into its internal structures, systems and processes, it remains in the first generation. When the objective of knowledge management expands to include competitors and the environment (vendors, suppliers, customers, etc.), the organization integrates external knowledge with internal knowledge and therefore widens the perspective of the organizational knowledge and moves to the second generation. When knowledge management is used to shape the environment, and learning itself becomes a value in the organization, the organization enters third-generation knowledge management.

Formulating a KM Strategy for Innovation

As organizations proceed towards implementation of third-generation KM, it becomes imperative to formulate a KM strategy that steers clear of the problems mentioned above in traditional implementation of KM programs.

Akin to the traditional SWOT (strengths, weaknesses, opportunities and threats) analysis, Zack (1999) describes a process of how an organization needs to align its knowledge resources and capabilities with the intellectual requirements of the strategy. A knowledge gap is defined as that between 'what the firm must know' and 'what the firm already knows' When the organization is concerned with bridging the internal knowledge gap, it embarks on a process of exploitation. When it is concerned with meeting the external/competitive knowledge gap, it is into exploration. Innovators are companies that integrate exploitation and exploration, and shape/lead the industry. In doing this, organizations can adopt either an aggressive strategy or a conservative one. The process leads to some key questions being asked. The Table 9.1 lists these questions and the corresponding actions (Zack, 1999: 143).

Table 9.1: Formulation of a KM Strategy

Step	Key Question	Action
1	How do you want to play the game?	Articulate desired or intended strategy
2	What do you need to know?	Articulate strategy–knowledge link
3	What do you know?	Create internal knowledge map
4	What is your internal knowledge gap?	Compare what you need to know and what you do know
5	What do your competitors know?	Create external competitor/industry knowledge map
6	What is your external knowledge gap?	Compare what you need know with what your competitors know
7	What is your learning cycle?	Assess your dynamic learning capabilities and intentions
8	What are your competitors' and industry learning cycles and capabilities?	Assess your industry's and competitors' dynamic learning capabilities and intentions
9	What is your learning gap?	Compare your dynamic learning capabilities with those of your competitors' and your industry

(Table 9.1 continued)

(*Table 9.1 continued*)

Step	Key Question	Action
10	What is your internal strategic gap?	Assess how your internal knowledge gap affects your current strategy
11	What is your external strategic gap?	Assess how your external knowledge gap affects your current strategy
12	What is your industry cycle strategic gap?	Assess how your dynamic learning gap affects your future strategy
13	What is your new, current, and future strategy?	Determine if and how your knowledge and learning gaps require a revision in strategy
14	What is your knowledge strategy?	Determine how aggressive you will be to close your knowledge gaps regarding – exploration vs. exploitation – internal sources vs. external sources

KM Implementation Strategy for Innovation

In order to successfully implement a KM strategy, an organization needs to understand what kind of knowledge it manages. Having understood this, the organization needs to find ways and means of converting one type of knowledge to another, escalating individual knowledge into organizational knowledge, and mapping the process of knowledge generation.

MODES OF KNOWLEDGE CONVERSION

Nonaka and Takeuchi (1995) differentiate two types of knowledge: tacit and explicit. Tacit knowledge is 'something not easily visible and express-ible. Tacit knowledge is highly personal and is difficult to formalize, making it difficult to communicate or to share with others. Subjective insights, intuitions, and hunches fall into this category of knowledge. Furthermore, tacit knowledge is deeply rooted in an individual's action and experience, as well as in the ideals, values, or emotions he or she embraces' (Nonaka and Takeuchi, 1995: 8). Further, they identify two dimensions of tacit knowledge—the technical dimension, consisting of informal skills and crafts that are hard to document, and the cognitive dimension, which encompasses schemata, mental models, beliefs and perceptions that are so ingrained in people that they are taken for granted.

Nonaka and Takeuchi (1995) have identified four modes of knowledge conversion within organizations: from tacit to tacit, tacit to explicit, explicit to tacit, and from explicit to explicit knowledge (Figure 9.3).

	To	
	Tacit Knowledge	Explicit Knowledge
From Tacit Knowledge	Socialization	Externalization
Explicit Knowledge	Internalization	Combination

Figure 9.3: Four Modes of Knowledge Conversion

Source: Nonaka and Takeuchi (1995: 62)

Sharing of tacit knowledge across individuals in an organization occurs through a process of socialization, where individuals new to the organizational context learn from their peers who are more experienced in the system. Experience sharing is more implicit where there is learning by observation, whereas explicit knowledge within an organization is shared through published documents, rules, procedures, and the like. The most important is the conversion of tacit knowledge to explicit knowledge and vice versa. The processes of externalization and internalization describe these knowledge transfers from tacit to explicit and explicit to tacit knowledge.

Externalization deals with the process of translating tacit knowledge into explicit concepts. Metaphors, analogies, figures, models, and the like are used to communicate tacit knowledge effectively. Metaphors help the knowledge consumer understand the knowledge in the knowledge provider's mind through relating to his or her own experience and other known concepts/contexts. In other words, it is a new way of experiencing reality.

Internalization, on the other hand, is closely related to organizational learning. It is a critical mode of knowledge conversion in terms of transforming individual learning and memory into organizational learning and memory. In this mode of transfer, knowledge generated through experience, clear documentation, manuals, and oral stories is firmly registered in the minds of the organization's members as shared mental models. It is not necessary for the individual to 'learn-by-doing,' in order to internalize the knowledge generated. Reading about and listening to others' experiences may itself generate adequate interest in the knowledge consumers, and facilitate tacit knowledge generation.

Combination is the process of sharing explicit knowledge within the organization. It involves systematizing and combining explicit knowledge through meetings, documents, telephonic conversations, or computer networks. Accumulation from different sources, and reconfiguration of existing information generates new explicit knowledge.

ESCALATION OF INDIVIDUAL KNOWLEDGE INTO ORGANIZATIONAL KNOWLEDGE

Nonaka and Takeuchi (1995: 70) emphasize that 'organizational knowledge creation is a continuous and a dynamic interaction between tacit and explicit knowledge'. This process starts with the 'sharing of tacit knowledge' that corresponds roughly to socialization. This sharing is facilitated through the creation of a field of interaction, where members share their experiences and mental models. The shared tacit mental models, when expressed in words and phrases, give rise to explicit concepts. This phase is known as the 'creating concepts' phase and corresponds to the externalization process. The concepts created are justified in the light of whether it is worthwhile for the organization to expend effort, time and resources on them. This phase, also known as the 'justifying concepts' phase, focuses on the internalization process. When the justified concepts are put to test in the form of an archetype (or a prototype), the organization enters the next phase that is, of 'building an archetype', the phase that corresponds to the combination process. The fifth and final phase of knowledge generation is known as 'cross-levelling of knowledge', which kicks off a cycle of knowledge generation based on the archetype generated. This new knowledge generation can happen either within the organization or outside it (among its customers, suppliers, competitors, affiliates, etc.) through dynamic interaction (see Figure 9.4 for a pictorial representation of the knowledge-generation cycle).

Innovation emerges when a dynamic interaction occurs between tacit knowledge and explicit knowledge. When an organization follows this conversion process and the knowledge-generation cycle, it graduates from second-generation KM to third-generation KM, as knowledge is now used to lead/shape industry/environment.

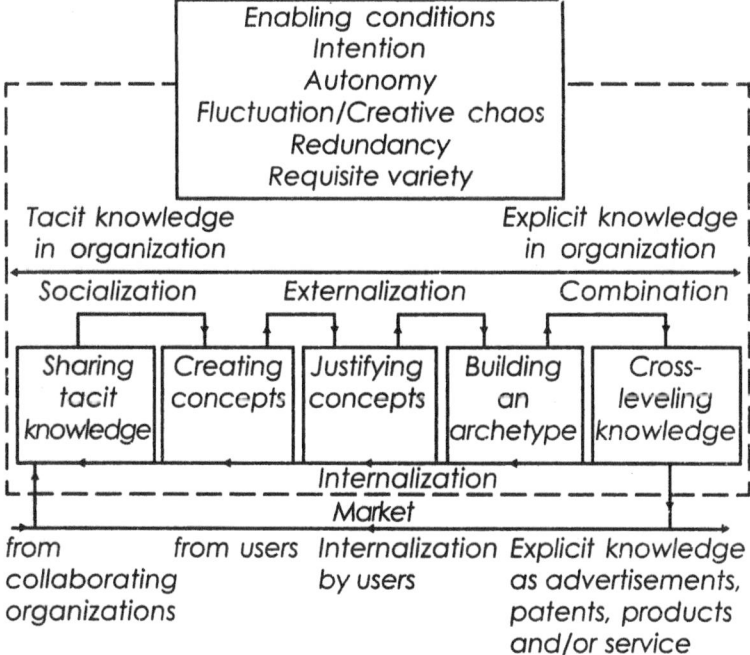

Figure 9.4: The Organizational Knowledge-creation Process

Source: Nonaka and Takeuchi (1995: 84)

KM OBJECTIVES

The primary objective of KM implementation in an organization so far has been to provide the backing of the entire organizational knowledge to the front-end employee. For instance, the KM strategy of Infosys Technologies Limited is that '... ensuring that employees in contact with the customer have the collective knowledge of the organization behind them' (Srinivasan and Shukla, 2000). The main aim here is to provide value to the customer as 'one giant brain'. Roger Siboni, KPMG deputy chairman and chief operating officer says, 'We need to provide our professionals with the knowledge of the entire firm—and deliver it to clients on demand, anywhere and at anytime' (Alavi, 1997).

While there is a clear need to minimize duplication of effort and 'reinvention of the wheel', as one of the prime motives of managing knowledge (first-generation KM), it is also seen that these initiatives were either targeted at creating and delivering extra value to the customer, or in generating competitive advantage (second-generation KM).

As organizations proceed towards implementing third-generation KM systems, we can see KM objectives that embody industry and environment leadership which goes beyond competitive advantage in the marketplace. For example, 'LeaseCo proactively searched for opportunities to build continually on what it knew about leasing formal dress apparel to appearance-conscious organizations. It became one of the most knowledge-able firms in the industry regarding this premium market. Buckman labs took a similar approach by focusing its learning to maintain and grow its superior knowledge of the pulp and paper industry' (Zack, 1999: 129).

Clearly, the broader the strategic objectives of KM, the further organizations move from first- to second- to the third-generation KM programs.

Leadership Support for KM Implementation

Leadership support is essential for successful implementation of any KM initiative. This was one of the significant lessons from the implementation of the pilot project at HP Consulting (Martiny, 1998). Also, in the case of McKinsey and Company, the CEO, Rajat Gupta's involvement in the Practice Olympics lends a lot of credibility to the exercise and the KM initiative in general (Bartlett, 1996). In almost all the cases documented in the literature, it can be seen that the evangelists of the KM program are from the top management.

The KM Implementation Process

KM implementation involves three significant decisions: about the knowledge architecture (how the knowledge is organized), about the systems and technology (what implementation structures and technologies are used to manage the knowledge), and about the people (how to create a culture of knowledge sharing and motivating people to contribute, disseminate and apply knowledge). These three decisions are similar to the key areas identified by Foy (1999) as content and information, technology, people, and process.

Knowledge Architecture

The knowledge architecture decisions include issues about how to gather, create, organize, disseminate and apply knowledge in organizations. Decisions like creation of databases, yellow pages, grouping of knowledge bases into functional and sectoral groups, etc. form part of the knowledge architecture. In sum, these decisions address the question of 'In what form is knowledge to be stored?' These decisions should be critically linked with the organization's business processes and its clients.

Systems and Technology

The decisions about systems include implementation structures and technology used for accumulation, review, administration, and access control of the knowledge base generated. Titles like Chief Knowledge Officer are being introduced and knowledge advisory committees etc. are being set up. It is also increasingly being recognized that ownership of the knowledge generated has to vest with the respective departments/ groups that have generated the knowledge base, rather than with a centralized database. However, there is a need for a corporate central department or group to streamline and evangelize these efforts.

As regards technology, firms have focused on the groupware, though intranets and other web-based technologies are also gaining ground. Technologies that provide real-time seamless integration of worldwide resources, both within and outside a firm, have simplified the sharing and application of organizational knowledge. These technologies have also provided enough scope for tapping and managing the tacit knowledge among geographically distributed employees through online and offline interactions.

People

Decisions surrounding the people-related issues are the most critical in any KM implementation. People have to be motivated, people have to create new knowledge, share their knowledge (both tacit and explicit), and apply the knowledge gained from others in their day-to-day working. A culture of knowledge sharing has to be institutionalized for harnessing individual knowledge in the creation of organizational knowledge.

Knowledge architecture and systems and technology should be aligned in such a way that knowledge creation and sharing becomes a part of the individual's regular work profile, rather than a specific demand from the KM implementers.

A typical KM implementation begins with decisions about knowledge architecture, then gradually moves to systems and technology, before deciding about the people-related issues. Most of these implementations are top-down because the top management has clarity about the knowledge management imperatives for the business as a whole. Next comes the setting up appropriate implementation structures (defining roles and responsibilities, creating departments, etc.) and augmentation of the technological infrastructure. Again, funds and support for this come from the top management, and unless the entire organization is convinced of the utility of the program, these systems will not be effective. A strict and timely alignment is, therefore necessary between the knowledge architecture and systems and technology. Also, it is imperative that all people-related concerns are addressed simultaneously: individual employees convinced of the utility, motivated to participate in creation, maintenance, application, and sharing of his or her own knowledge. For ensuring a sustainable advantage of a KM program, an organization needs to focus on all three decision areas simultaneously. Figure 9.5 represents the typical model of implementing these decisions.

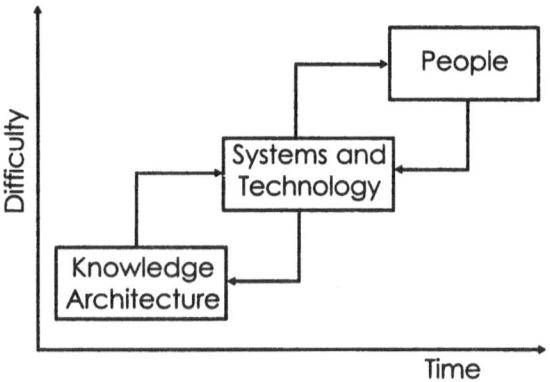

Figure 9.5: Decision Areas in KM Implementation

KM AS A CHANGE MANAGEMENT PROGRAM

KM is typically implemented as any other change management program. The issues that crop up in management of change surface in the implementation of KM as well. If an organization has implemented a successful change management program (like ISO certification, BPR, ERP, etc.), it would be helpful if KM implementation is modelled on the same lines. This lends a great deal of credibility and support to the initiative from the outset.

A highly successful way of implementing KM programs is by beginning on a small scale, and then scaling up to the whole organization. This helps in two ways: it tests the functionality, utility, requirements and expectations of the system, and acts as a good demonstration for groups that are not part of the pilot project.

Conclusion

This chapter focused on whether KM programs ensure innovation and creativity in organizations. We discussed the concepts of second-generation and third-generation KM as the organization graduates in its KM implementation. Directions were also provided on how to formulate and implement a KM strategy for promoting innovation.

First- and second-generation KM programs typically focus on exploiting internal knowledge and exploring external competitive knowledge, rather than on developing new knowledge for innovation. Our contention is that as organizations proceed from first- to second-, and then to third-generation KM, innovation and creativity can be fostered and sustained.

References

Alavi, M. (1997). *KPMG Peat Marwick US: One Giant Brain.* HBS Case 9-397-108 (Revised 1997). Cambridge, Massachusetts: Harvard Business School Press.

Argyris, C. and D.A. Schon (1978). *Organizational Learning: A Theory of Action Perspective.* London: Addison Wesley.

Bartlett, C.A. (1996). *McKinsey and Company: Managing Knowledge and Learning.* HBS Case 9-396-357 (Revised 1998). Cambridge, Massachusetts: Harvard Business School Press.

Beckman, T.J. (1999). 'The Current State of Knowledge Management'. In J. Liebowitz (ed.). *Knowledge Management Handbook.* Boca Raton, Florida: CRC Press, 1–22.

Cohen, W.M. and D.A. Levinthal (1990). 'Absorptive Capacity: A New Perspective on Learning and Innovation'. *Administrative Science Quarterly.* 35, 128–52.

Feldman, J. (1986). 'On the Difficulty of Learning from Experience'. In H.P. Sims and D.A. Gioia (eds.). *The Thinking Organization: Dynamics of Organizational Social Cognition.* San Fransisco: Jossey Bass, 263–92.

Fiol, C. and M. Lyles (1985). 'Organizational Learning'. *Academy of Management Review.* 10(4), 803–18.

Foy, P.S. (1999). 'Knowledge Management in Industry'. In J. Leibowitz (ed.). *Knowledge Management Handbook.* Boca Raton, Florida: CRC Press, 1–15.

Martiny, M. (1998). 'Knowledge Management at HP Consulting'. *Organizational Dynamics.* Autumn, 71–77.

McElroy, M.W. (1999). 'Double-loop Knowledge Management'. Knowledge Management Society of India. Available http://egroups.com/files/KMSI/Double-Loop+KM.pdf.

—— (2000). 'Managing for Sustainable Innovation'. Knowledge Management Society of India. Available http://egroups.com/files/KMSI/SustainInnovation.pdf.

Morath, F.A. and A.P. Schmidt (1999). 'Management of Knowledge as Interface Management: From Exo-worlds to Endo-worlds'. In P. Jackson (ed.). *Virtual Working: Social and Organizational Dynamics.* London: Rouletge, 193–205.

Nonaka, I. (1991). 'The Knowledge-Creating Company'. *Harvard Business Review.* November–December, 96–104.

Nonaka, I. and H. Takeuchi (1995). *The Knowledge-Creating Company: How Japanese Companies Create the Dynamics of Innovation.* New York: Oxford University Press.

Simon, H.A. (1991). 'Bounded Rationality and Organizational Learning'. *Organization Science.* 2(1), 125–34.

Srinivasan, R. and A. Shukla (2000). 'Knowledge Management at Infosys Technologies Limited'. IIML Case Series, 2000–02. Lucknow: Indian Institute of Management.

Van den Bosch, A.J., H.W. Volberda and M. de Boer (1999). 'Coevolution of Firm Absorptive Capacity and Knowledge Environment: Organizational Forms and Combinative Capabilities'. *Organization Science.* 10(5), 551–68.

Weick, K.E. (1969). *The Social Psychology of Organizing.* Reading, Massachussetts: Addison Wesley.

—— (1995). *Sense Making in Organizations.* Thousand Oaks, California: Sage.

Weick, K.E. and M.G. Bougon (1986). 'Organizations as Cognitive Maps: Charting Ways to Success and Failures'. In H.P. Sims, D.A. Gioia (eds.). *The Thinking Organization: Dynamics of Organizational Social Cognition.* San Fransisco: Jossey Bass, 102–35.

Zack, M.H. (1999), 'Developing a Knowledge Strategy'. *California Management Review* 41(3), 125–45.

10

Team-based Leadership for Non-governmental Organizations

MARY P. SEBASTIAN • SHIVGANESH BHARGAVA

Introduction

Public has great faith in non-profit organizations, because of their creditable achievements. They have successfully worked with the problems of poverty, illiteracy, exploitation and very often achieved what the government machinery failed to achieve. Though they help the government with their programs, more importantly they are central to discharging social tasks. The role non-profits play in integrating right values, and engendering a sense of worth and service is crucial to our society. It is noteworthy that many people are ready to devote time and effort for voluntary work after their full-time jobs. It is also true that many of our organizations lack the ability to integrate voluntary work successfully to meet their needs.

'A business supplies, either goods or services. Government controls. A business has discharged its task when the customer buys the product and pays for it, and is satisfied with it. Government has discharged its function when its policies are effective. The non-profit institution neither supplies goods or services nor controls. Its product is neither a pair of shoes nor an effective regulation. Its product is a changed human being. The non-profit institutions are human change agents. Their product is a cured patient, child that learns, a young man or woman grown into a self-respecting adult; a changed human life altogether' (Drucker, 1990). It is this job of voluntary organizations that makes these organizations indispensable in our society. Despite all the work the non-profits are involved in and their recognition of the need for good management and leadership, little that is so far available has been specifically designed for them. It is mostly borrowed from the business and management sciences which were made for the needs of the business world. Very often voluntary organizations see 'management' as a bad word, because they see it as business management while the success of the voluntary organization lies in its informal climate (Drucker, 1990). So a great gap exists between what is practised by voluntary organizations, their needs, and the theory developed to cater to these needs. This chapter tries to partially answer this need by explaining how to convert a non-government organization (NGO) into a team-based organization in the context of the problems it faces, with the effective intervention of the leader. NGOs, while concentrating on the service of society at large, have gone through different stages for improving the quality of their services. Leadership is a key factor in NGOs. The qualitative nature of the work makes the ability of the leader to direct very important. For proper time management and to avoid an unduly long planning period, a team-based approach to leadership will be helpful.

Leadership is often viewed of as a set of functions performed by a superior vis-à-vis his or her subordinates, such as task and interaction facilitation, goal emphasis, and nurturance or support. Leadership may be an important mechanism for the processes of socialization, organizational integration and institution building. The work of Sinha (1984, 1995) is particularly relevant to these processes. Various studies have looked into the suitability of various styles of leadership in different organizations and cultures. Essentially, Sinha (1995) has argued that in a culture prone to high dependency, a weak work ethic, and a strong bonding orientation, a firm, directive, but nurturant leadership (NT leadership style) is an essential first step in socializing the workforce into a culture of autonomy, work ethic and professionalism.

Singh et al. (Singh, 1982; Singh, Warrier and Das, 1979) have been championing the participative, democratic leadership style as the best style. Singh, Warrier and Das (1979) found that the authoritarian leadership style affected group productivity negatively, while democratic, participatory leadership affected it posititively. Similarly, the more democratic the style, the higher tended to be work satisfaction and group cohesion.

Those practising the authoritarian style tended to perceive the work culture as lacking in work ethic, while those practising the participative style tended to perceive a friendly, congenial work atmosphere. Equally plausibly, if the work ethic is perceived to be weak, managers will tend to practise an authoritarian style, and if the work climate is perceived to be friendly and congenial, they will tend to adopt a participative approach.

The above discussion clearly brings to the fore the issue of appropriate leadership in different settings, in the context of the Indian culture. Although this issue is dealt with by research in production organizations, research on leadership in the NGO setting does not address the problem. Hence an action research format is used in the analysis of leadership and teamwork discussed in this chapter to understand its implications in the NGO sector.

Understanding Teamwork

The work of NGOs is not easy to quantify. The highly qualitative nature of their work makes it difficult to practise teamwork in the same manner as in profit organizations. An honorary director of an NGO in Kerala feels that teamwork enables staff to take initiative as well as discourages tendencies of tale-bearing. The leader also learns from experience how to lead a team, supporting and directing without being the person who plans and the staff, the implementers. All the same leaders wanting to have a team-based organization in itself is a step in the right direction.

It is necessary to understand what is teamwork. There is a vast difference between organizations that 'do teams' and those that become team-based organizations. Committees, task forces, groups are not teams. A whole organization is also not a team. 'A team is a small number of people who use synergy to work together for a common end' (Tompkins, 1995). Synergy means combining the parts so as to have a whole that is greater than the sum of its parts. For example, once a team is working the end result will be $1 + 1 = 4$. This means that when all the qualities of the individual members are put together and the team is working, the final outcome is much more than expected.

Groups differ from teams in that they rely on the sum of the individual qualities and not on synergy. Groups do not pursue performance improvement, but rather share information and opinions and make ad hoc agreements to help one another and there is no predefined process. The only commitment of the members is to attend meetings. For a team to work, it is very important to understand the objectives and have an evidence procedure or points for evaluation so that one can know when goals or objectives are achieved.

Comparison of Two Organizations

Two organizations are compared here to understand the problems that may come in the way of an NGO converting to a team-based organization. Organization A is over hundred years old. Organization M is twenty-five years old. Both organizations have around a hundred employees. In the opinion of some other NGOs, organization M is doing better work than organization A. An attempt is made here to examine why this difference exists. To understand this, the working of the boards of NGOs was looked into.

Highly qualified individuals from 'the world of affairs' serve on non-profit boards. They are needed for their knowledge, skills and general competence. They are also needed for fund raising, for contacts, and, in part, for appearance's sake. Although it is difficult to devise a rigorous empirical test, Bowen (1994) suspects they are ineffective because they are underutilized. The boards of many organizations have highly qualified and highly placed individuals but their talents are not utilized. They are not involved in running of the organization because board meetings are seldom held. Giving a free hand to the employees is a mistake the boards make under the misguided belief that it is democratic leadership style.

The boards of NGOs are constituted of bureaucrats, ministers, executives others in important positions. Yet why are they ineffective? Taylor, Chait and Holland (1996) give various reasons for this. For instance, by a chief executive fears a strong board and hoards information, seeking the board's approval only at the last moment (Taylor, et al., 1996). This was noticed in organization A. The director of the NGO was trying to get her pet projects sanctioned which were not in line with the mission of the organization. For example, while interviewing the staff, one of the points that emerged was the need to give importance to grassroots-level activities. The said organization had adopted a slum for development and was doing quite well there. Despite this, it had not ventured into other slums. It was noticed that the emphases of the staff and the director were at loggerheads. The director was interested in activities like setting up a media centre and a computer centre, saying that would help the organization to move with the times. The organization was in the process of raising funds for construction; the director presented a proposal to the board and said it needed to be sanctioned immediately. Moreover, she said that the funding organization had insisted on media-related courses so that could not be deleted from the proposal. Although the board was divided on the issue, due to the urgency of the situation it sanctioned the proposal without reviewing or studying the pros and cons of the funding organization's requirements. One group felt that the funding organization's requirement should be met, while another felt that the mission of organization was more important and funds should be availed of with that in mind. Sinaga (1993) noticed that very often NGOs yield to the objectives of the funding organizations forgetting those of their own organization. It was felt that this was due to the financial constraints NGOs face. As a consequence there was very little involvement of the staff in decision-making. This was quite evident in organization A. Since organization M has a clear vision and mission, it does not change its work to suit funding organization's requirements. A funding organization can fund any of its activities.

NGOs are often dependent on the availability of funds and hence the funding organization. As a result, their staff are not aware of the vision and mission of the organization. Many NGOs are not clear even of their goals and in the absence of a target waste precious person-hours in discussions, planning, redrafting plans and so on.

Another reason for the board's lack of control is that members sometimes lack sufficient understanding of the NGO's work and avoid dealing with issues requiring specialized knowledge. In organization A, the board members do not involve themselves in the administration of the organization because board membership carries little personal account-ability. Also, the board members change every two years, hence it is easy for the director to run the organization with very little control of the board. In the absence of long-term knowledge of the organization's activities, a board might refine management's proposal, but rarely rejects any (Taylor, et al., 1996).

Non-profit organizations are directly accountable to their board of directors or to their funding organizations. Hence non-profits lack the guidance the market provides corporations. In the business world, customer satisfaction is very important. If customers are dissatisfied, the business will be affected. Those who receive services from NGOs are called clients or service consumers. Clients are satisfied if their expectations are met. Their reactions to the services provided by NGOs are not as revealing as the responses of consumers to products of for-profit organizations. Since NGO services are either free or subsidized, clients are more likely to forgive poor quality as well as ignore inefficiency (Herzlinger, 1994). Clients feel obliged to NGOs even if they have got only a minimum of help.

Organization M was started because the founders perceived a need. This need continues to be the focus of their work to date. Although organization A too continues to address one of the key reasons for its starting, its growth is not applaudable. Seeing the history of organization A one sees that many good activities were begun and stopped for various reasons. Treatment of drug addicts and counselling of women in remand homes were a couple of activities discontinued. Since the board members are elected annually, people with different ideas come to the board and an effort is made to put these ideas into action. But the sustainability rate is very poor. Activities being started and stopped could be one of the factors hampering the growth of organization A. Organization M has a clear idea about its mission and all its activities centre on that. So although there are various other social problems requiring aid, the NGO does not shift its focus. This type of focused work also helps the staff to be more creative, as well as satisfied with their work. In organization M at least one of the board members is present in the office every day and fully involved in overseeing every aspect of the NGO's work. Although this kind of direction, control and involvement may somewhat hinder the creativity of the staff from coming to the fore, it helps in effectiveness and efficiency.

Some organizations reward their executives with the kind of salaries and perks that are on a par with those of corporate heavyweights (Herzlinger, 1994). This trend reported in developed nations, is prevalent here too. Organization A provides furnished accommodation to its directors. Moreover, the vehicle of the organization is used for personal needs. During the interview, one of the employers mentioned how difficult it was to get dedicated staff these days as the main concern was salary. Herzlinger and Khasker (1987) in their study noticed that non-profit hospitals were providing too few services, particularly to the poor, who should be their reason for existence. Hence the authors felt that there was no need to exempt these organizations from tax. Most of the doctors employed by these hospitals, in addition to receiving a good salary, earn through private practice as well. Not only is the quality of service poor, the clients are ignored and the beds occupied by the private patients of these doctors.

This comparative analysis of two organizations has shown the role the board of trustees and clarity of organizational goals play in the effectiveness of an organization. The key leader of the organization be it the board of trustees or the director or anyone else, needs to be identified and given the task of introducing team-based leadership. The first step of the leader should be frame the objectives and goals, and the activities required to achieve them. This will also help in evaluation and knowing if and when the set goals were achieved.

A Case Study

In this case study, how organization A initiated team-based leadership is analyzed. It was easy to introduce teamwork in the NGO in Kerala because the director was an experienced leader of teams. But the transformation of organization A was a tedious task, given the resistances. A brief narration of these experiences is given below.

Lately the board of trustees (hereafter referred to as 'management') had felt that there was a lack of communication between the staff and management. The management felt that the staff were distancing themselves from the management and also feared that some of the staff were trying to take over the organization. Hence the management decided to get professional help to revert the situation. The consultant was a person with experience of working in NGOs in various positions. Initially, the consultant (Y) got a questionnaire filled by the employees and the management. Despite assurance of confidentiality, 'Y' found that the answers lacked depth and were not adequate to gauge or understand the problems in the NGO. Thereafter 'Y' spent time observing interactions, asking questions, and interviewing employees at various levels. It was found that there existed a rift between the director and the management. Some members of the management were supporting the director but the majority were unhappy with her functioning. In addition, the director had antagonized a few department heads.

Although organization A had regular meetings and training programs for the heads of the departments, nothing was done for the other employees. There was no structure to transmit the knowledge gained by the heads to their staff. Since there was conflict between the director and some heads of departments, 'Y' decided to conduct a workshop excluding the department heads. Representatives from each department (two or three) attended the workshop, which was fixed by the organization. A representative of the management too was present. The workshop was on 'teamwork'. To start with, members of the same department sat together, but they were divided into groups that had a mix of members of other departments. The participants were slowly brought to the topic of the strengths and weaknesses of the organization. Discussion revealed that there was conflict between them and the director and that they were not distanced from the management. Despite the presence of a management representative, they were ready to express their criticism of the management. While discussing the weaknesses, the points that came to the fore were the need for a grievance-handling procedure, the lack of proper communication, the inadequate importance given to grassroots-level activities, low involvement of management in administration and their inaccessibility to staff. It was later realized that there existed a form and a well-maintained procedure to pass on communication from management, board meeting, etc. to the heads of departments and their subordinates. Despite that, there were strong complaints about lack of communication. Thus it was evident that the procedure was not being effectively utilized. As a consequence the inaccurate messages were reaching the staff in the lower cadre about the decisions and actions of the management.

Another issue that emerged in the workshop on teamwork was the need for a structure to pass on the learning from workshops to others. So the participants were asked to share information from the workshop with others and do spadework for transforming the organization to a team-based one. They were informed that a different set of people would be called to the next meeting and proper communication was therefore necessary. Despite the fact that the issue had been raised by them, at the next meeting 'Y' found that the members of the group had discussed the workshop activities with only the few they were friendly with. Many had not conveyed what they learnt in the workshop to the heads of their departments. Since they were not used to such a practice, the participants of the workshop were diffident to share their learning. The same group was therefore called for the next meeting as well.

The department heads and staff representatives were invited to the meeting to formulate the mission statement. Staff representatives represent every level of the hierarchy and are active participants in such decisions as salary revision and policy changes. They were divided into three groups. Each group came out with quite a relevant and inspiring mission statement. The three statements were then compiled into a single statement. Subsequently the department heads set the goals for their respective departments for the year, up to a maximum of five years.

A different set of employees were called to plan the grievance-handling procedure. This was a mixed group comprising heads of departments, those who had attended the workshop on teamwork, and a few who had not. 'Y' was present at the meetings to direct the team as well as to help the members to focus on the agenda. Hardaker and Ward (1987) mention the importance of a neutral outsider to lead the discussions. Teams were similarly formed to discuss the other issues that came up in the workshop. All the teams were expected to pass on information to those who were not part of their team.

The meetings held in coordination with members of the management helped bridge the gap between the management and the employees.

Meanwhile, in a meeting with two heads of departments, as part of the grievance-handling procedure, it came to light that the director was highly autocratic, misused funds, carried tales to cause misunderstanding and fights between departments. Once the teams started functioning, she found it difficult to adjust as a member of a team. So she had to leave the job. Very often there are good workers who are not able to function as part of a team. These members should be helped to leave the organization.

The literature on leadership talks of the qualities of good leaders: a leader must be forceful but also sensitive, dynamic but also patient, not only an excellent speaker but also an excellent listener. Since a single individual cannot possess all these qualities, a good team is the solution. Teamwork not only helps to keep in check the bad elements, but also helps the creativity of all employees to function at its fullest. With a team running an organization, mismanagement of the organization's funds can be checked, director introducing her pet projects can be avoided, the mission of the organization becomes clear to everyone and all work toward achieving it. There is complete transparency of everyone's work.

Teamwork has been used in organization A to bring about organizational transformation. Since the staff and the leader have no experience of teamwork, it will take time to stabilise the climate in the expected form. Also, the director's opposition to teamwork had led to a lot of problems and uncertainty. She would pass contradictory information to the staff, leaving them doubting each other as well as the credibility of the team. Once this was brought out in the open, she was not ready to accept the responsibility for her actions. Such people cannot work as part of a team.

Another point NGOs should note while introducing team-based leadership is that the roles and activities of each of their staff is important at that point. Often since staff are so used to carrying out orders, it is difficult to make them talk, give suggestions or be creative. Those in the lowest levels of the hierarchy are the ones who will need maximum direction and support to talk and express their ideas. This is the test of the leader. If the leader/director knows the difference between directing and listening, the biggest block to teamwork has been levelled. However, the director needs to refine his or her ways of directing and leading so that goals are achieved more effectively and efficiently.

Conclusion

For any organization to be effective, good leadership is imperative. The leader's awareness of his or her flaws as well as abilities can help him or her to use them to build up the organization. A shift to accepting the challenge of creating team-based organization, can enhance the performance of an organization tenfold. This also leads to an organization where cooperation, trust, sharing of ideas are the thrust. For innovative and indigenous ideas to come to the fore, a team process is a must. It is also found that ordinary people have more common sense than the people working for NGOs as they are more in touch with reality. For their ideas to come to the fore, an opportunity should be created. Any process which empowers one man is dehumanizing. Teamwork is a process of humanizing administration'.

Team-based leadership is thus a powerful strategy in the effective management of the activities in an NGO. A leader who decides to convert the organization into a team-based one will realize the need for guidance. It is advisable to have discussions with organizations that are successfully carrying on teamwork. With experience, leaders will learn the intricacies of team-based leadership.

References

Bowen, W.G. (1994). 'When a Business Leader Joins a Non-Profit Board'. *Harvard Business Review*. September–October, 38–43.

Brody, R. (1993). *Effectively Managing Human Service Organisations*. New Delhi: Sage.

Drucker, P.F. (1990). *Managing the Non-profit Organisation: Practices and Principles*. Delhi: Macmillan India Ltd.

Hardaker, M. and B.K. Ward (1987). 'How to Make a Team Work'. *Harvard Business Review*. November–December, 112–19.

Herzlinger, R.E. (1994). 'Effective Oversight: A Guide For Non-Profit Directors'. *Harvard Business Review*. July–August, 52–60.

Herzlinger, R.E. and W.S. Khasker (1987). Who Profits from Non-Profits? *Harvard Business Review*. July–August, 67, 93–106.

Sinaga, K. (1993). 'Neither Merchant nor Prince: A Study of NGOs in Indonesia'. *Sociological Bulletin*. 42, 137–56.

Sinha, J.B.P. (1984). 'A Model of Effective Leadership Styles in India'. *International Studies of Management and Organization*. 14, 86–98.
—— (1995). *The Cultural Context of Leadership and Power*. New Delhi: Sage.
Singh, J.P. (1982). 'Improving Quality of Working Life in the Indian Context'. *Productivity*. 22, 13–20.
Singh, P., S.K. Warrier and G.S. Das (1979). 'Leadership Process and Its Impact on Productivity, Satisfaction, and Work Commitment'. *Decision*. 6, 259–69.
Taylor, B.E., R.P. Chait and T.P. Holland (1996). 'The New Work of the Non-Profit Board'. *Harvard Business Review*. September–October, 36–45.
Tompkins, J. (1995). *The Genesis Enterprise*. New York: Mc-Graw Hill.

11

Managerial Leadership and Power

G.S. DAS

Human society from the inception of civilization has confronted several dualities. One particular duality, which confronts us even today, is between freedom and conformity, empowerment and obedience. At different points of human civilization it was believed that conformity and obedience are the best forms of social governance. It was also believed that freedom and empowerment give rise to chaos and destabilization of the social order. Although this thinking basically reflects the pre-industrial mindset, it is not uncommon in present times to come across leaders in work organizations whose most important 'wish-list' happens to be conformity and obedience from their subordinates.

There is a definite reason for which people expect conformity and obedience from others. To some extent the reason can be traced in the meaning of these words: conformity is defined as an act of compliance, acquiescing or yielding or a tendency to yield readily to others, especially in a weak and subservient way; obedience is defined as the state or quality of being obedient or the act or practice of obeying dutifully, in other words, submissive compliance. Examples of conformity and obedience can be derived from any regimented social structure, such as a totalitarian state and military service. In such social structures there are problems aplenty. These structures have to deploy an enormous amount of resources to impose control and suppress human beings' eternal desire for freedom.

Work organizations too expect some degree of conformity and obedience from their members; and by their nature do not expect their members to behave like free human beings. Commitment and involvement are two expressions widely valued in organizations. The power process helps circumscribe idiosyncratic behavior and keeps it in conformity with the rational plan of the organization. Organisations for their survival also require the integration of the diverse activities of their members. The coordination and order thus created out of the diverse and sometimes conflicting interests and potentially diffused behavior of their members is largely a function of power. However, it is also true that the nature of commitment and involvement of the members depend upon the nature of the power used at the micro and macro levels in the organization.

Motivation for Power

Before getting into further discussion of power, it might be relevant to develop some understanding about why people want to have power, in other words, what are the motivations for power.

'Of the infinite desires of man', Russell (1938) said, 'the chief are the desires for power and glory'. In Galbraith's (1983) views, people abhor the existence of power, disavow its possession, but value its exercise. Much evidence reflects that people have a fundamental psychological need to control events that affect them, and that the loss of such control creates psychological distress. Perhaps the most compelling evidence relates to physical pain. Numerous laboratory experiments show that subjectively experienced pain is not merely an autonomic response of the nervous system, but stems from the loss of control over one's body that a physical trauma implies. When there is no sense of having lost control, pain does not develop.

In Horney's (1950) thinking, a person seeks power when anxiety coupled with the belief that the environment is out to take advantage of him or her. Here the need for power can serve two purposes: as an assurance against the nagging fears of being helpless and abandoned; and to express repressed hostility.

In discussing human growth, May (1972) said, 'Power is essential for all living things. To survive, man must use his powers and confront opposite forces at every point of his struggle.' The striving for power centres on the fact that human beings seek not only to survive, but also to maximize their own outcomes, and in doing so they come into conflict with fellow human beings likewise engaged. As a result power is sought not for its own sake but to help in the competitive struggle with others. Zeleznik (1970) too mentioned that competition for power is there in all social structures including business organizations.

There are at least three popular ways of explaining the motivation for exercising power. Adler (1927) saw the desire for power as the prime motivation of man. In Adler's view, the seeking of power is a compensation for an inferiority complex. Adler's theory was that one attempts to overcome feelings of inferiority by getting power. This theory permits power seekers to accomplish much for themselves and their organizations.

An increasingly accepted view is that power is an expression of instincts (Ardrey, 1962; Lorenz, 1966). On the basis of the theory of evolution, it is easy to imagine that particularly in the barbaric era those who successfully exercised power more likely survived and produced offspring. Thus, the desire to exercise power may be ingrained in man's genetic makeup. Lorenz and Ardrey, among others, have explained that the exercise of power is natural, even necessary.

The view of power as instinct, contrasts with Adler's compensation theory. While Adler attributed the compensation drive to early social experience of deprivation in one's life, the instinctual view maintains that the desire for power is more basic and is inherent in one at birth, even before social experiences. These two views of motivation for power, as springing from biological and social sources, can be complementary.

Besides a psychological perspective, a more 'everyday' view of the motivation for power is that its possession can provide more of what a person wants. In fact managers need power to move others, to entice others, to persuade and encourage others to attain specific goals or to engage in specific behavior; it is the capacity to influence and motivate others. Krausz (1986) argued, 'Power is the ability to influence the actions of others, individuals or groups. It is understood as the leader's influence potential' (p. 69). Verderber and Verderber (1992) argued, 'Social power is a potential for changing attitudes, beliefs, and behaviors of others' (p. 280). Weber (1954) defined power as 'the possibility of imposing one's will upon the behavior of others,' while Etzioni (1978) wrote, 'Power is an actor's ability to induce or influence another actor to carry out his directives or any other norms he supports.' Those in power have the ability and capacity to get others to do what they want them to do, thus enhancing capacity to act effectively. Tannenbaum (1962) believed effective leaders have the ability, through interpersonal influence, to cause their subordinates to attain specific personal as well as organizational goals. Hersey and Blanchard (1982) suggested that effective leadership influences the activities of an individual or group in their efforts towards goal achievement in a given situation.

These definitions of power focus on the way leaders successfully influence their followers to produce an effect. Therefore, motivation for power cannot only be traced in psychological framework but also in the organizational reality that successful leaders have to motivate people through their power towards greater accomplishments for themselves and their organizations.

How We React to Power

It is some forty years since the social psychologist Stanley Milgram studied the dynamics of obedience to authority. Milgram's studies have fundamental and far-reaching implications for our understanding of human behavior and, more particularly, the extent to which a person's behavior is determined by particular situational and organizational factors. Some salient features of the study that have special significance for the topic under discussion can be summarized as follows.

The Basic Experimental Design of Milgram's Studies

A stern-looking experimenter in a white coat greets a typical male subject volunteering to take part in Milgram's early experiments at Yale University in 1963. He finds that another subject has already arrived. The experimenter informs the two men that they are to take part in an experiment to discover the effect of punishment on learning and verbal memory. One subject will be the 'teacher' the other the 'learner during the session. The allocation of the respective roles is decided by lottery.

The two men are told that the teacher is to read pairs of words to the learner and then test the learner's memory by giving the first word of each pair and asking him to supply the second word. Incorrect answers are punished by an electric shock administered by the teacher by depressing one of thirty switches located on a 'shock generator' in front of him. These switches are arranged in a row and are labelled according to the voltage of electricity they transmit to an electrode strapped to the learner's arm. The first switch is labelled 15 volts, the second 30 volts, the third 45 volts and so on. The final switch is labelled 450 volts. There are also a number of descriptive labels on the switch panel. For example, 'Slight Shock' describes the 15–60 volt range and the 435–450 volt range is labelled 'XXX'.

The experimenter tells the teacher that he is to punish the learner's first recall error with an electric shock of 15 volts. The second error is to be punished by a shock of 30 volts, and so on until the learner has correctly memorized the list of word pairs.

Before the session begins, the learner is strapped to a chair; his arm is treated with an electrically conductive paste to which an electrode is then attached. He mentions to the experimenter that the learner has a mild heart condition. He is assured that the shocks, although painful, will not result in any permanent tissue damage.

Then the teacher is escorted to an adjacent room where the shock generator is situated. The experiment begins. The experimenter sits a few yards behind the teacher to remind him that increasingly severe electric shocks must punish every error.

During a typical session the learner makes an error in approximately three out of four responses and the teacher steadily increases the shock level. At 75 volts the teacher hears the learner moan 'ugh'. At 150 volts the learner calls out: 'Ugh! Experimenter, get me out of here. I told you I had heart trouble. My heart's starting to bother me now. Get me out of here, please. My heart's starting to bother me. I refuse to go on. Let me out.'

The experimenter ignores these pleas and urges the teacher to continue. At 210 volts, the learner demands to be let out. Still the experimenter urges the teacher to continue until all the word pairs are learned. At 300 volts prolonged agonized screaming can be heard and the learner shouts in desperation that he will no longer provide answers. The experimenter tells the teacher that silence represents an error and must be punished In the first two experiments 64 per cent of teachers administered the maximum shock of 450 volts. In fact, the learner was an accomplice trained to play the role and no electric shocks were administered. However, the actual subjects, the teachers, were completely unaware of this. As Milgram states:

There is overwhelming evidence that the great majority of subjeets, both obedient and defiant, accepted the victims' reactions as genuine. The evidence takes the form of: (*a*) tension created in the subjects; (*b*) scores on 'estimated pain' (*c*) subjects' accounts of their feelings in post-experimental interviews; and (*d*) quantifiable responses to questionnaires distributed to subjects several months after their participation in the experiment.

Greatly surprised by their initial findings, Milgram and his research team carried out numerous variations of the basic experimental design in order to ascertain the key situational factors governing the dynamics of obedience.

The results came as an unwelcome surprise both to the researchers and to many other presumably sophisticated observers. Most experts had foreseen that very few subjects would push the shock buttons all the way to the maximum. In fact, about 50 per cent followed orders to the hilt, even while believing that they were inflicting very severe electric shock on a screaming middle-aged man with a heart ailment. In addition, the person giving that order had no 'real' power. He was just a guy in a white coat running the experiment.

What these experiments suggest is that people have a strong propensity to obey authority. It is not just because of fear sanctions–like getting fired–that most of us obey orders. We seem to obey anybody wearing the simplest trappings of authority (in this case a white lab coat). Even if it is obvious that no significant sanctions could be imposed on us for refusal to obey, we fuss and complain, but to a disturbing and frightening extent, we also obey.

Perhaps, then, managers must be careful in assuming that their organizations run smoothly because they are such great managers, such effective users of power and authority. Rather, they run because subordinates were taught, long before they came to work, to obey authority. Maybe we as managers are not as masterfully authoritative as we would like to believe. Those people in fact would obey anybody. And if that is true, perhaps managers should be more concerned about how not to use authority than how to use it. Perhaps managers should encourage subordinates to question their authority and to think for themselves before they obey managers' orders. It is only through such learning experience that conditions can be created whereby people will learn to assume personal responsibility for their actions. This is an essential condition by which people can be transformed from being dependent to becoming independent and interdependent.

A considerable number of managers believe that it is easy to use authority. This is because they often confuse positional authority with authority: the two are not same. From this confusion arises the belief that it is very simple to exercise authority. Authority in the true sense originates from the word 'author', in other words creating. The person who started an enterprise is a creative person; he has more authority than the managers he has employed to achieve results through people. That is, the entrepreneur has authority, while the managers have positional authority. Positional authority is accompanied by some amount of coercion—and we cannot ignore the fact that exerting authority is often personally gratifying for superiors, and therefore attractive. Imposing discipline on others can be reassuring to those who need reassurance about themselves. Moreover, authority fits neatly with organizational superior's need, if any, to release the aggression arising from their own frustration. When parents spank a child they do not just want to change the child's behavior but also most likely provide themselves with an outlet for tension built up in them, by their boss, or spouse, or the troublesome child.

Similarly, authority is sometimes seen, perhaps properly, as a way for organizational superiors to guarantee their superiority. If subordinates know that supervisors can and will punish readily, they are likely to be respectful and submissive, at least in their presence. The reassurance derived from these visible demonstrations of respect may be a great distortion of true feelings, but it can be helpful to the superior's own uncertain psyche.

Positional authority has another advantage, that is, speed. A do-it-or-else order precludes the time-consuming dilly-dallying of feedback. But speed might be at the cost of both accuracy and morale. However, where the issues are not critical, speed may be worth its cost. Positional authority also has the advantage of imposing orderliness and conformity in an organization. Large numbers of people can be made to conform to fundamental regulations (manager must make sure that his people stay through the required eight working hours). Even though the great majority may conform without external threat, the superior has to ensure minimum conformity by all employees. Moreover, such enforced discipline looks efficient because it can be used on large number of people at the same time, even when one does not know much about those people.

Positional authority, which is rooted in the employment contract itself, is very limited in scope, since it obligates employees to perform only duties assigned to them in accordance with minimum standards does not make them exercise initiative. This shows that effective management is not possible within the confines of positional authority alone.

Power Beyond Authority

To instill obedience and conformity in the work situation managers have to go beyond authority and use power. Management writers (Baldridge, 1971; French and Raven, 1959; Hackman and Johnson, 1991; Kanter, 1977; King, 1987) have described the sources, types, and uses of power essential to effective leadership. Eight primary sources of power are: support systems, information, credibility, visibility, legitimacy, persuasiveness, charisma, and agenda setting.

Support systems include both formal and informal opportunities for networking. Information, the second source of power, involves not what one knows, but how fast one can gather information, which encourages power players to be good listeners. Power flows to those who have the information and know-how to accomplish organizational tasks. Credibility, the third source of power lies in how much respect one attains, because we rely on people who have established a history of experience and expertise. The fourth source of power, visibility, means taking on tough jobs so that people take notice. Legitimacy, the fifth source of power, works in concert with visibility and involves having respected power players commend one publicly; thereby creating acceptance among would-be doubters. The sixth source of power, persuasiveness, determines how successfully a person uses rational or emotional appeal. The ability to persuade depends on one's personality, the content of a task, motivation, and confidence. Charisma, the seventh source of power, constitutes many ethical qualities of leadership. It includes a leader's reputation, sincerity, trustworthiness, expertise and dynamism. The last source of power, agenda setting, rests in knowing when meetings will be held and accessing the group leader to put items on the agenda at just the right time. Two by-products of networks and alliances involve access to decision-making arenas and the ability to influence the agendas in those arenas. People or groups with access to agenda setting frequently represent their positions, while the interests and concerns of those not present can get distorted or ignored (Brown, 1986; Lukes, 1974).

Another typology by French and Raven (1959) is also well known. According to them, the five most commonly known types of power are coercive, reward, legitimate, expert, and referent. Coercive power lies in the ability to administer punishment or give negative reinforcements. Reward power rests on the ability to deliver something valued by the receiver. People who can deliver money, jobs, or political support have something other people want, and therefore become extremely powerful in organizations. Legitimate power lies in a person's position rather than in the person himself or herself. This type of formal power relies on position in an authority hierarchy. Occasionally, people with legitimate power fail to recognize that they have it, and then they may notice others around them accomplishing *their* goals. The fourth type, expert power, stems from a person's special knowledge and expertise in a given area. The last type, referent power, includes admiration and subsequent influence of a leader, and his or her acceptance by subordinates. Referent power is a little like role model power in that it depends on being respected, liked and held in high esteem. It usually develops over a long period of time.

Creating a positive operating climate entails choosing the most appropriate of the foregoing compliance-gaining tactics, which tend to lead to greater 'life' or job satisfaction (Plax, Kearney and Downs, 1986). McCroskey, Richmond, Plax and Kearney (1985) claimed that relying on expert, reward and referent power appeared to produce the greatest satisfaction, while reliance on coercive and legitimate power had the opposite effect. Rahim (1989) found legitimate power useful in gaining compliance, but satisfaction from supervisees decreased. Expert and referent power bases correlated with both compliance and satisfaction. Rahim (1989) also noted that effective leaders can 'enhance their referent power base if they learn to be considerate of their subordinates' needs and feelings, treat them fairly, and defend their interests when acting as their representative' (p. 555). Effective leaders combine the various bases and sources of power, electing to use them in appropriate situations. An effective leader rarely depends on only one source or base of power.

The increasing number and complexity of organizations in modern industrial societies requires large numbers of persons with a high level of technical and administrative expertise to play leadership roles. This demand reduces the suitability of recruitment on the basis of social status or family connections. Training centres for leaders established in universities, business schools, and training institutes, and the possibilities of a career in industrial leadership are getting evenly distributed across all strata of society. Management has now become a professionals' domain. Although these developments are most apparent in business and industrial organizations and in some government agencies, they are present in other types of organizations as well.

Most of these changes imply a rationalization of the power process in organizations consistent with Weber's (1947) bureaucratic model. However, further changes in the way leaders exercise power are likely to accompany this rationalization, and these represent a divergence from the classical bureaucratic model. Leaders may rely on discussion and persuasion rather than on command exclusively. Attempts may be made to elicit cooperation, sometimes by having organization members participate in making decisions that affect them in the workplace. The rising level of education of the workforce represents an important factor that contributes to this trend. In addition, the specialized skills that are frequently required of persons at all levels in modern organizations can sometimes place subordinates at a higher level of expertise in a particular area than their superiors. This alters the classical supervisor–subordinate relationship. Subordinates can have power over their superiors, as described by

Mcchanic (1962) in his classic article. Because most executives report to other (higher) executives and take orders from them, superiors influence subordinate managers' behavior. The role-set model suggests the way peers and subordinates influence the role behavior of managers. Beginning with Woodward (1958), research efforts have pointed towards the nature of the task as an important determinant of the boss–follower system. The implications of House and Dessler (1974), Stinson and Johnson (1975), and Osborn and Hunt's (1975) studies are that work designs affect managers' power. Engineered tasks govern the behavior of subordinates and superiors alike through work design over which neither has direct control. Organizational structure, policies, and procedures prescribe what managers and other workers must do in given situations.

Additionally, professional managers are more inclined than their predecessors to adopting the human relations approach to control in organizations. At the same time, socio-political developments have led to the introduction of schemes of co-management and of workers' councils, with varying degree of success. These developments may not be fully consolidated in any contemporary society, but incipient support is found in many organizations for less authoritative and autocratic control than was customary in the past.

Taken together, these developments imply the growth—actual in some places, potential in others—conceptions of the power process in organizations.

First, a change has taken place in the analyses of the bases of power. While coercion has played a prominent role in traditional analysis, consistent with the presumed conflict between leaders and followers, a contemporary variation in the concept of power relates to assumptions concerning the mutuality–unilaterality of control. A view common among traditional analysts is that the control process is unilateral: one leads or is led, is strong or weak, controls or is controlled. Contemporary analysts, on the other hand, are more likely to consider relationships of mutual as well as unilateral power: of followers influencing leaders, as well as vice versa.

Moreover, traditional analysis of social power assumes that the total power in a system is a fixed quantity and that leaders and followers are engaged in a 'zero sum game': an increase in the power of one party must be accompanied by a corresponding decrease in the power of the other. Some social scientists are now inclined to question the generality of this assumption. The total amount of power in a system may grow, and leaders and followers therefore enhance their power jointly. Total power may also decline, and all groups within the system may suffer a corresponding decrease.

This scenario leads us to believe that managerial interdependencies are a reality today in work organizations. While successful managers are powerful persons, they are dependent upon their subordinates, peers, bosses, customers, suppliers, government regulators, and others to enable (or permit) them to do their jobs effectively. They therefore operate in a network of complex interdependencies in which they are often as much or more dependent than the other party or parties. The sources of the interdependencies are numerous, sometimes extending beyond the organizational boundary.

The foregoing supports the assertion that managers are not unilateral power holders in organizations. There are forces both within and outside the organization that limit managerial actions and create interdependencies. This being the case, the answers to the questions 'How do managers manage their dependencies?' and 'How do managers react to situations in which they are not particularly powerful?' are vital to an understanding of the power dynamics of organizations. The work of Emerson (1962, 1972a,b), with its emphasis on the relationship between power and dependencies, has promise as an approach to answering these questions.

Emerson's Power-dependence Model

A person or group cannot have power in isolation; power must be in relationship to some other person or collectivity. The relational aspect of power is especially clear in Emerson's (1962, 1972a,b) theoretical development of the importance of dependency relationships in the total power constellation. Emerson suggests that power resides 'implicitly in others' dependency'; that is, parties in power relationships are tied to each other by mutual dependency.

Emerson (1962, 1972a,b) views social power as the result of dependency, and formulates the relationship as:

$$Pab = Dba$$
$$\text{and}$$
$$Pba = Dab$$

Where P is power, D is dependency, and a and b are two entities (individuals, groups, organizations, etc.); that is, the power of actor a over actor b is equal to the dependency of actor b upon actor a. At the same time, the power of actor b over actor a is equal to the dependency of actor a upon actor b.

Emerson believes dependency is influenced by two factors: intensity of demand and the number of supply alternatives. One's dependency is directly proportional to one's demand for what the other supplies. At the same time, one's demand is inversely proportional to the availability of the valued item from alternative sources. Emerson (1972a,b) also identifies cohesion in a relationship as being the average dependency in that relationship. Using his notation, cohesion would be written as:

$$\frac{Dba + Dab}{2}$$

Emerson (1962) argued that in an unbalanced power relation, where dependencies are unequal, the weaker member tries to resolve that imbalance to overcome the 'tensions involved in an unbalanced relation'. Combining two variables—supply and demand—and two actors, Emerson identified four possible ways a low-power actor in a relationship can equalize power in that relationship, calling these 'power-balancing operations'. In the first and second power-balancing operations, the low-power actor can reduce his or her own dependency while leaving the other's dependency low by: (i) reducing his or her own demand for what the other supplies, and (ii) increasing his or her alternative sources for what the other supplies. Both operations cause the total power and cohesion in the relationship to decline because the total dependency declines.

In the third and fourth power-balancing operations, the low-power actor can increase the other's dependency while leaving his or her own dependency on the other high by (iii) increasing the other's demand for what the low-power actor supplies, and (iv) reducing the other's alternative sources for what the low-power actor supplies. In both operations, the total power and cohesion in the relationship increases because the total dependency increases.

This approach to dependence and power facilitates understanding managerial power. It obviates the necessity of viewing power as some generalized attribute of a person, and leads to the assumption that net power results from a set of relationships between the constituents of the task or role. Thus an individual may be relatively powerful in relation to those who receive his or her output or vice versa; or an individual may be relatively powerful in relation to the input and output sectors, a situation which may generate countervailing power. The very nature of the managerial job requires interdependence of personnel and sub units. That interdependency among individuals, groups and technology ensures continuance, development, and growth of an organization is a reality. This theory has attracted considerable attention of researchers of social power. Emerson's model seems particularly appropriate to examining managers' reactions to dependency by focusing on their choice of power-balancing operations.

A further advantage of this theory of power is that it does not rest on any assumption of intent or usage. Moreover, this power-dependence concept provides an important escape from the 'zero-sum' concept of power (Persons, 1960), which assumes that in a system composed of A and B, the power of A is power at the expense of B. By viewing power in the context of interdependence the possibility of A and B becoming increasingly powerful with regard to each other. This means that increasing interdependence may result in increased net power. It is this possibility on which coalition rests.

Let us come back to Emerson's four power-balancing operations to examine them in greater detail.

STYLE ONE
In the first power-balancing operation, the low-power person reduces his or her motivational investment in goals mediated by the high-power person. These goals may be either foregone or postponed, but they are not acted upon. In organizations, this can be seen in those who minimize their dependence on others, and who ignore or evade attempts to influence them. The self-satisfaction inherent in the adoption of this style is the individual's feeling that he or she calls no one boss.

STYLE TWO
In the second power-balancing operation, the low-power person finds alternative sources for the gratification of his or her goals. In organizations, individuals who prefer this power-balancing style will predominantly meet their dependency needs off the job or in parts of the organization not associated in a routine or official manner with their job. It would seem that such individuals are relatively common in the 'deal-end', 'no- future' jobs. Others who find satisfaction in this style are those who seem to avoid feeling overly dependent on any single source of need gratification, thus spreading their dependencies among many sources so that each source has relatively little power.

STYLE THREE

In the third power-balancing operation, the low-power person endeavors to get the high-power person to increase his or her motivational investment in goals mediated by the low-power person. Organizationally, this style is used by those individuals who are trying to make themselves indispensable to the organization through hard work and who, in Emerson's terms, 'confer status' or flatter the high-power person or otherwise befriend their superiors. The satisfaction that these individuals derive from the use of this style would include feelings of loyalty to their superiors and to the more selfish ones related to doing that which is most likely to further their career.

STYLE FOUR

In the fourth power-balancing operation, the low-power person attempts to deny the high-power person access to alternative sources of gratification for the goals mediated by the low-power person. Operationally, in organizations, this is done by forming coalitions with other low-power persons in the form of unions, professional associations, or informal pressure groups. Less formally, forming a wide network of friends among one's organizational peers can also do it. Persons using this as their basic style seek to assemble a countervailing power of equals or colleagues. The satisfaction they derive from this style is that of the 'democratic idea', the notion that one's peers are the only legitimate source of control over one's activities.

In a study involving a large number of managers (Das and Cotton, 1988) it was observed that Indian managers demonstrate a distinct tendency to adopt style three. Findings also support that style three is more functional in the organizational context. The applicability of Emerson's theory of power can be demonstrated by analyzing a case from the author's personal experience. This case has a special significance from the standpoint of the banking profession. Going by the author's experience, a career banker feels good and significant so long as he or she is in 'operational banking'; in staff positions bankers often feel undervalued.

Example 1

The organization in this case is a large commercial bank located in south India. The bank has always had a comfortable market position in the country, with a conservative, traditional approach to investment and loan decisions.

Human resource activities such as recruitment, training, job assignments, and rewards were rather routine. There was an emphasis on long service and corporate loyalty. Job-move decisions were made by the senior management based upon what they felt was best for the bank.

In the 1990s, the banking scenario in India changed fundamentally. What had been the 'right type' of banker became out of place, with the uncertainty, and the emerging needs for risk-taking, conflict management, and individual creativity and accountability. There was a burgeoning of new types of services and organizational subunits, such as financial services, venture operations, leasing activities, and subsidiaries, calling for differentiated employee skills, career paths, and rewards. The chairman of the bank thought that a novel and proactive personnel function was essential to the organizational changes necessary for future success.

A young fast-track manager was chosen to head the personnel function. He had grown up in the city, tough and street-smart, and put himself through college as an employee of the bank. Though just in his mid-30s, he had ten years' service with the bank, an important loyalty factor in this organization. With a background of systems and operations, he had credibility with the task-oriented managers of the line units, such as commercial lending. His personal style was affable and cooperative, but at the same time, no-nonsense, thorough, and blunt. He was well aware of the change taking place in banking, and he had a vision of what the new organization should be like. He was also aware of the low-power role of personnel and the need to negotiate with and influence the line organization.

In the sections that follow, we will describe various strategies that he used to manage dependencies, thus increase his power.

Capitalizing on personal power. As has been said, the banker's personal credibility was critical. First he was a 'fast tracker', a 'star' in this system. He had 'practical' experience in systems and operations. He was mainstream. He was not an 'HR' type. He had gone to one of the good respected Catholic colleges in the city. His physical qualities reinforced his interpersonal style: tall, trim, ruggedly attractive; immaculately, and conservatively dressed; tough; able to 'bore in' to the other person in conversation with intense concentration; a dynamic, persuasive, somewhat down-to-earth speaker. While forceful, he could also 'read' people beautifully.

A major advantage in his negotiations was his ability to diagnose the motives and interests of the adversary and to generate win-win solutions to help meet many unstated aims. In short, he had good perspective-taking ability, a critical factor in effective conflict resolution. He showed many of the 'face-to-face' qualities such as expertise, creation of dependencies, persuasion, and creation of obligations.

Exploiting Relational Power.   Of course, the most important source of power this individual had was the support from his chairman, who had been and still is his mentor. This relationship does not translate into unconditional support on every issue, but it does mean access to the top and a good opportunity to influence at this level. Others' perceptions of this identification with the CEO greatly enhanced this person's power.

He is also well connected to the network of other formal and informal leaders in the organization (he is one of the 'old boys', a 'right type'). In addition to the relationships formed by 'growing up together' in the bank, he has also consciously worked at developing good working relationships with key line managers. Over time, a history of mutual respect and trust has developed.

Thinking strategically.   A critical starting point was having a clear sense of the organization's mission and strategy (which came from the chairman). To think strategically, the banker initiated several important activities. First, realizing that there must be a strategy for one's own function, that fits with the organization's mission, he created a personnel role and a personnel function that would create the organization of the future. Second, it was necessary to have different sub-strategies for each of the three organizational levels. In this case, the HR strategy for the institutional level was to influence the chairman and the top management to adopt new personnel policies and to introduce human resource considerations into the business plan for operations. At the managerial level, his strategy was to develop modern personnel systems (such as selection and performance appraisal), and to work with line managers to implement these systems branch- and region-wise. At the operational level, the strategy was to gradually replace staff that had been 'dumped' in personnel either because they had failed elsewhere or because they were 'good with people'. New staff would have to be trained as personnel specialists or they would be high potential management trainees in rotation from 'mainstream' departments.

What did he do to influence top management?   Specifically, how did this institutional-level influence take place? First, there was the process of 'educating' top management. This took the form of direct personnel influence, through discussions of critical cooperation problems and key personnel moves. It was also done through the strategic use of outside consultants. Another variant here was his role as counsellor to the chairman. He developed plans and programs of involvement of top management in human resource issues. Another strategy was to influence top management to influence future top management (i.e., today's 'fast-trackers').

Just as strategy and policies have far-reaching and long-term effects, the culture of an organization, its pivotal norms and values, permeates all thinking and action in the system. Recognizing this fact, he developed strategies for impacting the culture. By recognizing that the present culture would greatly impede the necessary changes, the personnel head attempted to influence the culture. A series of climate surveys revealed the current cultures in the various units of the bank. Managers were left to take action on the survey results, and thus a whole network of line management 'change agent' was created throughout the bank. The culture was also affected through new selection and induction practices.

What did he do to influence information systems? At the managerial level, new information systems greatly enhanced the key role of personnel. A uniform, bank-wise performance appraisal system and with all reports maintained by personnel, affected a critical aspect of line management: the administration of rewards. The organizational surveys, mentioned earlier, constituted a key information system, feed back from which had a considerable impact on line managers. Publications such as employee newsletters, and periodic reports to employees, shareholders and outside constituents also became effective means of communicating and promoting management's objectives. A critical type of power being the power over a person's career, the personnel head created a new function, internal placement, which was responsible for internal job transfers.

Co-opting external support by using boundary role. Central to many of the strategies was the effective utilization of the boundary-spanning function of the HR activity. Because part of the HR role is to interact with external agents such as government organizations, placement agencies, and professional associations, the HR manager often used the demands and pressures from external agents to support the HR agenda.

Strategic use of personnel's resources. As the various resources of the personnel function were being created, they became in part resources for use in enhancing personnel's future negotiating power. These resources were given with a message: The personnel function intends to be an integral part of the running of this business. And, in fact, this is what has happened.

Unlike many bankers, who either go for the withdrawal (style two) or collegial (style four) power-balancing style in such a situation, the banker in this case decided to adopt style three. His effort was to get the high-power persons (in this case the top management and other line bankers) to increase their motivational investment in goals mediated by him. This was made possible by using strategic thinking and meticulous planning. Managers who use such strategies to enlarge their power grow in the long run; for them all situations, which man may consider as loss of power, are actually potential sources of power.

Empowerment: Losing Control for Better Management

In the current-day competitive environment organizational leaders have to show results to demonstrate their effectiveness. For this, it may be necessary for managers to look beyond authority and power. Rather, they need to be more concerned with encouraging self-efficacy belief in their subordinates to ensure that the latter assume personal responsibility than merely ensuring obedience from their subordinates. This is only possible by learning new skills of empowering people.

Empowerment can improve employee motivation and job satisfaction, with the knock-on benefits of customer satisfaction and retention. In the new world of business, the traditional management model of 'the manager in control and the employees being controlled' does not work. Instead, managers have to search for ways to empower the workforce. Bureaucratic managers limit people, limit themselves, and limit their organizations. The shift from a bureaucratic to an empowering management calls for massive and difficult change organization wide. It demands a thorough understanding of both the nature of empowerment and the mechanics of moving from bureaucracy to empowerment.

Empowering is beneficial in the work situation, as researchers have observed that deprivation of power generates hostility, suspicion and a lack of commitment. Empowering subordinates contributes to managerial and organizational effectiveness. It has been observed that empowered subordinates develop a sense of competence, voluntarily share their superior's responsibility, participate in the change process, and assume personal responsibility.

Empowering subordinates has taken various forms in India over the years; for instance, involving employees in decision-making, or, in other words, participative forms of management. In participation, power is shared. Sharing power is a lower form of empowering. The first attempt to involve workers in management was made by TISCO as early as in 1918. Subsequently, in 1921, the government of West Bengal urged industries to set up workers' committees as a remedial measure against industrial unrest. Subsequently, different mechanisms were developed to democratize the work environment in Indian organizations. Noteworthy among them were work committees set up in 1947, joint management councils, set up in 1957, workers' directors set up in 1970, and the shop and joint councils set up in 1975.

In recent years, the concept of quality circle has become quite popular in work organizations in India. The concept has many elements which lead to empowerment. For example, allowing a group to find solutions to their own problems rather than depend on others presents distinct possibilities of increasing their sense of efficacy, leading to empowerment. However, there are some basic differences between the concept and practice of participative management and quality circle. While the former has always come as a part of legislation or a government scheme, quality circle is more voluntary in nature, and so far there is no government directive on it. It is nonetheless necessary to remember that quality circle, too, like participative management, has encountered severe setbacks. Although both these traditional ways of empowering enhance the feeling of self-efficacy among organizational members, the approach is basically formal and structured. At the same time there is a growing demand to know about the other ways of empowering people at the work place, because of its inherent benefits.

It is possible to empower through informal social processes as well. In their study on corporate success, Singh and Bhandarker (1990) highlighted the importance of empowering leadership used by successful corporate chief executives. They observed that an empowering management style reduces anxiety, increases security and confidence, and encourages people to accept change and actively participate in it. In the authors' case studies the primary concern of all the five chief executives was not to make people do something but to make the process of their doing it possible, enabling them, and enhancing their sense of competence. The mechanism used for empowering was not systems and procedures but primarily informal social processes.

One informal social process of empowering is the mentor–protégé relationship. Studies strongly indicate that this relationship can be instrumental in supporting both career advancement and personal growth (Kram, 1985; Levinson, et al. 1985; Phillips-Jones, 1982). Mentors basically perform two types of functions: career-enhancing functions and psychological functions. The former include sponsorship, coaching, facilitating exposure and visibility, offering challenging work, and protection, while the latter include role modeling, confirmation, counseling and friendship. Whereas career functions enhance the possibility of career advancement, psychological functions enhance the sense of competence, clarity of identity, and role effectiveness of a protégé. Mentors, through interpersonal relationships, enable protégés to develop and grow in their organizational life. In some cultures, for example the Japanese, the relationship between superior and subordinate fulfils all the requirements of the mentor–protégé relationship.

Based on Bandura's (1977, 1986) self-efficacy model, Conger and Kanungo (1988) demonstrated that empowerment in the work situation helps enhance the feeling of self-efficacy among organizational members. However, their stress is on ensuring that the informal social process of enhancing self-efficacy beliefs be meshed with formal organizational policies and practices.

The essential task of a leader is to continuously develop an organization where the constituents put shared values into practice. Credible leaders strengthen constituent competence and confidence. This enhances the team, department or organization's ability to perform and meet promises and builds the credibility of the leader. Available empirical evidence (Das 1997) suggests that empowering supervisory behavior promotes role innovation and a sense of involvement among subordinates. Even at the work-unit level, task performance appears to be better in units with empowering supervisors.

Empowerment is not just 'giving people the power to make decisions'. In fact, they already have the power to make intelligent decisions to help the company operate more effectively. It is self-efficacy belief and competencies that are the essential milestones of empowerment. In a factor analytic study (Das, 1992) it was observed that for empowering subordinates, managers have to basically demonstrate three sets of behaviors. The first set has been described as 'giving exposure, visibility, and protection', and the second set as 'facilitating career advancement'. Both sets of behavior are oriented towards developing subordinates and helping them in career advancement. The third set, 'acceptance and encouragement', has the potential to enhance interpersonal bondage. The following examples show how these dimensions can actually manifest in managerial behavior.

Example 2

I was told by a large number of banker friends that how superiors can empower their subordinates can be learnt from Mr Shah, Deputy General Manager (Planning) in a leading Indian commercial bank in Karnataka. In course of discussion, Mr Shah said, 'If you want to know my strategy of empowering go and ask that fellow sitting in the right corner of the room. When he first joined this bank twelve years ago as probationary officer I was his reporting authority; I was then only a chief officer in the regional office. Now I am DGM, and he is chief officer. By now he has acquired doctorate in macro-economics'.

Dr Bhatnagar clearly remembers his experience of working under Mr Shah. He recollects Mr Shah saying, 'In your work you have two bosses, one is me and the other is yourself. It is important to remember that you must do your work in such a way that both your bosses are happy, since that is important for you. If you do good work I will give you a good report that will help you in the long run. However, you should also find ways and means of doing things that make you happy'.

Dr. Bhatnagar recalls that initially there was a fear of committing errors or deviating from the usual way of doing things. However, Mr Shah made it clear that 'errors are accepted so long as actions are there. The spirit of experimentation was primarily due to Mr Shah's, encouragement, admits Dr Bhatnagar. 'After twelve years he is again, my boss and he is DGM. Even now I find that he does not hesitate to share credit with me. He often takes me to high-level meetings, where my presence is not an official requirement. At these meetings Mr Shah encourages me to provide explanations or clarifications when needed'. Another aspect, which Dr Bhatnagar wanted to mention in this connection, was the sense of pride Mr Shah had about him, in spite of a knowledge gap between the two. In his own words, 'You see I am a doctorate in macro economic planning, and I have also published in good journals, whereas my boss is only a graduate, although he has considerable business experience. On many technical matters he asks for my opinion without any hesitation. I know that he has mentioned to people the benefits he derives from my knowledge.'

Example 3

When Mr Bedi assumed charge as regional manager of Bangalore region he followed a unique style. 'He used to organize fortnightly meetings with all the branch managers. At these meetings he was interested not only to know about the business progress but also about what problems we were encountering', recalls a branch manager. 'Mr Bedi would convert each problem, faced by us, into a project and ask us to talk to our people at the branches to find possible solutions. In subsequent meetings we were expected to present our ideas, based on feedback received from branch people, on how we were planning to tackle the problem. Not only Mr Bedi but the other branch managers present were also free to give suggestions.' 'These meetings helped our regional manager to maintain a solid evaluation of the progress of all the projects within his region, as well as gave all the branch managers a chance to garner appreciation and support from him and from their peer managers. At one such meeting a branch manager shared his anxiety about losing business to a rival and aggressive bank about to open a branch close by. The branch was going to be more spacious, with state-of-the-art interiors and fully air-conditioned. There was no comparison between the competitors' proposed branch and this one.'

Mr Bedi suggested returning to his branch and discussing what could be done: this was a Project for him. In course of time the branch manager came up with an idea, which was successfully implemented.'

'The idea was very simple. On the occasion of a religious festival he sent all important clients greetings accompanied by a rose. These clients were very rich people, and the branch manager thought no other gift would be attractive to them, which he could afford. It turned out to be a marvelous marketing strategy, very cheap (fifty paise per client) and highly effective. After receiving the greetings a large number of customers called on the manager and expressed their appreciation for his gesture. In a subsequent meeting, the regional manager requested the branch manager to share in detail how he tackled the project. 'Three months later, the concerned branch manager received a congratulatory letter from the zonal manager. In that letter the zonal manager mentioned that he had learnt about this incident from the regional manager, Mr Bedi'.

Three main learning points emerge from this incident. First, it is necessary for the superior to keep close contact with field-level functionaries, because this provides plenty of feedback to both and support to the junior. Second, such interactions give an opportunity to receive praise and encouragement from superiors and the peer group. Third, they demonstrate to other employees how to be innovative in different situations and also encourages them to act accordingly.

When asked 'how much control they have on their subordinates, superiors like Mr Shah and Mr Bedi tend to say that when employees have agreed to do their job and also know that they will be held responsible, they will control their own work'. Further, they feel that if subordinates are not controlling themselves, they have apparently failed to see the importance of their task'. Many superiors equate empowering with losing control. They often overlook the fact that being affiliated to national level unions, and their job knowledge, employees can create difficulties for superiors if they want to. A superior is thus dependent on the goodwill of subordinates, and they cannot be forced to do things unless they want to. An empowering superior recognizes all these factors and consciously develops strategies to lose control for better management.

Power Maturity as a Value

People who demonstrate a need to always be 'one up' take every available opportunity to point out or try to prove that they are better than you, more capable than you, more worthy than you, smarter than you, etc. They feel that the only way for them to 'win' is for others to lose. They regard power to be finite. Consider the following example:

Example 4

A rural branch manager feels upset, threatened and slighted when farmers or agriculture borrowers who come to his branch go to the Agriculture Officer instead of coming to him. The branch manager, who feels that his power is being diluted by the agriculture officer's popularity or influence with the rural clientele, creates problems for the agriculture officer.

The branch manager is jealous of his lead bank officer who is junior to him, because other banks in the district headquarters consult him. The lead bank officer also has direct contact with the district collector; the regional manager of the bank also seeks his help for various liaison works. The branch manager feels insecure.

From the psychological perspective, people like the branch manager undervalue their own inherent worth. They are more concerned about their position relative to that of others and preoccupied with their own value and potential without thought for others in the organization. So they think power is finite and limited. They may therefore engage in more win–lose or lose-lose activity than is called for. Often they may find it necessary to justify power abuse, hence further undervaluing their self-worth.

In sharp contrast to those who feel that power is unlimited and can be shared by all, those who believe the amount of power available is expandable or infinite will tend to create more win-win outcomes. In attempting to empower others, they empower themselves. They believe that they become more effective in the process of making others more effective.

A win-win outcome is one in which all those involved in a situation or transaction benefit. For instance, when a manager uses his or her power to promote a qualified subordinate, the outcome is win-win, because the productivity of the manager's Unit increases, and the employee benefits from a better position. Now consider the following example:

Example 5

The branch manager organizes a function for the launch of a new deposit scheme by the chairman of the bank. The chief secretary of the state and other VIPs also attend the function. The entire arrangements and coordination are done by a team headed by the accountant. Having given directions, the branch manager remains in the background, allowing ample scope for his juniors to do well. He also accords public recognition to the team members by inviting them to the dais for being given mementos by the chairman.

To him, power is unlimited and by sharing it with others, he increases his power still further.

Example 6

The branch manager always allows staff meetings to be presided over by the sub-manager and accountant. He makes everybody understand that administrative is vested with the triumvirate. All issues appear to be resolved by the troika. In this participative process, even though all the decisions are taken by him, the branch manager creates the illusion of power being shared. And in this process, the other two feel powerful (empowered). This helps in the smooth running of the branch, and leaves the branch manager free to concentrate on business development.

These are the people who have a strong sense of self-confidence, and they feel good about it. They do not believe that their self-respect depends upon being best at everything; they can benefit from and enjoy interactions with those who can outperform them. They have a tendency to create opportunities for learning and growth for self and others. They show a distinct tendency to use power ethically. As a result, they are more likely to expand their abilities.

Unethical use of power may help a leader gain in the short term, but in the long run this behavior can cause the leader to become a detriment to the organization and force the organization to move against him or her. It is a common observation that leaders with an abrasive personality—though often of high intelligence, are perfectionist—pushing for accomplishments and consistently doing a superior job—do not work well with others, are usually unsuccessful in motivating subordinates. Leaders of this type often fail to live up to their potential, rarely rise very high in organizations, and have trouble delegating work or empowering others. Such leaders need to be trained to use power in a mature manner.

At this stage it will be useful to clarify what is meant by power maturity. When making a case that organizational leaders must have power and that those who do not must be empowered, some discussion about power abuse and misuse is essential. From the perspective of psychoanalytic tradition, the tendency to abuse or misuse power is linked to psychological maturity. In this context the theory proposed by Stewart (1975) comes quite handy. Based on an individual's level of psychosocial *development*, and patterns of psychosocial *orientation*, Stewart proposed four stages of development. Although continuity is assumed from stages one to four (i.e., stage four reflects a higher level of development than stage three, state three higher than stage two, and stage two higher than stage one), each stage stands on its own. Each stage is unique in terms of dealing with relationship to authority, other people, and feelings, as also action orientation. McClelland (1975) observed that managers with high maturity level tend to be effective in their organizations by creating an encouraging work climate. Sometimes stage-one-oriented leaders appear to be better than those of stages two and three, because of their charismatic nature. However, they tend to create feeling of dependency in their subordinates. In contrast, a stage four leader is oriented to develop his subordinates, create a culture and systems. His believes that if he wants to have power he will empower all those who work with him. For this, he will let them work on their own and support them at every step so that they learn from their own experiences rather than from him alone. Leaders of this type operate from high maturity level and contribute to independence and inter-dependence.

Leaders who use power in a mature manner by become powerful depending more on personal power than their job title, or credentials, to mobilize resources, inspire creativity, and instill confidence among subordinates. They become more powerful as they nurture the power of others. They empower spontaneously and naturally. Often, they act more as a colleague than boss, relying on influence, respect and relationships to work with employees. Empowering managers seek to share power: they give power, and then hold those they have empowered, accountable. They recognize and reward people for their accomplishments, contributions and ideas. They encourage participation, solicit input, and involve people in decision-making, giving credit where it is due. They reward those who make the greatest impact towards achieving organizational goals, rewarding results rather than processes. Leaders with maturity care about people and avoid dominating them.

It is the characteristic of a dominant personality to seek power. A dominant personality lives in a world in which manipulations guide his existence. The mastery of an experiential flow hinges on their ability to use techniques and skills to reduce diffuse events to organized and smooth running sequences. The excessive need for freedom and a sense of happiness in dominant personalities leads to an artificial imposing of a belief in the manipulability of situations that is obsessive in nature. This pattern arises from an excess of dominant energy and vigor. However that does not mean that people with dominant personality make poor leaders. In fact we need dominant personality in leadership positions, provided they have attained a level of maturity.

Conclusion

In this chapter I have attempted to make a case that leaders have to gain power for effective role performance. In the process of gaining power, besides conventional bases, the significance of managing dependency has been highlighted. Although acquiring power is important for a manager leader, equally important is to create an empowering environment. In reality, effective leaders increase their personal power by empowering others in the organization.

It is a fact that powerful people abuse power. That is not because they have power but due to their lack of maturity. Developing maturity can restrict human beings' natural tendency to misuse and abuse power. Towards this end power maturity training has immense potential. Institutions of leadership development among managers require to build in such training into their curriculum.

The guiding principles of an independent maturity can be found only through self-knowledge and self-control. Leaders need to be trained to develop a cognitive frame where there is no ostracism, only selective withdrawal, and no punishment, only selective indifference.

References

Adler, A. (1927). *The Practice and Theory of Individual Psychology*. New York: Harcourt Brass.

Ardrey, R. (1962). *African Genesis*. New York: Anthenium.

Baldridge, J.V. (1971). *Power and Conflict in the University*. New York: Wiley.

Bandura, A. (1977). 'Self Efficacy: Towards a Unifying Theory of Behavioural Change'. *Psychological Review*. 84, 191–215.

Bandura, A. (1986). *Social Foundations of Thought and Action: A Social Cognitive View*. Englewood Cliffs, NJ: Prentice-Hall.

Brown, L.D. (1986). 'Power Outside Organizational Paradigms. Lessons from Community Partnerships'. In S. Srivastva and Associates. *Executive Power: How Executives Influence People and Organizations*. San Francisco: Jossey-Bass.

Conger, J.A. (1988). Kanungo R.N., 'The Empowerment Process: Integrating Theory and Practice'. *Academy of Management Review*. 13(3), 471–82.

Das, G.S. (1997). 'Determinants and Consequences of Role Innovation'. *Indian Journal of Industrial Relations*. 33(2) October.

——— (1993). 'Development of an Empowering Scale: Item Analysis and Factor Structure'. *ASCI Journal of Management*. 22(2–3), September–December.

Das G.S. and C.C. Cotton (1988). 'Power Balancing Styles of Indian Managers. *Human Relations*. 14(7), 533–51.

Emerson, R. (1962). 'Power Dependence Relation'. *American Sociological Review*. vol. 27.

——— (1972a). 'Exchange Theory; Part 1: A Psychological basis for social exchange'. In Berger, J., Zeldith, M., and Anderson, B. (eds.). *Sociological Theories in Process (Vol. II)*. Boston: Houghton Mifflin.

Emerson, R. (1972b) 'Exchange theory; Part 2: A Psychological basis for social exchange'. In Berger, J., Zeldith, M., and Anderson, B. (eds.). *Sociological Theories in Process (Vol. II)*. Boston: Houghton Mifflin.

Etzioni, A. (1978). 'Comparative Analysis of Complex Organizations'. In D. Hampton, C. Summer and R. Weber (eds.). *Organizational Behaviour and the Practice of Management*. Glenview, Ill: Scott Foresman and Company.

French, J.R.P. and B. Raven (1959). 'The Bases of Social Power'. In D. Cartwright (ed.). *Studies in Social Power*. Ann Arbor: University of Michigan, Institute for Social Research.

Galbraith, J.K. (1983). 'Anatomy of Power'. Boston: Houghton Mifflin.

Hackman, M.A. and C.E. Johnson (1991). 'Leadership: A Communication Perspective'. Prospect Heights, Ill: Waveland Press.

Hersey, P. and K. Blanchard (1982). *The Management of Organizational Behavior*. Englewood Cliffs, NJ: Prentice-Hall.

Horney, K. (1950). *Neurosis and Human Growth*. New York: Norton.

House, R.J. and G. Dessler (1974). 'The Path-Goal Theory of Leadership, Some Post Hock and Apriori Tests. In J.C. Hunt and Larson, LL. (eds.). *Contingency Approaches to Leadership*. Carbondale, Ill.: Southern University Press.

Kanter, R.M. (1977). *Men and Women of the Corporation*. New York: Basic Books.

King, A. (1987). *Power and Communication*. Prospect Heights, Ill: Waveland Press.

Kram, K.E. (1985). *Mentoring at Work: Developmental Relationships in Organisational Life*. Illinois Scott. Foresman.

Krausz, R. (1986). 'Power and Leadership in Organizations'. *Transactional Analysis Journal*. 16, 85–94.

Levinson, D.J., C.N. Darrow and E.B. Klein (1985). *Seasons of a Man's Life*. New York: Knopf.

Lorenz, K. (1966). *On Aggression*. New York: Harcourt Brass and the World.

Lukes, S. (1974). *Power: A Radical View*. New York: Macmillan.

May, R. (1972). *Power and Innocence*. New York: Norton.

McCroskey, J.C., V.P. Richmond, T.G. Plax and P. Kearney (1985). 'Power in the Classroom: Behavior Alteration Techniques, Communication Training and Learning'. *Communication Education*. 34, 214–26.

McClelland, D.C. (1975) Power: The Inner Experience. New York: Irvington Publisher.

Mechanic, D. (1962). 'Sources of Power of Lower Participants in Complex Organisations'. *Administrative Science Quaterly*. 7.

Milgran, Stanley (1974). *Obedience to Authority: An Experimental View*. New York: Harper and Row.

Osborne, R.N. and J.G. Hunt (1975). 'An Adoptive-Reactive Theory of Leadership—The Roles of Macro Variables in Leadership Research'. In Hunt J.G. and Larson L.L. (eds.). *Leadership Frontiers*. Ohio: Ohio State University Press, Kent.

Parsons, T. (1960). *Structure and Process in Modern Societies*. New York: The Free Press of Glencoe.

Philips-Jones, L.L. (1982). *Mentors and Proteges*. New York: Arbort House.

Plax, T.G., F. Kearney and T.M. Downs (1986). 'Communicating Control in the Classroom and Satisfaction with Teaching and Students'. *Communication Education*. 35, 379–88.

Rahim, A.M. (1989). 'Relationship of Leader Power to Compliance and Satisfaction with Supervision: Evidence from a National Sample of Managers'. *Journal of Management*. 15, 545–56.

Russell, B. (1938). *Power—A New Social Analysis*. New York: Norton.

Singh, P. and A. Bhandarker (1990). *Corporate Success: Transformational Leadership*. New Delhi: Wiley Eastern.

Stewart, A.J. (1975). *Psychological Maturity Scale*. Boston: Dept. of Psychology, Boston University.

Stinson, J.E. and T.W. Johnson (1975). 'The Path Goal Theory of Leadership, A Partial Test and Suggested Refinement'. *Academy of Management Journal*. 18(2).

Tannenbaum, R. (1962). 'Control in Organizations'. *Administration Science Quarterly*. 7, 236–57.

Verderber, R.F. and K.S. Verderber (1992). *Inter-act Using Interpersonal Communication Skills*. Belmont: Wadsworth.

Weber, M. (1947). *The Theory of Social and Economic Organisation*. New York: Oxford Univeristy Press.

Woodward, J. (1958). *Management and Technology*. London: Her Majesty's Printing Press.

Zaleznik, A. (1970). 'Power and Politics in Organizational Life'. *Harvard Business Review*. May–June, Issue 110012, 13–26.

12

Effect of Empowerment in Indian Industries: An Empirical Analysis

K.S. GUPTA

Introduction

The environment is undergoing critical changes the world over. In India similar patterns of change started in the 1990s with economic reforms. This has resulted in a greater pressure on organizations to deal with competition, consumer awareness, globalization, diversification and professionalism. The liberalization, privatization and globalization of the Indian economy were bound to have a significant impact on business organizations. The competition spurred by the reforms led corporates to adopt a market-oriented approach to be quicker in their responses. The impact of economic reforms on industries led managements to search for better alternatives for survival and growth of organizations.

Running through the research literature on organizational behavior and the operations of many successful organization is a common theme that emphasizes the power of confident people, passionately committed to meaningful goals, acting in accordance with their own higher values, taking risks and demonstrating initiative and creativity in the service of these goals. This theme of individual well-being is now being expressed in terms of empowerment. The process of empowerment is a highly powerful device. In certain situations, it can be introduced without any turbulence, in others it takes a lot of time. Hence the mantra which can ensure organizational success is 'employee empowerment' (Dwivedi, 1996).

Definition Empowerment

There are as many definitions of the term empowerment as have thought and written on it. The term has been used with a limited focus and understanding. With the objective of providing a holistic view, empowerment is defined as: 'the process of sharing power and providing an enabling environment (by removing hurdles) in order to encourage employees to take initiative and decisions to take actions at all levels to achieve organisational and individual goals' (Gupta, 1999).

Need and Objective of the Study

Empowerment is still in an embryonic stage, with its definitions as the process of sharing power and providing an enabling environment. However, the need for empowerment of employees has been felt for the last three decades with the changes in business scenario, technology, trade union movements and environmental protection movements, human behavior in organizations has changed a lot and employee empowerment has gained strategic importance for competitiveness. The measuring instrument developed by the author for the study is to understand the implications of different interventions on empowerment and to ascertain whether empowerment could be used as an organizational development intervention in organizations.

Tool Used

The empowerment framework and measuring instrument (Gupta, 1999) were used for collecting responses from four selected organisations. The data is given in Table 12.1. The variables have been grouped as empowering variables and consequences (outcome variables).

Empowering Variables

The variables were grouped under empowering variables depending upon their characteristics (Gupta, 1999). These variables are, Respect for Team Member (RTM), Top Management Attitude to Human Resource (TMA), Opportunities for Learning Application (OLA), Open Communication (OC), Organizational Support for Innovation (OSI), Responsive Superior (RSR), Opportunities for Self -development (OSD), Low Formalization (LFN), Performance-linked Feedback (PLF) and Autonomy (AMY).

Table 12.1: Mean Empowerment and Consequence Scores: Four Cases

Organization Group Name Variable	PVT ORG1 FR	PVT ORG1 RR	PVT ORG2 FR	PVT ORG2 RR	PVT ORG3 FR	PUB ORG4 FR	PUB ORG4 RR
Empowerment							
AMY	3.38	3.40	4.09	3.92	3.94	3.66	4.12
LFN	3..04	3.25	3.19	3.20	3.26	2.29	3.50
OC	3.20	3.50	3.59	4.27	4.02	3.67	4.05
OLA	2.48	2.60	2.76	3.50	3.10	2.92	3.50
OSD	2.82	3.25	3.83	4.00	4.05	3.66	4.25
OSI	2.84	3.00	3.14	3.58	3.56	3.25	4.00
PLF	2.78	3.20	3.21	3.39	3.77	3.22	3.90
RSR	3.40	3.40	3.80	3.80	3.94	2.11	2.25
RTM	2.78	3.00	3.20	3.55	3.75	2.93	3.41
TMA	2.96	3.25	3.52	3.40	3.92	3.31	3.97
Consequence							
JIT	3.00	3.20	3.38	3.05	3.78	3.11	4.00
OCT	3.70	3.90	4.00	3.95	3.76	4.16	4.37
RS	3.24	3.50	2.76	3.25	3.68	2.03	2.00
SE	3.28	3.50	3.71	3.75	3.89	3.25	3.50
WES	3.60	3.80	3.83	4.01	3.77	3.89	4.31
Mean							
EMP	2.95	3.19	3.40	3.70	3.77	3.26	3.84
CQS	3.43	3.58	3.65	3.70	3.77	3.54	3.95

FR: First Response.
RR: Repeat Response.

Consequences

The factors grouped under consequences are influenced by the empowering variables. There are Self-efficacy (SE), Organizational Commitment (OCT), Work Environment Satisfaction (WES), Role Satisfaction (RS), and Job Involvement (JIT).

Methodology

The case approach was used for this study. Four organizations agreed to participate in an in-depth analysis to study the effects of interventions the organizations had undertaken on the level of empowerment. They were labeled as:

- ORG1: obtained a low score of 2.95 during first response and 3.19 during repeat response on empowerment.
- ORG2: obtained high score 3.40 during first response and a higher score of 3.70 during repeat response on empowerment.
- ORG3: obtained high score of 3.77.
- ORG4: obtained higher score of 3.26 during first response and the highest score of 3.84 during repeat response on empowerment.

ORG1, ORG2 and ORG3 are private organizations while ORG4 is a public sector organization. Initially, in 1997, only three organizations, namely, ORG1, ORG2 and ORG4, were planned for study. In mid-1998, ORG3 also expressed its willingness to participate. Variable-wise empowerment and consequence scores for all the four organizations are summarized in Table 12.1. In organizations ORG1, ORG2 and ORG4 the results of data collected as pre-intervention score (shown as FR in Table 12.1) were discussed with the divisional/HR heads and they were requested to decide upon and implement a few interventions to improve the level of empowerment. Data were again collected during the last quarter of 1998 to analyse post-intervention results. In the case of ORG4 the data were collected in mid-1998.

Interviews of some team leaders and members were conducted to understand their perceptions of the interventions and their effects on empowerment scores. Discussions were also held with the HR heads of these organizations to validate the views of the respondents. It is evident from Table 12.1 that the score in consequences as a result of different interventions in all four organizations are higher in Repeat Samples. The following are the results of the study of the four organizations.

ORG1

Top management started looking at human resource as the tool and technique to remain at the top in terms of market share. As a result, an HR department was established at the corporate level in 1996. The department organized a brainstorming session of top-level executives of the company to set directions for the future. Also, an employee's satisfaction survey (HR health) was conducted. The result was an eye-opener. In spite of the company being a market leader, the employee satisfaction level was found to be very low.

At the end of 1996, empowerment responses were collected from the middle-level executives of the company. From Table 12.1 it can be seen that the score on opportunities for learning application is the least (2.48) and the score on autonomy is highest (3.38) among all ten empowering variables. The score on the job involvement is least (3.00) and that on organizational commitment the highest (3.70) among all five outcome variables. The results of the survey confirmed a similar trend.

The score on all the empowering variables in first response is lower than the mean scores of the sample (959 responses) and is less than the score of the other three companies, ORG2, ORG3 and ORG4. This clearly indicates that an absence of conscious effort on the part of management resulted in a lower empowerment score and higher dissatisfaction level in the organization.

In 1997 the management of ORG1 decided to conduct a biennial survey of employee satisfaction, and a review of welfare practices, higher education sponsoring scheme, participation in training and learning programs conducted by other group companies, performance appraisal in key result areas, celebration of birthdays and marriage anniversaries at the department level, social get-togethers and annual picnics with families at the plant level and emphasis on fast and effective decision-making, as HR interventions. Repeated responses were collected from the same respondents in end 1988 to find out the changes as a result of the interventions. (See Table 12.1 and Figure 12.1)

The results of the repeat responses from samples taken in end 1998 (Table 12.1) showed improvement in empowerment and consequences.

OPPORTUNITIES SUPPORT FOR INNOVATION

There were no direct efforts made by ORG1 to encourage innovation (except in the area of research and development). Therefore the change in score on organizational support for innovation is low. Autonomy and opportunities for learning application showed small changes and responsive superior showed no change post interventions. Some of the factors that showed marginal improvement are discussed below.

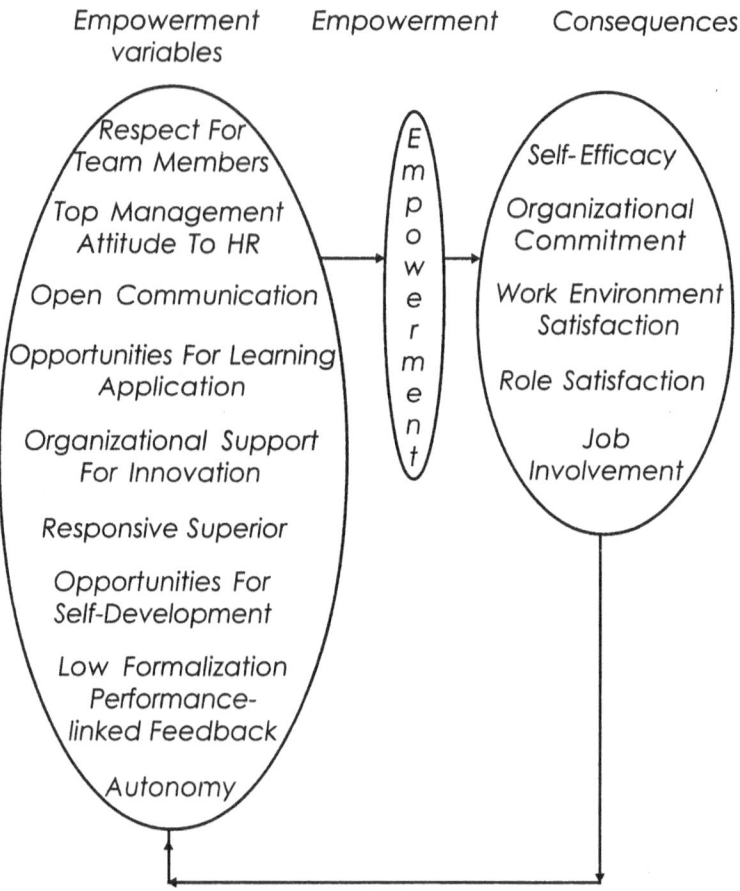

Figure 12.1: Framework of Empowerment

TOP MANAGEMENT ATTITUDE TO HUMAN RESOURCE

A company-wide employee satisfaction survey indicated a positive change in top management attitude to human resource. The company also sponsored a study on benchmarking of the best HR practices. Moreover, top management reviewed the welfare practices and made efforts to improve them.

OPEN COMMUNICATION

An information manual for all employees and an induction manual for new incumbents was prepared. A personnel manual for functional heads and product manuals for old and new product knowledge were also prepared. In addition, half-yearly open house discussions improved information sharing and thus created an environment for open communication.

PERFORMANCE-LINKED FEEDBACK

Open communication contributed to discussions on company performance and the importance of feedback for improving individual and group performance. This brought about an improvement in employees commitment, work environment satisfaction and self-efficacy.

OPPORTUNITIES FOR SELF-DEVELOPMENT

Top management initiated an employee development program by implementing a sponsoring scheme for obtaining higher qualifications and learning through participation with other group companies. Management also decided to provide need-based training of minimum 48 hours per year. The introduction of a key result area- based performance appraisal system shifted the responsibility of learning and developing to individuals.

RESPECT FOR TEAM MEMBERS

To develop a feeling of 'oneness', the company introduced activities like department-level celebration of employees birthdays, participation in competitive quiz programs and games, and picnics and get-togethers with family members.

LOW FORMALIZATION

Employees dealing closely with clients were given flexibility in using policies and procedures with the aim of bringing about an increase in customer satisfaction.

ORG2

A multinational, multi-location, multi-product company, ORG2 serves customers in the areas of electric power generation, transmission and distribution, industrial and building systems and rail transportation.

The company had a multiple-layered hierarchical structure with centralized decision-making on major issues and was governed by structured rules, procedures and policies. In 1996, in order to provide more transparency, the company conducted a survey (involving all employees) to get feedback on improvements required to meet the challenges.

Based on the results of the survey, the company decided to implement the following interventions:

- Adaptation of company-wide values which are supreme for organization
- Modification of policies and procedures in consonance with organizational values
- Reduce the 12-layer hierarchical structure to a 4-layered one
- Shift performance assessment from individuals to teams in the form of business units
- Focus on developmental appraisal rather than performance appraisal on individual level
- Deputation to training and development programs (based on individual needs) selected by the individual
- Providing more autonomy to functional managers
- Improvement in transparency and open communication.

The results of the repeat responses (RR) from the sample taken in mid-1998 are shown in Table 12.1.

ORGANIZATIONAL SUPPORT FOR INNOVATION

The participants expressed a strong opinion that the company supported the adoption of best HR practices in order to maintain its growth. They exemplified situations in which they had had opportunities to experiment with new ideas and risk taking. Barring a few unsuccessful ones, most of their attempts had been successful which further encouraged them to use innovative ideas. The company also had a suggestion scheme and quality circles through which employees were encouraged to experiment and promote innovation.

OPEN COMMUNICATION AND TOP MANAGEMENT ATTITUDE TO HUMAN RESOURCE

The chairman of the company meets all recruits during training to encourage them to have open discussions by breaking the barriers of hierarchy. During discussions only first names are permitted to be used. This encourages open communication in the organization and thus builds up transparency.

Periodic communication meetings at various levels, team-based working systems, bottom-up processes for budgeting and planning, periodic cultural and employee surveys are some examples of the efforts at improving company-wide open communication. These were supported by periodic plant-level and national-level meetings of top management with unions, open-door policy and profit centre concept in order to encourage open communication. A decentralized structure, cross-functional team approaches, task-based teams, customer focus programs and benchmarking were a few interventions used for improving role satisfaction.

OPPORTUNITIES FOR SELF-DEVELOPMENT AND PERFORMANCE-LINKED FEEDBACK

Open communication helped provide continuous feedback on performance-related areas to all concerned. Performance appraisal was called developmental appraisal. Non-performance was viewed as an opportunity for identifying the areas for improvement and development. Opportunities for self-development were plenty and individuals had to undergo training for a fixed number of days in a year (eight days at present). The decision on the choice of training program was taken by individuals.

The opportunities for application of learning following the training were supported by the superiors. Individuals were also supported in experiment learning. Post-training, participants had to present an action plan about the learning and its application to the top management. A top-level executive was assigned the responsibility to provide all support for application of learning. Dealings with the external environment, interaction with parent business units, training programs in India and abroad are some more examples of opportunities for self-development in the organization. The performance-related feedback to the individual, a part of developmental appraisal, was carried out in a free and non-threatening manner, an excellent environment to improve self-efficacy.

AUTONOMY AND RESPECT FOR TEAM MEMBERS

There was total freedom in decision-making and execution of plans. During discussions, middle-level executives cited several examples of real situations in which they were free to take decisions and act upon them.

This they said gave them a sense of satisfaction. They also said that similar freedom was provided at all levels of the organization. The teamwork approach adopted by the company was one of company-wide values and thereby any sacrifice on individualism was acceptable. Respect for team members was also extremely high in this company. Informal discussions with the concerned persons was very common in the teams. Any Decisions about the work were taken only after consultation with all the team members.

RESPONSIVE SUPERIOR

Decisions were taken at each level and not passed on to someone at the top. Since teame-working and decision- making were the main focus, decision-taking was an easy and effective process.

LOW FORMALIZATION

The policies and related procedures were used flexibly and as guidelines to achieve the business unit goals. Customer service engineers were given broad guidelines to serve the needs of customers. The internal customer concept, which focuses on satisfying the needs of internal customers, was practised throughout the company. This helped develop customer-oriented policies and procedures.

ORG3

ORG3 is a company engaged in diversified activities in manufacturing and has marketing offices and regional offices all over India. The organization has a turnover of Rs 1,000 crore and employs 5,000 people. With a modest beginning as a tractor manufacturing unit in 1959, over the years the company expanded its activities and entered into technical collaborations with foreign companies.

The company established a separate consultancy services unit in 1991. This unit was aimed at offering its experience to Indian industry for 'managing change'. It provided not only theoretical solutions but competitive strategies that work through tried-and-tested 'hands on' expertise.

The company provided a number of welfare measures for its employees and their families like canteen, transport and recreation as also educational, insurance and medical facilities. The organization works on strong values and at does not compromise on them. There was strong evidence and numerous examples to prove the value orientation of the organization. One of the company's values was client satisfaction, the ultimate goal of the organization.

Interventions in ORG3

Based on the discussion of the result of empowerment responses with the HR head, this company implemented some interventions (in 1996). These contributed towards a high empowerment score. The interventions used to improve empowerment are given under each of the variables.

ORGANIZATIONAL SUPPORT FOR INNOVATION

There was complete freedom to experiment. Assessment was made to develop individuals and not to admonish them. The nature of task (consultancy) itself calls for finding new ways to satisfy customer's needs.

TOP MANAGEMENT ATTITUDE TO HUMAN RESOURCE

The organization considered people as its assets and gave human values utmost importance. Even in the case of higher level appointments, subordinates were involved. Appointments could not be made until the acceptance of all the team members was obtained. Everyone played an active role in the implementation of strategies and solutions through close interaction with clients. Everyone was provided relevant and vital international exposure for widening his or her knowledge and gain competitiveness. Innovative human resource practices such as building trust, consistency in day-to-day actions, open-door policy, same canteen for all and non-compromise on basic ethics at all levels of the organization were used to promote organizational values and attitude of top management to human resource.

OPEN COMMUNICATION

Open-door policy was in practice with a view that nothing is confidential. Any top-level person visiting a plant made sure that he or she met all the employees there. The organizational structure was flat to increase the communication speed, accuracy and adequacy of information. There were ample opportunities for discussion. The feedback mechanism operated directly and indirectly. Once a year the whole organization went on an annual learning conference. Senior-level professional management committee met four times a year to discuss group strategies and future plans.

PERFORMANCE-LINKED FEEDBACK

There was a continuous feedback mechanism. A 360-degree assessment was used for promotion. Feedback to the individuals on their performance was provided continuously using both formal and informal channels.

OPPORTUNITIES FOR SELF-DEVELOPMENT

Top priority was given to individual development, with training playing a vital role. For example, interventions such as a separate budget for training, compulsory training of 20 person-days for an individual per year and cross-functional and cross-business exposure were used as opportunities for individuals' self-development.

The boss alone did not determine future action but peers were also involved. The uncle concept of mentoring was practised in which an experienced elderly and unrelated person had a say in case a wrong course of action was being taken by boss. In this mentoring system, a newcomer to the company was put under an unrelated senior-level person in company along with the boss who acted as his mentors. The uncle-mentor was responsible not only for developing the person through guidance but also for empathizing in case of failure.

AUTONOMY

A great deal of autonomy was given, since it is a basic requirement of any consultancy company. Customer focus and customer satisfaction were the sole criteria of performance assessment. There was no concept of casual or sick leave. Stemming from the belief that people have to meet family and society responsibilities, full freedom was given to take leave.

RESPECT FOR TEAM MEMBERS

Recruitment of a new member in a particular group was decided by the group members. Similarly, the contribution to internal customers was rated and promotion depended on multiple ratings along with rating by the departmental head. Therefore everyone had a say in the performance-appraisal process. This fostered respect for team members and encouraged proper working in a team. It does not however eliminate the need for individual performance appraisal

RESPONSIVE SUPERIOR

Where the direct customer was involved, response was faster. Decisions related to customer service were taken quickly, while in other areas the time-frame for decision-taking was two to three days.

LOW FORMALIZATION

Some activities were formalized. Barring a few rules and regulations, the focus of the organization was on customers (internal and external) and peer satisfaction.

ORG4

ORG4 is part of a large and vertically integrated 55-year-old public sector organization. The unit studied was established in 1951. This organization is a leader in aerospace and defence sector supplies. Quality standard is its prime concern. It has a fully equipped facility to manufacture components with a high degree of tolerances. It supplies precision castings and forgings to defence, aerospace, and many public and private sector organizations.

Post-interventions' mean empowerment score for this organization is the highest, except the score in open communication (ORG2 scored highest), score in opportunities for learning applications (equal to ORG2) and score in responsive superior (lowest among all four organizations). The lowest score in responsive superior reflected in a lower score in role satisfaction. Self-efficacy is also lowest among the scores of the three organizations.

ORGANIZATIONAL SUPPORT FOR INNOVATION

Being a strong research and development-oriented organization, ORG4 had very good support for innovation. The suggestion scheme worked as a support for individual innovation and the quality circle approach was used as a support for team innovation. Ownership was guaranteed through encouraging and supporting all technocrats to present papers in various technical and techno-managerial conferences, workshops and seminars and also to participate in training activities as trainers.

TOP MANAGEMENT ATTITUDE TO HUMAN RESOURCE

Open-door policy and easy approachability helped communicate the favorable attitude of the top management to human resource. Team members were encouraged to talk about their family problems, which not only helped in their solution but also improved the trust among team members.

OPEN COMMUNICATION

Open door policy encouraged open communication. Frequent and regular meetings at all levels, involving employees in suggestions schemes, quality circles, etc. were the forums which helped increased open communication. The information flow was very good. People were given the required information and free communication was ensured.

PERFORMANCE-LINKED FEEDBACK

Open communication and team approaches provided a platform for continuous feedback wherever rewards were directly related with performance. Both formal and informal channels were utilized for providing regular feedback on an individual's development.

OPPORTUNITIES FOR SELF-DEVELOPMENT AND LEARNING APPLICATION

The organization provided ample opportunities for self-development. Individuals were sponsored for training programs on the basis of the need felt by them. Subsequent to training programs the learning was shared with others and support was provided for experimentation, application and transfer of learning.

AUTONOMY

Everyone in the organization was given maximum autonomy within the broad framework of a public sector organization. Total freedom was given for decision- making regarding work and getting results.

RESPECT FOR TEAM MEMBERS

Everyone had a say in the team and was free to present his or her views to team members for arrive at decisions. During unit head and other departmental meetings, detailed discussions were held before any decisions were taken. Due consideration was given to the views of all members of the team.

Responsive Superior

Being a public sector unit, the impact of control and command ran very deep in the minds of the people. In spite of all the interventions people were still hesitant to take decisions. They continued to look up to pass on the onus. Of late, decision-making has been encouraged by suitable individual development and providing support in the case of failure.

Low Formalization

Formalization was quite low. Rules were taken as guides. Procedures were followed to achieve the results and to fulfil the minimum organizational requirements.

Conclusion

The outcome of these interventions is seen in the improvement in the score of all the five outcome variables in ORG1. In ORG2, the result of all the interventions mentioned above is a higher score on empowerment, which enhances organizational commitment, job involvement, self-efficacy, work environment satisfaction and role satisfaction.

In ORG3 the participants in the study had very high work environment and role satisfaction. The score in work environment satisfaction is higher than that in role satisfaction because of the autonomy of functioning, respect for team members, and good attitude of top management to human resource. Good opportunities for self-development and learning applications resulted in better outcomes such as increased job involvement, better self-efficacy and increased organizational commitment along with higher satisfaction.

The interventions used for top management attitude to human resource had an impact on organizational commitment. The interventions for improving openness in communication resulted in an improvement in work environment satisfaction. The development appraisal and matrix structure improved job involvement. Opportunities for self-development and performance-linked feedback resulted in better self-efficacy. Higher role satisfaction was an outcome of the interventions for autonomy and respect for team members.

In ORG4, the outcome of the interventions was that people in the organization developed a very high degree of job involvement, which increased the organizational commitment and self-efficacy. These ultimately enhanced work environment satisfaction. The postponement of decision-making and some organizational constraints were responsible for scoring lowest in role satisfaction.

The results of the study are summarized below:

- The instrument shows its discriminating capability by indicating the improvement in score of empowering and consequence variables as a result of different interventions used by different organizations.
- Improvement of the score of empowering variables has also shown an improvement in the score of the outcome variables.
- The organizations can use the instrument for measuring the level of empowerment and decide on the interventions to improve their performance.

References

Dwivedi, R.S. (1996). 'The Concept and Process of Empowerment: *Udyog Pragati.*' *Journal of National Institute of Industrial Enginering.* 29(3), July–September.

Gupta, K.S. (1999). 'Empowerment: A Conceptual and Exploratory Study'. Unpublished Ph.D Dissertation of Indian Institute of Technology, Mumbai.

13

Building a Value-based Corporate Character: The Wipro Experience

R. PADMAJA • MANISHA SINGH

Values are variously defined in literature as individual attributes. They are the inner beliefs that govern an individual's behavior in any given situation. Values represent an individual's ideas about what is desirable and not desirable, right and wrong, good and bad. In short, values represent what an individual thinks 'ought to be'. Rokeach (1973) defined values as an enduring belief that a specific mode of conduct or end state of existence is personally or socially preferable to an opposite mode of conduct or end state of existence.

Values are acquired early in life through the process of socialization involving agents such as family, school and religion. Significant experiences in later life also help in fine tuning an individual's beliefs. Values, thus acquired, become the most deeply ingrained part of an individual's personality.

When organized hierarchically, values become a value system, which helps in decision-making and resolving conflicts. This value system creates conviction and willpower that helps in making difficult choices even in critical situations.

When values take the form of a collective consciousness among members of an organization as to what is desirable and right, they become organizational values. Once espoused, organizational values form a framework that surrounds the functioning of the organization including interactions among members, policies and ways of conducting business.

Values also set norms of behavior for individual members and clarify what is desirable. Without organizational values, members will follow their own respective personal value systems which influence a manager's perception of the problems of the individual and his or her subsequent decisions and solutions, perceptions of others, and thus interpersonal relationships (England, 1974) and the selection of corporate strategies (Guth and Taigiuri, 1965). The personal value system plays an important role in life including every aspect of work life. This results in behavior which may or may not be in tune with the organization's expectations of its members. Organizational values, on the other hand, provide a common framework for behavior. Most importantly, core values provide guidance for accomplishing organizational objectives and create an identity for the organization. According to Bob Haas, chairman and CEO of Levi Strauss, 'Values provide a common language for aligning a company's leadership and its people ... there is no way that any of us in management can be around all the time to tell people what to do. It has to be strategy and values that guide them.'

When all members of an organization hold the same principles and put them into practice it results in increased efficiency. In addition, the practise of values lends credibility to the business organization, which is central to the long-standing success of any company. The importance of having core values is reflected in the findings of the pioneering study on excellent companies by Peters and Waterman (1982). They claimed that every excellent company they studied was clear on what it stood for and took the process of value shaping seriously. They felt it was impossible to be an excellent company without clarity of values and right sort of values.

Ethical Versus Business Values

An analysis of the value statements of some companies revealed two types of values—business values and ethical/human values. The purpose of business values is to facilitate the organization's business growth and success. Ethical/Human values, on the other hand, have the larger purpose of maintaining a harmonious world and contribute to the development of mankind. Some ethical and business values are:

Ethical/Human values	Business values
Serving society/nation through industry	Being the best
Respecting people as individuals	Business growth
Integrity	Profitability
Harmony and cooperation	Quality
Humility	Productivity
Simplicity	Customer satisfaction
Fairness and openness	Innovation
Commitment	Optimum utilization of resources

It is important for an organization not to get carried away with business values and neglect ethical/human values. Striking a balance between ethical and business values enables the organization to survive, grow and at the same time contribute to people and society. In fact, this will help the organization to succeed in the long run, as it gains a reputation which gives it a competitive advantage and helps it to have trusting relationships with all stakeholders. Donaldson (1994) quotes two studies which reveal that ethical values also help an organization's success. The first, presented in the *California Management Review* of 1990, shows that over a seven-year period, most corporations that demonstrated a concern for ethics also tended to show the highest growth and profits. The second was a landmark survey done by Johnson and Johnson, which tracked companies over a 35-year period, from the 1950s to the 1980s. The findings showed that the company's ethical reputation influenced the high stock market value of its shares.

Integrating Values into Organizational Life

Organizations need to spend considerable time and effort for the espoused values to actually become a way of life in the organization. Obviously, values become important only when an organization's members accept and practise them. It is a challenge for the management to make values a reality in the minds of people, as each individual member comes from a different background, carrying different personal value systems. How should organizations handle this difficult task? To begin with, they must ensure that every member practises, that is, adheres to the values. But in the long run, the only way to sustain a value-based culture is by helping individual members to imbibe and internalize the values and make them personally committed. It is increasingly being realized by top management that the real test facing them is shaping and rooting organizational values.

Values help an organization create a corporate character. They instill a feeling of pride among its members. Corporate values give a sense of community and act as the binding factor that holds an organization together.

The Wipro Example

'When you accumulate virtue with continued practice, you do not see the good of it, but in time it will function. If you abandon right and go against truth, you do not see the evil of it, but in time you will perish', reads a Zen scroll of the ancient Chan communities. At Wipro Corporation, this ancient wisdom goes beyond mere truism to being a passionately held article of faith. Indeed, Wipro's success in its businesses vindicates this strong and even stubborn adherence to a value-based approach in all its endeavors. There is no dearth of organizations today which have articulated vision, mission or value statements. What makes Wipro unique is the quiet conviction and near fanaticism with which Wipro employees live the Wipro values daily.

From a small vegetable oil business with sales of Rs 4 crore to Rs 2,373 crore (sales) infotech major, values have been like the steady and infallible North Star guiding Wipro on its journey. As Wipro's chairman, Azim Hasham Premji is quoted 'I had seen such hard times, that I wanted to build something that would have the strongest foundation possible. I wanted it to be pure. Initially, it was almost an aesthetic sensibility. Only later did I realize what a powerful business advantage integrity could be.' Initially articulated as Beliefs in 1973, the four Wipro values, namely, Human Values, Integrity, Innovative Solutions and Value for Money (Box 1), simply represent Premji's attempts to institutionalize and implement an implicitly held business philosophy, which flows from his family ideology. These beliefs form the foundation for conducting business. As enunciated in one of the Beliefs booklets, as the Wipro Corporation diversified into services, technology products and consumer products, it was these Beliefs that provided a strong sense of identity for the company. As one senior leader at Wipro told the authors, Wipro considers Beliefs enunciation as a significant landmark in its history, besides diversification into IT, attaining the Software Engineering Institute

(SEI) Level 5 certification and its Six Sigma initiative. Wipro's pursuit of its values has enabled it to ensure a coherence and control in a diversified, de-layered set-up, while simultaneously providing the social cohesion necessary to undertake new ventures and try out new ideas. More than anything else, it is these values that have enabled Wipro to emerge as an organization with a strong corporate character.

Box 13.1

Wipro's Promise Statement: 'With utmost respect to Human Values, we promise to serve our Customer with integrity, through a variety of Innovative, Value for Money Products and Services, by Applying Thought, day after day.'
The four values encapsulated in the Promise Statement are:

- Human Values—We respect Customers as individuals, recognize that they have different needs and continually strive towards satisfying those needs to improve the quality of their lives.
- Integrity—Our individual and business relationships are governed by the highest standards of Integrity.
- Innovative Solutions—We constantly research and develop superior Products and Services that meet the ever-changing needs of the Customers.
- Value for Money—We Promise to serve the Customers with continuous improvement in quality, cost and delivery of our Products and Services.

The Study

A study of Wipro was taken up to identify the factors and processes involved in building a value-based organization, for Wipro has a long-established corporate identity of values. For this purpose, a semi-structured interview schedule was designed focused on tracing the value path, communication of values and values in practice. In-depth interviews were conducted with thirty-two Wipro executives at different levels, from project manager to executive corporate vice-president.

Factors and Processes Involved in Integrating Values into the Organization: Learnings from the Wipro Experience

The processing of the data revealed the following factors and processes that helped Wipro institutionalize and internalize its corporate values and make them a way of organizational life.

Founder/Owner's Ideology

Core values arise from the founder/owner's deeply held convictions regarding the right way to conduct business. They are a reflection of historical behavior in the organization. In Wipro, as a senior executive shared with the authors, Premji believes that the strongest legacy his father left him were his values. His father was also known to be a man of strong principles. Raised in a family that believed in high thinking rather than high living, the Premjis never flaunted their wealth. Wipro today exemplifies the same values. The study shows that Wiproites do not believe in flamboyance, revere simplicity and are proud of their down-to-earth nature and middle-class values. Because these values arise from the organization's history and the owner/founder's deeply experienced philosophy, the core values are authentic and not a reflection of contemporary management fashion, inspiring members of the organization to buy into that vision.

Firm Belief

Ultimately, there is true acceptance and ownership only when each individual experiences the core values as fundamental truths that are time and context invariant. According to MacGregor (1997), highly successful organizations do not simply proclaim a set of values; rather they immerse their employees in the ideology to an obsessive degree. This is true of Wipro too. In the words of Dilip Ranjekar, Executive, Corporate Vice-President, 'Wiproites are fanatical about their values.' The passionate conviction of the senior management percolates down to all levels. The authors believe that this conviction comes because of a twofold emotive and logical appeal in the Wipro values. The emotive appeal comes from the enlightened self-interest and the logical appeal from the ability of Wipro's top leadership to persuade employees that following values makes perfect business sense. Wiproites firmly believe that their high stock valuation is partly because of their reputation for being true to values. In fact, the Wipro values permeate even to employees' personal lives because of their strong faith in them. It is this conviction that provides the thread of continuity, enabling new entrants to assimilate the Wipro values faster. In the absence of this firm belief, the process of internalization and institutionalization will not be complete.

Articulation

Articulation is the process of making explicit the values that already exist implicitly. Identifying the values practised internally and their implications for customers externally help members understand the behavior expected from them. Further, they help define each statement and spell out its implications on the conduct of each employee to elicit the particular behavior required (Mathias, 2000). Involving employees in the process of identifying and articulating value ensures their acceptance of and commitment to the values.

Originating from the Premji family's business philosophy, the tacit beliefs, embedded in Wipro's history were articulated as belief statements in 1973. These values have remained the same throughout, with some refinement from time to time. For example, the belief on 'being close to the customer' was incorporated in 1982. A customer perception survey was carried out in 1997, and after consulting a cross-section of key employees, the beliefs were set out in the form of four values. Massive one-day workshops were conducted at various locations to communicate these to all the employees. The values, thus articulated, were brought out in a belief booklet that gives the meaning of every belief and a series of action policies that show the values in action. To make these values customer centric a promise statement was evolved. Today, Wipro gives a Promise booklet to every employee. The booklet enunciates the Promise, explains every value, and gives a series of thought-provoking questions that can be used to reflect on the application of that value.

Through this process of fine tuning, Wipro has articulated its values in such a way that they are not only internally consistent but also externally validated, and from which employees can derive clear standards of performance in terms of value addition to the customer, as well as clear expectations of desirable behavior in the workplace.

Communication

Apart from an implicit understanding of values and their demonstration in day-to-day practice, wide publicity and explicit discussion are required to facilitate institutionalization and internalization. At Wipro, every new entrant learns about values directly from Premji when he takes a session on beliefs as part of the induction program and get the opportunity to seek clarifications from the chairman himself. When questioned about their first introduction to Wipro values, most employees mentioned induction training and the Beliefs booklet. They are also given a Promise booklet in addition to the Induction Manual, which explains exactly how they must conduct themselves in business. Apart from this, employees have access to online information on the company's intranet. All this ensures that the organization has an education system in place to communicate its values in detail.

Another important practice related to communication is that the immediate supervisor or human resource representative talks to the person about values on the day he joins. In fact, every opportunity is utilized to build an understanding of Wipro values; the authors had first-hand experience of this when they were requested by a senior manager to allow a new entrant to sit in during the interview so that he would be able to better appreciate Wipro values. Also, each part of the organization has its own experiences regarding value practices, which get communicated down the line. Combined with displays of the Promise statement in all the Wipro offices, apart from appearing on all documents, communications, brochures, films, presentations, visiting cards and mouse pads, these explicit communication efforts are reinforced through implicit means.

Initial Socialization

New entrants learn the values of the organization through initial inter-actions with other members of the organization. An interesting practice at Wipro is that when a person joins the organization, everyone con-cerned—that is, other members in the role set— spend time with him or her till everything falls in place. Care is taken to explain matters in detail and issue-based guidance is provided. This is not an organized or formally planned process but a natural one. In the absence of a formal mentoring system, senior members make conscious efforts at the individual level to mentor, coach, sensitize, develop and provide guidance to new members. This initial socialization process, according to Schein (1992), is an informal method, quite powerful, but chancy as it assumes that the older organization members hold the stated values of the organization. This drawback can be dealt with and the process can be made more effective by making it a planned informal process with the trusted older members taking part.

Enlightened Self-interest

Values will only be internalized when they actually mean something to the person concerned. We are all raised on stories and legends that emphasize the importance of following the right path and leading a value-based life. It is in the process of growing up that we start compromising. However, working at Wipro gives every individual an opportunity to listen to his or her inner voice. They gain intrinsic satisfaction by doing things the right way. As Premji says, 'There are personal benefits. You sleep better. You wake up in the morning and look at yourself in the mirror and feel good. You don't have to keep looking over your shoulder.' Wiproites realize that the organization gives them an opportunity to practise the values they were taught early in life. This creates a sense of well-being and inner peace. The absence of inner conflict helps individuals de-stress. Individual members' commitment to the values increases as they acknowledge the personal benefits that accrue therefrom.

Continuous Feedback

Living a value-based life has a self-perpetuating effect. This is true at all levels, including the individual, organizational and national. Once credibility is established, individuals or organizations continuously strive to live up to the image they have created through their conduct. However, care should be taken that this does not lead to complacency, which can lead to stagnation. The solution to this problem, derived from the Wipro experience, is continuous evaluation of the practise of the value system. The feedback mechanisms used at Wipro include the following:

- Customer satisfaction surveys conducted periodically to assess how customers rate Wipro's practise of the values.
- Rating from customers about the way individual departments are practising the values.
- Employee perception surveys to get ratings from organizational members about the practise of the four values.

- At the individual level, 360 degree appraisal to elicit how each individual member practises these values.

It is important to note that there is a black-and-white approach regarding integrity. The company's stand is very clear: whatever the cost involved, Wipro never compromises on integrity. Violation of this value by any individual member, in whatever position he or she is, leads to separation. The above-mentioned procedures are in place to assess the actual practise of values in the everyday functioning of the organization. These methods help the organization to keep track and take corrective measures immediately in case of deviation. This continuous evaluation also reiterates the organization's commitment to the practise of values.

Systems and Policies

Systems and policies play a major role in the ownership and acceptance of values, albeit indirectly. Value-driven management implies that plans, decisions, actions and rewards are all governed by a value focus (Ginsburg and Miller, 1992). The organization simply must demonstrate its values to its members through rules and policies (MacGregor, 1997). This is a very powerful way of demonstrating commitment to the values. At Wipro, a flat organizational structure and the use of common canteens and common buses clearly demonstrate the values practised. Additionally, values are embedded in all Wipro's systems and policies.

- Recruitment   Strictly merit-based recruitment with an emphasis on identifying individuals with the right values and attitudes is prevalent. One-third of the application form is devoted to getting information about the applicant's values. Wipro might compromise on the candidate's competence but not on his or her values and attitude.
- Performance Appraisal   Adherence to values is an important consideration in evaluation of performance. Appraisal forms consist of a section on the individual's observance of values. Any deficiencies in the practise of human values, innovative solutions and value for money are treated as developmental needs.
- Personal Development   The practise of promoting employees if they are sixty per cent ready for the job reflects Wipro's faith in individual growth. Policies like reserving 5 per cent of manpower costs for training, provision for one-year sabbatical after five years

of employment enabling employees to further their education, tie up with technical and management institutions to sponsor employees on courses reflects Wipro's belief in continuous education and growth of employees.

- Reward Systems Compensation is benchmarked against the best in the world. Violation of values, especially integrity, leads to immediate separation. In case of violation of human values, attempts are made to help the person by providing him or her with counseling services; however, lack of improvement leads to separation. Humaneness is practised even in separation. The individual in question is asked to resign and the reasons are not made public.
- Mission Quality Projects Wipro takes up quality as a mission. Its Six Sigma project, initiated in 1998, aims to provide customers quality services benchmarked against the world's best. In 1998 Wipro became the world's first software services company to achieve CMM Level 5 certification from SEI of the US.
- Innovation Council The council has been set up to ensure innovative solutions and products. Heavy investments are made in research and development.
- Availability Service Wipro believes in the 'customer-in' approach as opposed to the 'product-out' concept. That is why the annual maintenance contract on Wipro's PCs has now been converted to an 'availability service', whereby the customer is assured of the machines functioning ninety per cent of the time—the customer need not pay if it falls below the time assured. This policy reduces customers' overheads.

Another interesting practice at Wipro is that the company does not make soft promises to customers. Whatever is being offered to the customer is made official, so that the customer knows what to expect from the transaction. And Wiproites never shy away from customers' calls: good or bad, the news is shared immediately, thus building a trusting customer relationship.

As Bell (1999) says, an individual learns more about the values of an organization from its personnel policies than from any other single source. The HR policies at Wipro are geared towards meeting the needs of employees (Box 13.2) and helping them fulfil their aspirations. However, if required, Wipro goes beyond the set policies in order to live the values. For example, there were several instances of individual medical expenses taken care of by the company, even when these exceeded the entitled limit.

Box 13.2

- One of the clerical staff was suffering from leukaemia and Wipro paid Rs 16 lakh for his treatment at Apollo Hospital. This was much beyond the medical benefits the employee was entitled to. Unfortunately and ironically he died, but of a different cause.
- Wipro ruffled many feathers in industry when it decided to pay overtime to workers on their total pay package as against the usual practice of calculating overtime on Basic and DA. In spite of stern admonitions from managerial circles, it has implemented this decision in four out of five factories, and is in the process of doing so in the fifth.
- The relative of a very senior manager at Wipro applied for a job. However, the HR manager concerned did not consider the candidate fit and decided not to recruit the person. The HR manager did not face any repercussions.
- Wipro is a safe place for women. An employee who sent an offensive e-mail message to a female colleague was fired by the company.

All these systems and policies serve as original mechanisms to demonstrate the organization's commitment to core values and bring a high level of integration in the its total practice.

A Culture of Ethics and Human Values

Corporate culture simply means a way of life in an organization. Values and beliefs form the core of the culture, whereas norms, stories and behavior reflect these values. At an organization like Wipro, where values form the foundation from which everything else including business objectives and strategies flow, it is important to have a culture that reinforces these values. The realization of the importance of culture is reflected in the fact that the chairman's office (called the Executive Corporate Council) is involved in building culture and values for the organization.

Certain practices in everyday life managers at all levels, including Premji, reflect how the culture supports the values. These practices include simplicity, an absence of flamboyance, and an informal, open and apolitical work environment where only merit counts. An achievement-oriented environment with enough flexibility is created where opportunities for personal growth are also provided. There are no symbols of hierarchy, no one carries anyone's bags and no one goes to the airport to receive anyone including the chairman. These practices reflect human values. Further, constructive discontent, questioning the status quo and taking a stand is encouraged. People are allowed to plan their own schedules, and opportunity is given to them to contribute in a completely different area if they want to. These practices encourage innovative solutions and creativity. All members, including top management, travels economy class and stay at value-for-money hotels in the process of minimizing the cost to the customer.

Box 13.3

- Wipro refused to pay a bribe of half a million rupees to a government official who was threatening to delay a shipment of computer hardware during the last quarter of the year. The official was trying to take advantage of the fact that Wipro's customers would be unable to depreciate their orders if the shipment was delayed until the next fiscal year, but to no avail. This incident cost the company $4 million in lost profits.
- When Wipro launched its first PC, in 1985, there was a new central excise officer who did not allow the consignments to move without a bribe. However, he relented after five or six weeks when he was told that the chairman never greases a palm.
- In yet another incident, Wipro's refusal to bribe bureaucrats responsible for issuing licences was met with disbelief. It took a long time for them to accept that the company was not bluffing and that it takes its integrity very seriously.
- In another instance, it took Wipro eighteen months to get a dedicated power station activated because of its refusal to bribe. This cost the company an enormous amount the plant had to be run for twenty months on captive power.
- A trade union leader using the usual rhetoric tried to incite workers against the Wipro management. To his surprise, the workers became incensed and defended the organization, saying that they were proud to be part of it.

At Wipro, folklore and stories (see Boxes 13.2, 13.3 and 13.4) are used to develop and maintain the culture. These stories spread and pervade the organization basically because they grow out of the leader's actions and demonstrate the meaning.

Leader as a Role Model

The effective management of values must have its centre in the intentions and actions of the leader. Consistency in words and deeds extending even to the leader's personal life makes a powerful statement about how seriously the organization believes in its core values. The leader's role as stated by Premji 'is to be a clear role model. That has a massive multiplier effect. If you can be trusted to adhere to the values you have espoused, you will be surprised how many people can be trusted to do the same, but if you slip or compromise, the whole thing unravels quickly.'

Premji clearly sets a personal example regarding the practise of all Wipro values. Apart from taking a clear and firm stand on integrity, he demonstrates the other values too through his actions. One of the managers shared with the authors that Premji encouraged him to express his disagreement in a plan review meeting with all the top management present even though he was a new entrant and the juniormost in the team. Besides being a role model, Premji is also involved in articulation and communication of values and creating a culture of ethics.

The Wipro experience clearly shows that a critical value-mass can be created with one person who believes in the values strongly, influencing the culture creation. To put it in the words of a Wipro executive, 'Premji is the biggest institution for values in Wipro.' Stories (see Box 13.4) about his actions demonstrating values circulate at Wipro, inspiring others to follow the same path.

Box 13.4

- Premji asked a union leader to leave the company because he submitted an expense account for first-class travel when he had actually traveled second class. Although this resulted in the first-ever union strike at Wipro's corporate office, lasting four weeks, he did not relent.
- Early in his career, Premji fired two of the company's top executives because they failed to live up to his standards

---

of integrity. It was a difficult decision to make because they were high-performing executives whose services were essential since the business was not in good shape at the time.

- In a now-famous incident, an HR manager circulated an e-mail to colleagues for parking in the space reserved for the chairman. Premji replied within five minutes saying that no notice should be taken of that mail and that the space would have been his had he come on time.

Wipro demonstrates that articulating the value statement, clarifying its behavioral implications, clear communication, continuous feedback, value-based systems and policies, an ethical culture and inspiring leadership, together help an organization create a value-based corporate character.

Some Insights

However, everything is not smooth sailing for Wipro. There is a concern among some employees that there needs to be more warmth at the workplace. Some also feel that after its heady success experiences, Wipro must devote considerable effort into continuing to remain humble, for it is this that helps it maintain a strong value-based culture that binds the organization together. Moreover, as Wipro tries to fulfil its vision of being among the top ten global software service providers, it will need to internalize its values among a growing number of fresh entrants. It needs to be seen how these concerns will be addressed.

One unique feature of Wipro is that the company's core values have never changed over the years; they have though undergone some fine-tuning. In the words of Collins and Porras (1992), 'In a visionary company, the core values need no rational or external justification. Nor do they sway with the trends and fads of the day. Nor even do they shift in response to changing market conditions.' This observation is appropriate for Wipro Corporation.

Wipro has also managed to strike a balance between ethical values and business values. In fact, customer satisfaction surveys rated Wipro the best on its ethical values. Some Wipro managers shared with pride that customers tell them they do business with the company because of its integrity and concern for the customer—proof that these values help gain a competitive edge in the market.

This does not stop Wiproites from introspection. There is an ongoing process of questioning and reflection at all levels that enables Wipro to grow. As Dilip Ranjekar, Corporate President, Wipro India Limited, says, 'Continuous dissatisfaction has been the hallmark of Wipro.' For example, Wipro employees have rated the organization low on innovative solutions and value for money. These are seen as potential areas for growth.

This process of self-evaluation applies to all areas of organizational functioning. In yet another example, the authors found the Executive Corporate Council deeply involved in changing the 360-degree appraisal form, from the previous year's broad-spectrum approach to one tailored to reflect responsibilities at the top, middle and senior management levels.

Whatever the challenges, Wipro is clear about its values-based stand. To quote Premji, 'To meet the future, we are prepared to change everything about ourselves, except our beliefs, as they alone guide, govern and bind us together as an organization.' It is this conviction and approach that has enabled Wipro to create and sustain a value-based corporate character.

References

Bell, W.F. (1999). 'The Impact of Policies on Organizational Values and Culture'. Retrieved on 17 March, 2000 from the World Wide Web: http://www.usafa.af.mil/JSCOPE99/Bell99.html.

Champy, J. and N. Nohria (2001). 'The Arc of Ambition: Defining the Leadership Journey'. Cambridge, Massachussetts: Peseus Books.

Collins, J.C. and J.I. Porras (1994). Built to Last. London: Century Business.

Donaldson, T. (1994). 'Ethics in Business'. In T.A. Mathias (ed.). Corporate Ethics. New Delhi: Allied Publishers.

England, G.W. (1974). The Manager and the Man—A Cross-cultural Study of Personal Values. Minnesota: Industrial Relations Centre, University of Minnesota.

Ginsburg, L. and N. Miller (1992). 'Value-driven Management'. Business Horizons. 35(3), 23–27.

Guth, W.D. and R. Taiquirie (1965). 'Personal Values and Corporate Strategy'. Harvard Business Review. 123–32.

MacGregor, D.A. (1997). *Breaking the Phalanx.* Westport: Praeger.
Mathias, T.A. (2000). 'Values the Bedrock of Successful Business'. *Management and Labour Studies.* 25(3), 211–19.
Peter, T.J. and R.H. Waterman (1982). *In Search of Excellence: Lessons from America's Best-run Companies.* New York: Harper and Row.
Rokeach, M. (1973). *The Nature of Human Values.* New York: Free Press.
Schein, E.H. (1992). *Organizational Culture and Leadership.* San Francisco: Jossey-Bass Publishers.

14

Emerging Global Concepts of Ethics and Leadership Effectiveness

R.C. SEKHAR

Stucturalist Analysis as a Complement to Empirical Research

Should we look for some pervading philosophy to explain the history of leadership? An enormous amount of empirical micro-level research in the West has inconclusively tested a scattering of hypotheses in psychological traits and behavioral charactersitics (Bass, 1989; Burns, 1978). This can be described as 'positivist research'. But there is now a growing need to see if it all fits into a holistic pattern that covers all aspects of social reality. Those who like to see an overall pattern in social reality may be called structuralists, for instance, Joanne Ciulla (2000). Karl Marx and Fredrick Engels (1976) much before her were more ruthless structuralists; to them all that has happened in history has been driven by overweaning structures, and history makes leaders, not vice versa. They, however, wrote before the spate of empirical research, which made obsolete many of their 'explanations and predictions'. Post-modernists see no point in straining analytical powers to discover any such pattern.

This chapter describes the variety of influences on the values of society and styles of leadership. These are better understood with cross-fertilization from philosophy, political economy and sociology, which makes for a more broad-based view and is another way of conceding the holistic structuralist concept of leadership. Ciulla's (2000) understanding of current-day leadership needs is thus firmly rooted in 'structures' built on the concept of 'virtue'—as propounded by Plato, Aristotle or St Thomas Aquinas, and nurtured and cultivated by culture, integrated with ideas of 'social democracy', the product of the Age of Enlightenment, refined by the pluralism of the twentieth and twenty-first centuries, the economics of free choice provided by market systems, and, finally by the availability of freedom of speech and information from a free press.

This chapter explores Indian structures and their role in the future of leadership as stated by Sekhar (2000: 360):

> 'To understand the current trends and styles of leadership in India ... we need to understand social and political aspects, as these are inextricable, inter-woven with ethics of organizations both in their internal and external dealings ... mutual learning between industrially developed nations and developing nations needs to be fostered. ... The sources of its living ethical and leadership traditions are to be found in some very influential philosophic writings, some explicit writings on statecraft and ethics, the varied tribal lore ... the political institutions consciously developed recently under the influence of American, French and Soviet revolutions and the more spontaneous movements having similar democratic and egalitarian inspiration.'

The Paradox of the Popularity of Aristotle in the West and the *Bhagavad Gita* in India

There is undoubtedly a strong wind in favor of Aristotle, Plato and St Thomas Aquinas in the West and the *Bhagavad Gita* in India. This growing popularity is a strange paradox, as both Aristotle and the *Gita* are highly anti-egalitarian and anti-democratic, and inconsonant with the idealism ushered in the world since liberty, equality and fraternity became the clarion call. Aristotle was an unabashed supporter of slavery and the *Gita* affirms the caste system. Both see the role of leadership in preserving the status quo in social norms (Hardee, 1968; Radhakrishnan, 1983: (p. 93, quoting ch. I, sloka 41 of the *Gita*). As Thomas W. Smith (2000) says, 'for an Aristotelian, virtues are understood with reference to the specific practices and communities they sustain.' Further, whereas work ethics is considered a desirable outcome of modern leadership, Aristotle avoided work ethics in all his deliberations; in fact, he had utter contempt for those who soiled their hands (Gordon-Childe, 1942: 223).

The reason for the strong revival of interest in these sources of leadership norms lies elsewhere. While ignoring these features of Aristotle and the *Gita*, modern revivalists realize that both of them have a profound understanding of the importance of 'virtue' as an essential ingredient of effective leadership. This is different from much of the moral philosophy of 'social democracy', 'plualism' and 'social contract', which dominated most thinking before the wave of 'virtue ethics'.

The prime purpose of moral philosophies of the nineteenth-century enlightened modernism was to distinguish between good and bad outcomes, as in the utilitarianism of Bentham and Mill (Mill, 1897), and good and bad acts by developing the criterion 'never do unto others what one would not like done to oneself (Kant, 1985). Moral leadership could therefore be judged by these factors. Aristotle on the other hand was less concerned about these 'formulae', as Robert Solomon (1993) puts it: 'Aristotle thought it was good judgement or phoronesis that was of the greatest importance. Good judgement rather than abstract formulation was a product of good education and upbringing ... abstract ethical theory actually discourages and distracts from the need to make judgements.'

Burn's (1978) classic work on leadership noted that the most effective leaders had a strong moral vision, but a careful reading of his questionnaires and responses would show that he was unconsciously measuring the leaders' Aristotelian quotient of 'virtue ethics'. MacIntyre (1981) was the most influential among the revivalists of Aristotelianism. Badaracco Jr. (1998) most explicitly denigrates the earlier moral criterion of Bentham, Mill and Kant, the products of modernity and the Enlightenment, and embraces the 'virtue ethics' of Aristotle.

Let us now turn to the *Gita*. Unlike Aristotle, who was oriented towards analysis, the *Gita* lays a strong emphasis on work ethics and action (ch. II, sloka 47; ch. III, slokas 4–5). It is therefore to be expected that the *Gita* would be morally concerned with outcomes as well. Following earlier Indian traditions, it sees the importance of the teleological approach of the greatest good for the greatest number. It is also aware of the approaches of doing unto others only that which can be accepted to be done to oneself, described as 'universalization'. But it sees that these two approaches may conflict with each other: while it is unethical to kill the near and dear ones or the teacher who nurtured them, one may resort to it for the preservation of the overall good. Thus it is the leader who is capable of resolving this conflict. The *Gita* most explicitly lays down the criticality of the ethics of the leader in the scheme of things (ch. III, sloka 21 details the concept of *raj rishi*, the leader who is also a sage), but enjoins that the person who takes the decision does so without selfish motives (*nishkama karma*) (ch. III, sloka 19) and in a balanced manner (*sthitaprajna*, as described in slokas 54–55 and ch. XVIII, sloka 63). Importantly, it details the process of self-discipline through yoga, which can enable one to perform this difficult task. It is in the concept of a virtuous person who can take a balanced view that it converges on Aristotle's virtue ethics expounded in the Nichomachean Ethics (e.g., Bk 2, ch. 2.11: 20–23 which says cryptically that what is destroyed by the excess is preserved by the mean). This means that extreme ideological positions do not adequately represent a reflective and virtuous mind and that the essence of virtue is to take a balanced unbiased view.

Both Aristotle and the *Gita* have been attacked by Marxists (Gordon-Childe, 1942; Kosambi, 1964) precisely on what they consider the amoral approach of 'virtue ethics' (there is nothing right or wrong but the leader's thinking makes it so). They blame it on class contradictions of the societies of the time. As mentioned earlier, the Marxists are ruthless structuralists and their arguments are understandable. But current thinking holds that the 'ambiguities of virtue ethics of leaders' are not necessarily the product of a society with class contradictions. Rather, it may be a more universal value which makes for effective leadership irrespective of the specific condition of a society, the ancient slave-ridden Greek one or a caste-ridden Indian one.

Having said this, one must hasten to note that historical evidence does indicate that the concepts of 'virtue ethics' and '*sthitaprajna*' have, more often than not, supported the reality of the suppression of people's rights through Western imperialism or indigenous Indian exploitation. These concepts lend themselves easily to power play (Sekhar, 2000). While the moral reasoning using the lightly criticized formula approach (Solomon, 1993) contained some guidelines for preserving basic human decency, the balanced virtue approach of Aristotle and the *Gita* can blur the distinction between right and wrong and be irrational and myopic in reality. It has prevented people seeing the point of view of the adversely affected, which in Greece were the slaves, and in India the lower castes.

The Gurus of India and the West: Some Empirical Evidence

In a logical extension of the need for a 'dispassionate person' to fit the role of the leader, Indian traditions place strong reliance on the leadership of 'gurus' and 'raj gurus' (guru is the Sanskrit word for teacher).

A sample of 4000 respondents from a cross-section of Indian society, who answered a questionnaire administered by the author, ranked the teacher as ethically far ahead of all other classes of professions. Interestingly, a small sample tested by the author in the US also held teachers in high regard but not to the extent as in India. Further, Hosmer (1987) also reported that dispassionate ombudsman in the West, who could be described as Western versions of raj gurus, being used in ethical arbitration However, it is important to remember that gurus can be polemical and aggressive—hitherto more common—or they can be reflective and facilitating, the ancient tradition of Gautama Buddha (Sekhar, 1997, 1999). The latter stance is now being recognized as functionally more appropriate in the cyber age of knowledge management. Thus it is apparent that the ideas and perceptions of teachers as role models for moral leadership have a high degree of similarity across the world.

The Dark and Bright Side of Realism

Some modern thinkers, especially in business, view leadership as a series of techniques and skills that help leaders get their jobs done. One can describe these thinkers as belonging to the realist schools. They are realists only in a vulgar sense, as any method which is not manipulatory and does not exploit to one's advantage the infirmities and frailties of human beings is condemned as unrealistic. The arch-priest of this is the European Machiavelli. Kautilya, who wrote the *Arthasastra* in the pre-Christian era lived long before Machiavelli, gives an even more exhaustive description of the ways in which a leader could manipulate his adversaries. He legitimated his ideas by repeatedly asserting that the leader (the king in his writings) did everything for the people's good: In another of his writings the leader (king) is ascribed to be the propounder of the Indian concept of the greatest good of the greatest number; to achieve which end, manipulation is permissible.

In Chanakya's *Niti Darpanam*, ch. 3, verse 11, Kautilya says (Tantrik Yogi Ramesh, 1997: 31): 'Sacrifice the person for the sake of the family, a family for the village, a village for the state'.

The influence of Kautilya on the thinking of Indian leadership is immense. Even though they may privately believe in Kautilya's style of leadership as it would legitimize many of their actions, they would not like to admit it openly, because India has chosen more honorable paths to leadership as embodied in its Constitution and its laws.

The Refined Versions of the Realist Systems Schools in the West and India

A version of realism quite contrary to the one described in the foregoing is to view human beings pragmatically as they actually are with their strong communitarian instincts and culture. Leadership in these circumstances is very different. Bharthrihari, the Indian poet-king of the sixth century AD (*Neetishataka*, sloka 65) recognized that most persons are well-intentioned: it is the function of leadership to ensure that they are not sorely tempted due to a bad system. Much before Bharthrihari, Thiruvalluvar of south India in his Tamil ethical classic, the *Kural*, propounded an ethics of leadership which enjoined the creation of conditions for productive activity in agriculture and trade by ensuring a relationship of trust between people.

Modern schools of transaction cost economics (Williamson, 1996) believe that much of creative leadership consists in developing laws, proper property rights and contracting practices which will induce people to work together in trust and avoid 'opportunistic behaviour'. Cultural conditioning by leadership to achieve the same purpose is noted by Couto (1999) by creating 'social capital'. More than formal and visible binding force of contracts, invisible social norms produce values more easily and spontaneously. This social capital, though intangible, is a potent asset which stimulates value in all transactions in that society. Social capital is defined by Putnam (1993: 167) as: 'features of social organisations such as trust, norms, and networks, that can improve the efficiency of society by facilitating coordinated action'.

The phenomenon of good people combining badly to do self-destructive disastrous deeds has now been addressed by institutional economics (Birdman, 2001; Williamson, 2001; Cooter, 2001) the main concern of which is to establish proper systems in India. Thus, in the opinion of these institutional economists, it is inadequate structures and systems that make good people produce bad outcomes. In their opinion, it is good leadership that helps develop appropriate structures and systems which enable people to play an honest part in society.

Thus both the West and India have prevalent beliefs and practices that are realistic not in the cynical sense of Kautilya and Machiavelli, but in the more positive sense of using the pragmatic forces of communitariansm aided by skilful and imaginative leadership.

Several Facets of Myths and Rituals

It is virtually unanimously admitted, even in the West, that styles of leadership are not determined only by rationalist arguments such as have been advanced so far in this chapter. As Guttorm Floistad (1999: 61) puts it: 'To be a leader... requires a fairly thorough knowledge of cultural changes... some models are the same from one culture to another; other models differ according to culturally dependent customs and rituals.'

Be that as it may, there is a great paucity of academic research in this area. Marxists (Kosambi, 1964) have tried their best to fit it all into a deterministic structuralist explanation; but these have fallen by the wayside. Freudian analysis has tried to see only the impact of individual psychology Kakar, (1978, 1996). Social psychological explanations are more difficult to capture. As Spanish sociologist Ortega Y Gasset says, this would need a patient and detailed acquaintance of the vigencia of a people (Marias, 1955). Nevertheless, as a broad generalization one may say that pragmatic evidence is that the triggers for these developments are 'behavioral patterns driven by natural selection and value systems across the globe centered around egalitarian tribal instincts' (Fredrick, 2000: 471–73).

Activist Leadership

The historical origins of activist leadership in the country was to correct injustices in society that legal remedies were too slow to correct. Activism, used not for the destruction of the old order but towards social cohesion and community effort for building a new order has emerged as a necessary complement to orderly participative processes. Participatory democracy and activism are likely to grow together rapidly in the future. These increase social capital (Couto, 1999; Sekhar, 1997, 2000b).

Leaders as Arbitrators in a Fractured Society

The popular Tamil movie *Ezhavadu Manidan* (The Seventh Man) expounded a theory made originally by Lenin—that a leader would sometimes prefer to be an outsider. In India this has a certain appeal. When society has strong caste schisms, all groups prefer to have an outsider as a leader to avoid bias. This could happen in organizations as well.

We should not however, allow cultural patterns and the differences between cultures to obscure the common thread that runs through all of them. As Anna Marta Gonzales (2000) puts it, 'distinct modes of perception do not constitute diversity of virtues. They are modes of action and vary in cultures but show the same disposition of the agent.'

The succeeding sections will explore the distinct Indian modes of perception. Since, it is a very poorly researched field and hard data are difficult to get by, most of the information is anecdotal. Anecdotal literature on management processes in India is peppered with analogies from mythology to guide thinking (Dutta, 1997).

Indian Legends in Leadership

McKim Marriot (2000) has captured the ways in which the same rituals in the same location at different times were used for very different social purposes. One ritual earlier used as an instrument of inclusion of one section of society and exclusion of some other sections was ten years later used for including everyone. It seems that the objective of the ritual was to bring about social cohesion and the same symbolism could be used to justify and legitimize segregation and later support inclusion of everyone in society. This is a typical example of a spontaneous transformation of old rituals.

There are several examples of similar transformations in India too.

On the other hand, Badri Narayan (2001) describes the rise of 'bahujan politics propping counter literature by negation of brahminical literature'. Forced efforts were made to make erstwhile villains like Ravana the new heroes and erstwhile examples of devotion symbols of the exploited like Ekalavya or Bali. These were held out as negative lessons for the future, as they ought to have risen in revolt against exploitation. These are projected as potential role models for leaders of the future.

One may reflect on why spontaneous transformations seem to be more socially sustainable than forced transformations. Is it that the former provide more mutually acceptable forms of social relationships?

With this background, we will take a bird's-eye view of Indian mythology as a source of leadership styles.

The Rama Legend

One of the most profound legends that provides a role model for leadership is the Rama legend. Rama was compassionate and sensitive to people's needs. He cared for every one of his citizens individually. The legend has been modified down the centuries to suit the times, but the basic ethical features have remained more or less the same. Recent empirical work on leadership styles shows that this style is still prevalent in India, even though its extent is not firmly established. Sinha (1995) has labeled this as the 'nurturant task' leadership style.

The Krishna Legend

In contrast to the Rama's legend, the Krishna's legend depicts a more pragmatic perspective, one which is achieving even in adverse conditions. Again, this style appears to be gaining in popularity in current-day environment of India which is turbulent and riddled with conflict. There are echoes here of platonic strictures for good leadership to be not only moral but also practical. This legend is likely to become even more widespread in the coming years when competitive forces are released by social upheaval caused by processes of correcting caste imbalances and inequities.

The Hanuman Legend

The pattern of sub-leaders provided by tribal allies of the dominant hegemonic races is a central part of the legend of the monkey-king Hanuman. Sociologists (Sabharwal, 1995) have noted that this phenomenon was not unusual until recent times. It could be observed in the pattern of larger companies hiring a cluster of persons who formed a cohesive and homogeneous group under a sub-leader. Its popularity will rapidly decline with changes in the old power equations and rise of democratic ethics. Sub-leaders and main leaders will have totally different power relationships in the coming times. The manner in which plural populations will be handled is also likely to be very different.

The Impact of Islam

Popular cinema in India has a profusion of populist leadership from mythology. Political leadership of the day has used this as a rich resource to build up their image. But Islam and its egalitarianism has certainly left its mark in India. It had several offshoots typically in the form of Sikhism and the Kabirpanthis.

MOTHER GODDESSES

Mother Goddess' legends have a strong hold in India. When male gods have failed, mother goddesses have come to the rescue. But different goddesses have been variously loving (Annapurna), angry and fierce in establishing ethics (Durga or Kali), or alternatively whimsical and vain (Manasa). The response to the author's questionnaire from over fifty Indian women managers has shown that their behavior could range over all these aspects. With growing female education and affirmative legislation for positions of authority for women, women leaders will have a very important say in the future. Perceptions conditioned by these legends and women's self-perception will affect behavior. Research on this issue has so far been inconclusive and further work is needed. Incidentally, two of the most powerful leaders in India in recent times have been women, Indira Gandhi and Mother Teresa.

Modernity and Social Contract

The years after India's independence have seen a rapid advancement of social contract and the rights concept of ethics. Inspired by the American, French and Soviet revolutions, they are now enshrined in the Indian Constitution. Their widespread adoption has been emboldened by trade union activism and other activist movement in the country. Field studies (Mitra & Singh, 1998) and (Reddy & Sekhar, 1992) have shown that the ethos of democracy has taken firm root in the country. But the leadership styles described earlier in the chapter, even if not contractual in nature, have been used in a contingent manner to support democratic processes. Traditonal views have helped followers in developing trust in leaders who they hope will use their power in a fair manner. People want leaders who recognize the plural character of society and be willing to protect it. Sometimes followers choose an 'outsider' as their leader because he or she is likely to be unbiased in adjudicating conflicts. Current practice combines the advantages of the 'self-discipline' and 'virtue ethics' leadership traditions with the powerful ethics of social control.

Significantly, the great modern Western philosopher of social contract and pluralism, John Rawls uses nothing of 'virtue ethics'. He had a very important criterion for establishing the ethicality of such a social contract, which he describes as the 'veil of ignorance'. He suggested that social contracts would get biased if everyone knew how they would be affected by it, and therefore, when entering into such a contract one should pretend that one is not aware of how it will affect one's fortunes. That would be the best way of honoring Kant's criterion of universalisability. Donaldson and Dunfee (2000: 438) realised that this stipulation could be impractical. Would it be more practical to practise *nishkama karma* as suggested by

Hannah Arendt (1961) and the *Gita*? As stated earlier, the philosophy of Aristotle and the *Gita* enjoins entering into such a contract with a 'virtuous mind' and a spirit of 'nishkama karma' respectively. Normatively, post-modernists of the right would say that is effective leadership. But as Sekhar (2000) points out, the facts on the ground are that the self-righteousness of the Western imperialism has often ignored the 'social contract' aspect of the expectations of their leadership behavior, the Bhopal gas tragedy being one typical example. Similarly in India, the credibility of the indigenous leadership being anchored only on 'virtue ethics' is therefore seriously jeopardized.

The Impact of Marx and Post-Marxist Concepts of Leadership in India

As noted, leadership theories flowing from the 'Enlightenment' or 'virtue ethics' have one major lacuna: they ignore the problem of power. Marx and Engels (1976), independent of their structuralist leadership theory of determinism, had a compelling compassion for the underprivileged and worked on the assumption that this would effectively cope with the problem of power; history showed that it could not. Post-modernists of the left such as Foucault (1998), have therefore been so wary of misuse of power that they would be suspicious of the very concept of leadership or of structures and systems.

Though, it would be impossible for post-modernists to credibly construct any social interaction where the need for leadership, structures or systems will vanish, their warning is of immense importance to leadership practices.

As Sekhar (2000) points out: 'Whereas the basic remedy is the cultivation of good intentions, a synthesis of social contract theories of Western ethical thinking and the concepts of Nishkama Karma and Sthitaprajna of India would enable one to steer one's way through'.

THE FUZZY LOGIC OF OPTIMISTIC PRAGMATISM

A description of the varieties of influence on Indian leadership styles could be anchored on a philosophic approach implicit in the terms 'optimistic pragmatism'. Optimism has a positive impact in our doings in a difficult world. Pragmatism means we would choose to tackle issues as they came along rather than try to derive an answer from a preconceived philosophy. There is also an implicit understanding that social processes in India and abroad have an uncanny way of developing several pathways to achieve social cohesion and socially desirable progress. This process is facilitated if one understands how each one these pathways works. Academic research will be helpful if it recognizes the reality of good intentions all round and the richness of solutions if collectively designed and implemented. But, dealing with these matters, would mean dealing with much fuzzy logic, which Kosko (1994) has described as inevitable. Reducing everything to a literal reductionist logic may be severely dysfunctional. The process is one of trial and error.

Conclusion

India is in the stream of progress to a global society of the future, which maintains the basic universal ethic recognized all over the world. This universal ethics can be called a happy amalgam of virtue and democracy. Efforts to design effective leadership can come for a collective wisdom emerging all around the world and in this we can have mutual learning between the West and India.

References

Arendt, Hannah (1961). 'Truth in Politics'. In H.Arendt, *Between Past and Future*. London: Viking Press.

Badaracco, Jr. (1998). 'Building Character'. *Harvard Business Review on Leadership*. Boston: Harvard University Press.

Naryana, Badri (2001). 'Heroes Histories and Booklets', *Economic and Political Weekly*. 13 October.

Bardhan, Pranab (2001). 'The Nature of Institutional Impediments to Economic Development'. In Satu Kahkonen and Mancur Olson, *A New Institutional Approach to Economic Development*. New Delhi: Sage. pp. 228–24.

Bass, B.M. (1989). *Stodgill's Handbook of Leadership*. New York: Free Press.

Burns, J.M. (1978). *Leadership*. New York: Harper and Row.

Ciulla, Joanne (2000). 'Trust and Future Leadership'. Draft paper.

Cooter, Robert (2001). 'Law from Order: Economic Development', and the 'Jurisprudence of Social Norms' in Satu Kahkonen and Mancur Olson, *A New Institutional Approach to Economic Development*. New Delhi: Sage. pp. 245–68.

Couto, R.A. (1999). *Making Democracy Work Better*. University of North Carolina Press, Chappel Hill.

Donaldson, Thomas and Thomas Dunfee (2000). 'Ties that Bind'. *Business and Society Review*. 105(4).

Dutta, Sudipto (1997). *Family Business in India*. New Delhi: Sage-Response.

Floestad, Guttram (1999). 'Ethics in Visioning and Modelling by Leaders', in S.K. Chakroborty and S.R. Chaterjee (eds.). *Applied Ethics*. Berlin: Springer Verlag.

Foucault, M. (1998). *On Power*. In L.D. Kreglman (ed.). *Politics, Philosophy and Culture*. London: Routledge Kegan Paul.

Fredrick, William (2000). 'Ties that Bind' A Review, *Business and Society Review*. 105(4).

Gonzales, Anna Marta (2000). 'Teaching Ethics in a Pluralistic Society'. Proceedings of International Conference on Teaching Business Ethics, IESE, Barcelona.

Gordon-Childe, V. (1942). *What Happened in History*. London: Penguin.

Hardee, W.F.R. (1968). *Aristotle's Ethical Theory*. Oxford: Clarendon Press.

Hosmer, L.T. (1987). *Ethics in Management*. New Delhi: Richard Irwin.

Kakar, Sudhir (1978). *The Inner World: A Psycho-Analytical Study of Child-hood and Society in India*. Delhi: Oxford University Press.

—— (1998). *The Indian Psyche*. New Delhi: Penguin.

Kant, I. (1985). *Foundation of Metaphysics and Morals*. London: Longman (Reissue).

Kosko, Bart (1994). *Fuzzy Thinking*. London: Harper Collins.

Kosambi, D.D. (1964). *The Civilization and Culture of India*. New Delhi: Vikas.

MacIntyre, A. (1981). *After Virtue*. London: Duckworth.

Marriot, McKim (2000). 'Hindu Rituals as a Means of Social Change'. Proceedings of the Sixteenth European Conference on Modern South Asia, Edinburgh.

Marias, Julian (1955). *Structure of Society*. Alabama: University of Alabama Press.

Marx, Karl and Fredrick Engels (1976) *Communist Manifesto*. In *Collected Works*. vol. 6. Moscow: Progress Publishers (Reissue).

Mill, J.S. (1897). *Utilitarianism*. London: Longman Green.

Mitra, S. and V.B. Singh (1998). *Democracy and Social Change*. New Delhi: Sage.

Putnam, R.D. (1993). *Making Democracy Work*. Princeton: Princeton University Press.

Radhakrishan, S. (1983). *The Bhagavad Gita*. London: George Allen and Unwin.

Rawls, J. (1993). *Political Liberalism*. New York: Columbia University Press.
Reddy, Pratap and R.C. Sekhar (1992). 'Collective Controls and Civic Culture Ambience'. Proceedings of the International Conference of Cooperatives, IRMA Anand, India.
Sabharwal, Satish (1975). *Wages of Segmentation*. New Delhi: Orient Longman.
Sekhar, R.C. (1997). *Ethical Choices in Business*. New Delhi: Sage-Response.
───── (1999). 'Intellectualism of Sankara and its Impact on Indian Management'. Tenth Sankara Darsana Conference, Delhi Management Association.
───── 'A Direction to the Ethics of Multinationals'. Sixteenth Intertnational Colloquim of Business and Economic Ethics. IESE Barcelona.
───── 'Trends in Ethics and Styles of Leadership in India'. *Business Ethics: A European Review*. 10(4).
Sinha, J.B.P. (1995). *Cultural Context of Leadership*. New Delhi: Sage.
Smith, Thomas W. (2000). 'Ethics and Politics'. *American Political Science Review*. December.
Solomon, Robert (1993). Corporate Roles Personal Virtues: An Aristotealian Approach'. In *Applied Ethics*. E.R. Winkler and J.R. Coombs (eds.). London: Blackwell Publishers.
Tantrik, Yogi Ramesh (1997). *Ethics of Chanakya*. New Delhi: Sahni Publications.
Tharoor, Sashi (1989). *The Great Indian Novel*. New Delhi: Penguin.
Williamson, Oliver (1996). *The Mechanism of Governance*. London: Oxford University Press.
───── (2001). 'Dictatorship, Democracy and Development'. In Satu Kahkonen and Mancur Olson, *A New Institutional Approach to Economic Development*. New Delhi: Sage.

15

India Transiting to the New Millennium: Kurt Lewin Remembered

UDAI PAREEK

In India in the twenty-first century, we are looking around for inspiring and reflective contributions of visionary thinkers of the past who shaped both thinking and action. One such thinker relevant to today's India is Kurt Lewin. We shall examine here Kurt Lewin's seminal contributions to theory and action, and their relevance to the major issues before India.

Kurt Lewin made significant contributions both to psychological theory and application of theory to action. In fact, Kurt Lewin's famous statement 'there is nothing so practical as a good theory' (Lewin, 1943) is a significant contribution towards forging closer links between theory and action: Designing actions based on sound and tested theory, which in turn should be formulated with an insight into the dynamics of action. He stated that 'close co-operation between theoretical and applied psychology ... can be accomplished in psychology as it has been accomplished in physics, if the theorist does not look towards applied problems with highbrow aversion or with fear of social problems, and if the applied psychologist realises that there is nothing so practical as a good theory' (Lewin, 1943).

Kurt Lewin died at the age of 57. He had experienced the fascist regime of genocide and been greatly agonized over the consequences of fascist thinking and action, personally because several of his family members and friends had been murdered, and, more importantly, because it was so pervasive in its effect on the large societies. In addition to his contribution to the theories and applications of psychology, in his personal behavior as a scientific leader and colleague was also significant, as recorded by his daughter and his student and later his colleagues (e.g. Miriam Lewin, 1922; White, 1922). Deutsch (1992) saw the great potential of Lewin's metatheory: 'in my phantasy, it also seemed to be a vehicle for integrating Einstsin, E. Freud and Marx—Einstein's way of theorising, Freud's influence on psychological dynamics, and Marx's emphasis on social influences upon psychological processes.'

Kurt Lewin's Major Contributions

We shall consider Kurt Lewin's contributions under five main groups.

Emphasis on Values

Kurt Lewin brought strong value orientation to psychology. He believed that science should serve society, and this was possible only when scientists had strong value orientations, because a science dealing with people and society could not be value free.

Faith in Democracy

Kurt Lewin migrated from Germany where he had witnessed the rise and devastating role of fascism. He was emotionally agitated with the evils of authoritarianism, and in his world-view democracy was the desired form of living. He saw authoritarianism not only as a personality problem, but the problem of the working of the group, group dynamics. The democratic way of working (climate) could be understood by studying different climates. The famous study of group climates (Lewin, Lippitt and White, 1939) showed that democratic climate, as contrasted with autocratic climate, was quite different from *laissez-faire* climate. This pioneering study led to a large number of studies in organizational climate and their practical application in work organizations.

Kurt Lewin also pioneered what can be called 'democratic social engineering'. Milgram's (1963) famous experiments on changing food habits by involving housewives in the decision to modify eating patterns have been called 'democratic social engineering' by Graebner (1987). Democracy does not mean that influence is not exercised; it means that such social influence is without 'deceit or trickery'. Kurt Lewin saw the paradox of democracy—how much and in what form one should exert influence in order to move from or out of autocracy to democracy: 'To investigate changes towards democracy, a situation has to be created for a period where the leader is sufficiently in control to rule out influences he does not want and to manipulate the situation to a sufficient degree. The goal of the democratic leader in this transition period will have to be the same as of any good teacher, namely, to make himself superfluous, to be replaced by indigenous leader from the group' (Lewin, 1987: 137). Graebner (1987) has raised ethical questions on social engineering. Rosenwein and Campbell (1992: 126) have proposed that 'democratic achievement of collective action requires majority/plurality amplification devices' (for example, public education and mobilization efforts), and further comment that such efforts are 'both moral and desirable so long as the rights of outvoted minorities to continue to organise and communicate are preserved'. Lewin's experiment, Rosewein and Campbell suggest, should be interpreted as a process of this kind.

Uses of Sciences

Kurt Lewin had strong faith in the use of science to solve problems. He believed that all social issues could be addressed through scientific methods. He believed in both the efficacy of and promoting the use of experiments to generate empirical data to deal with social problems. Two traditions emerged from this emphasis: one of social experimental psychology (simulating and experimenting with variables), and the other of action research (dealing with social issues in a scientific way by involving the affected people as partners in this research). The former (experimenting with variables) has flowered into creative experiments in the areas of obedience and conformity (Milgram, 1963), focus of control and conditioning (Seligman), attitude change (Festinger) inartistic motivation (Deci), and cooperation and competition (Deutsch).

Action research has made a much wider impact on practitioners and facilitators or interventionists. Kurt Lewin suggested six main characteristics of action research (as summarized by Bargal, Gold and Lewin, 1992: 8).

(i) A cyclic process of planning, action and evaluation.
(ii) A continuous feedback of the research results to all parties involved, including the client.

(iii) Cooperation between researchers, practitioners and clients from the start and throughout the entire process.
(iv) Application of the principles that govern social life and group decision-making.
(v) Taking into account differences in value systems and power structures of all the parties involved in the research.
(vi) Using action research concurrently to solve a problem and to generate new knowledge.

Holistic Framework

Kurt Lewin rejected 'the traditional atomistic, positivist, reductionism, Watsonian behaviourist philosophy of science for psychology' (Bargal, Gold and Lewin, 1992). White (1992) thinks that Lewin rejected the simplistic S-R approach. He emphasized the importance of a holistic framework. This emphasis has several aspects which later contributed to new developments.

Kurt Lewin stressed the need to study a situation in its totality, rather than the parts independent of each other. His contribution to the concept of field theory has significant implications for a proper understanding of social phenomena and for designing interventions to deal with social issues.

Gold (1992) distiguishes between Lewin's metatheory and the specific field theory. There were six metatheoretical rules developed by Lewin.

(1) Constructive method: This emphasized constructs which in Lewin's terms were to be 'genotypical' as compared to the 'phenotypical', the latter being a description and classification of things as they appear.
(2) Dynamic approach: This emphasized a systemic approach, the element of a situation being parts of the system.
(3) Analysis: Taking a part as a whole basic Gestalt principles, that is, change in any part would affect other parts. Lewin's field theory is in fact an elaboration of this principle.
(4) Contemporaneity: According to this, only current conditions explain the experience or behavior. Lewin deemphasized historical concepts of causation, although he did not deny the significance of the past in creating current conditions.
(5) Methodical representation of psychological phenomena: This stressed the need to formalize theory by making it methodical and logical.

(6) Psychological approach: According to this, psychological phenomena should be explained by psychological conditions. Gold (1992) takes the last approach as the basis of elaborating the concept of field theory. According to him, the implications of field theory are that the troubled and troublesome must change (for example, destitute must utilize more resources, criminals must stop harming others and themselves). The importance of intervention lies in providing them access to these courses. The application of field theory would emphasize identifying the barriers to their goals and then reducing these barriers. However, this would mean changing the conditions so as to reduce the current state of barriers. Such changes are necessary in the environment. The field theory, therefore, does not deal with their psychology of transformation, but with interventions which would help them find ways of changing the entire context. Such interventions must be in the total situation.

According to Diamond (1992), the underlying method of the field theory must be motivational calculus, psychological forces commensurate and expressed in effective terms. This has contributed to recent developments in the decision theory, an alternative paradigm to the economical rational choice models, when applied to social policy and counters biased and misleading implications of such models.

The holistic framework resulted in the emergence of systems thinking in psychology and other fields. Systems thinking has been taken up as a major concept by various schools of management. The latest emphasis is reflected in the concept of organizational learning. In fact, Senge (1990) regarded systems approach as the most important of the five disciplines: Systems Thinking, Personal Mastery, Mental Models, Shared Vision, and Team Learnings and he named his book 'The Fifth Discipline', which lays great stress on systems thinking.

Concept of Dynamics

Kurt Lewin emphasized the need to understand phenomena which were in a kind of flux rather than being stationary and permanent. He developed several concepts and their application to social problems. The most popular concept in understanding social change was that of the 'quasi-stationary equilibrium'.

Force field analysis as an application of the dynamics theory meant analyzing the forces which were keeping such an equilibrium, and developing a strategy of increasing positive and reducing negative forces. Related to this concept was the concept of the three stages of the change process: unfreezing, moving and re-freezing. These concepts led to a large number of studies and practical implications of improving and accelerating the change process. These three stages were later elaborated by psychologist and sociologists.

One of the most important contributions of Kurt Lewin was the concept of figure and ground. According to this concept the perception—e.g., phenomena change—depending on whether the elements are treated as a figure or ground. In order to understand a particular phenomenon, it is necessary to understand the context that gives it meaning; without its context the phenomenon does not have any meaning. The most popular concept in understanding social change was 'quasi-stationary' equilibrium force field analysis. It is an application of the dynamics theory and meant analyzing the forces which were keeping such an equilibrium, and developing a strategy of increasing positive and reducing negative forces.

According to this concept, the individual can be understood as a figure in the context of ground of a group. An understanding of individual psychology would, therefore, require an understanding of the psychology of the group to which an individual belongs. The extended use of this concept was the concept of person–environment fit.

A great deal of use was made of Lewin's concept of dynamics in education. The application of this concept made possible the study of classroom as a dynamic system and understanding children by examining the social forces surrounding them. Maruyama (1992) states that the implications of Lewin's concept are important in active involvement of students in their learning, cooperative learning, and constructive ways of treating conflicts in the educational sector.

The Current Indian Concerns

As discussed below, it is clear that Kurt Lewin's idea and methods are quite relevant to the current Indian concerns. The three primary concerns today relate to values, ways of managing transformation and (the changes are so fast that they are assuming the proportion of transformation), making research relevant to social reality. All these concerns were Lewin's basic concerns. Let us look at some of the issues India is facing today.

Fragile Democratic Ethos

Although India is committed to democracy, its democratic social life is threatened by feudalism and authoritarism. The feudal mentality has been deep rooted in Indian culture, endangering the fragile democratic proces. The same is true of authoritarianism, which takes the form of narrow communalism, factionalism, casteism, etc.

Attempts are made to divide people, and those who grab power try to scuttle democratic decision-making. Democratic processes need to be promoted in most organizations, starting from schools to work and government organizations. A renewed emphasis on democratic decision-making and decentralization with wider distribution of power is needed. Additionally, there is a need to demonstrate through research and experiments the superiority of the democratic process and its advantages to all concerned.

Managing Diversity and Differences

India has a rich variety of languages, food, practices, etc. This unique richness, which is a very valuable heritage, must be respected, maintained and advanced. Some propagate that this unique aspect is our weakness. Lewin's contribution led to the development of ways of managing adversity, and these are relevant to India. In fact, all great thinkers have emphasized India's diversity as our strength. Mahatma Gandhi, for example, embodied such diversity in his own personal life. Social scientists need to understand the Indian model in its proper perspective as one of rich diversity. There have been attempts to understand such uniqueness in terms of 'synergic pluralism' (Pareek, 1992: ch. 48).

Lack of Systemic Thinking

Most good work being done in India today is done in isolation. Greater attention must be paid to total system development. We may not be able to solve problems by good isolated work; such good attempts may be wasted in the long run. For example, the problem of growing population requires to be understood as a part of the larger 'system' of development. The systems approach will help decide both priorities and sequential planning to get the best results from such synergy.

Decreasing Concern for Values

Although the younger generation is brighter, morally bolder, yet, regretfully, the concern for values is diminishing. Society cannot live value free.

It is necessary to develop a strong value orientation and help people—from children to adults—debate on values important for our society. There is an increasing concern for personal gain rather than for sustaining values. There seems to be more self-seeking, reflected, for example, in careerism among the young. While advancement of one's career is a legitimate pursuit, the concern for values should not go down as a result of over-concern for career. Learning from Kurt Lewin, social scientists should work to reinforce the value of integrated democratic living which binds people in a society.

Lack of Meaningful Research

Most social research in India is sterile and isolated. There have not been any serious attempts at application of social research to the urgent problems in society. Lewin's greatest contribution was to make research serve the social cause. Today, more action research is needed. Action research would mean involvement of practitioners in the research process, maintaining as much rigor of research as its practical implications. A great deal has been said in various places on this aspect.

Facilitating Change

The significant implications of Lewin's contributions are change management, and facilitating change in organizations and society. An understanding of Kurt Lewin's ideas would help design change that transforms society. Since Lewin's ideas have been further advanced in understanding how transformational changes can be designed, we need to learn from the experiences of other developing countries that have been able to transform themselves into vibrant nations. In their role in facilitating the process of change, social scientists would require a more thorough understanding of Kurt Lewin's theories and applications and further evolve them for application to India.

References

Bargal, D., M. Gold and M. Lewin (1992). 'Introduction: The Heritage of Kurt Lewin'. *Journal of Social Issues*. 48(2), 3–13.

Deci, E.L. (1975). *Instrinsic Motivation*. New York: Plenum Press.

Deutsch, M. (1992). 'Kurt Lewin: The Tough Minded and Tender-hearted Scientist.' *Journal of Social Issues*. 48(2), 31–34.

Diamond, G.A. (1992). 'Field Theory and Rational Choice: A Lewinian Approach to Modelling Motivations'. *Journal of Social Issues*. 48(2), 79–94.

Festinger, L. (1957). *A Theory of Cognitive Dissouance*. Evanston, Illinois: Row, Perkerson.

Gold, M. (1992). 'Metatheory and Field Theory in Psychology: Relevance or Elegance?' *Journal of Social Issues*. 48(2), 67–78.

Graebner, W. (1987). 'Confronting the Democratic Paradox: The Ambivalent Vision of Kurt Lewin'. *Journal of Social Issues*. 43(3), 141–46.

Lewin, K. (1993). 'Forces Behind Food Habits and Methods of Change'. *Bulletin of the Research Council*. 108, 35–36.

Lewin, M. (1987). 'Kurt Lewin and the Invisible Bird on the Flagpole: A Reply to Graebner'. *Journal of Social Issues*. 43(3), 123–39.

—— (1992). 'The Impact of Kurt Lewin's Life on the Place of Social Issues in his Work'. *Journal of Social Issues*. 48(2), 15–29.

Maruyama, G. (1992). 'Lewin's Impact on Education: Instilling Co-operation and Conflict Management Skills in School Children'. *Journal of Social Issues*. 48(2), 155–56.

Milgram, S. (1963). 'Behavioural Study of Obedience'. *Journal of Abnormal and Social Psychology*. 6–7, 371–78.

Pareek, U. (1993). *Beyond Management*. New Delhi: Oxford and IBH.

Rosenwein, R.E. and D.T. Campbell (1992). 'Mobilzation to Achieve Collective Action and Democratic Majority/Plurality Amplification'. *Journal of Social Issues*. 48(2) 125–38.

Seligman, M.E.P. (1991). *Learned Optimisim*. New York: A.A. Knoff.

Senge, Peter, M. (1990). *The Fifth Discipline: The Art and Practice of the Learning Organization*. New York: Currency Doubleday.

White, R.K. (1992). 'A Personal Assessment of Lewin's Major Contributions'. *Journal of Social Issues*. 48(2), 45–50.

Notes on Contributors

Editor

Shivganesh Bhargava is Faculty at the Indian Institute of Technology (IIT), Mumbai. He has been a member of the faculty of the Indian Institute of Management (IIM), Lucknow and the universities of Jodhpur and Bhopal. He has over 30 research publications of international and national repute including the *International Journal of Human Resource Development and Management,* the *Journal of Social Psychology,* and the *Journal of Experimental Social Psychology* and has contributed to over 70 international and national seminars, conferences, symposiums and workshops. He is the recipient of the ISCA Young Scientist and MPCOST Young Scientist Awards. His areas of teaching, research, training, and consulting interests are in organizational behavior and people management.

Contributors

Vineet Basotia is Research Associate at the Satya Sai Institute of Higher Learning, Bangalore.

Asha Bhandarker is Faculty in the area of organizational behavior at Management Development Institute (MDI), Gurgaon. Trained as a psychologist, she has done extensive research work on leadership and organizational behavior. Her main areas of research, teaching, training and consulting are corporate leadership, strategic management and organizational development.

G.S. Das is Senior Faculty at the International Management Institute (IMI), Delhi. He has been involved in both academic and administrative capacities in different management institutes of the country. Global business is his main area of research and consulting.

Garima Garg completed her postgraduation in management at the Xavier Labour Research Institute (XLRI), Jamshedpur.

K.S. Gupta is Faculty at the Academy of Management of the Staff Training Institute of Hindustan Aeronautics Limited, Bangalore. He obtained his doctorate from IIT, Mumbai and his main area of research, training, and consulting is empowerment.

Venkat R. Krishnan is Faculty at the Xavier Labour Research Institute (XLRI), Jamshedpur. His broad area of teaching, training, and consulting is organizational behavior.

Mohit P. Kumar is Faculty Associate at National Institute of Bank Management (NIBM), Pune. He obtained his doctorate from IIT Mumbai.

R. Padmaja is at present in the USA. Prior to this she was associate with Centre for Organizational Development (COD), Hyderabad.

Udai Pareek is a retired Larsen and Toubro Professor of organizational behavior at IIM, Ahmedabad. He is the author of several books and articles in journals of repute such as the *Journal of Social Issues*. At present, he is Advisor at the Indian Institute of Health Management Research, Jaipur.

M. Radhaswamy is Senior Faculty at the Satya Sai Institute of Higher Learning, Bangalore.

Sumita Rai is Research Associate at IIM, Lucknow. She obtained her Ph.D. from IIT, Kanpur. Leadership is her main area of research.

Mary P. Sebastian obtained her Ph.D. from IIT, Mumbai. At present, she is Program Officer, Population Development Council, New Delhi. Her research is in the areas of management of NGOs and human service organizations.

R.C. Sekhar is Professor Emeritus at the T.A. Pai Institute of Management, Manipal. He has been in the field of management for over three decades and is the author of several books on the subject of ethics in business and leadership.

Archana Shukla is Faculty at IIM, Lucknow. Prior to this, she worked at the Department of Psychology, University of Allahabad and Center for Organizational Development (COD), Hyderabad. Her areas of teaching, research, training, and consulting are organizational structure and design, team building, knowledge management and group dynamics.

Arvind K. Sinha is Faculty and Chairman of the Department of Humanities and Social Sciences, IIT, Kanpur. Prior to this, he was associated with the Department of Psychology, University of Allahabad and A.N. Sinha Institute of Social Studies, Patna. He has done extensive research work in the area of leadership in India.

Dharni P. Sinha is at present Director General, Consortium for Strategic Management and Organization Development (COSMOD), Hyderabad and a member of the Board of Governors of IIM Bangalore and IIM Lucknow. Dr. Sinha was also Principal of the Academic Staff College of India (ASCI), Hyderabad. His main consulting and research areas are organizational development and strategic leadership.

Manisha Singh is a staff member with Center for Organizational Development (COD), Hyderabad.

Pritam Singh is Director, IIM Lucknow. Prior to this he was Director, Management Development Institute (MDI), Gurgaon and Dean, IIM, Bangalore and Administrative Staff College of India (ASCI), Hyderabad. His main areas of research, teaching, training, and consulting are strategic management, organizational development, corporate growth, managing creativity and innovation, culture building and knowledge management.

Shailendra Singh is Faculty at IIM, Lucknow. Prior to this, he was faculty at Sri Ram Center, New Delhi and Ram Manohar Lohia University, Faizabad. His areas of teaching and research are organizational behaviour and PMIR, managerial stress, coping strategies, mentoring, emotional intelligence, competence building, education management and managerial effectiveness.

R. Srinivasan is Faculty at IIM, Lucknow. His areas of interest include IT strategy, competitive strategies, internet organizations, management of change, mergers and acquisitions, strategic management, knowledge management, virtual organizations, management of NGOs and voluntary organizations, electronic commerce, marketing research management of internet (dotcom) organizations, knowledge management, and team behavior.

Index